FRAUD
INVESTIGATION

FRAUD INVESTIGATION

—— FUNDAMENTALS FOR POLICE ——

by

RUSH G. GLICK, L.L.B.

Chairman
San Diego and Los Angeles Chapters
The American Society for Industrial Security
Member
State Bar of State of California

and **205892**

ROBERT S. NEWSOM, L.L.B.

Commander, Detective Bureau
San Diego Sheriff's Department
Instructor, Miramar College

With a Foreword by
C. ALLEN GRAVES, PH.D.
Department of Criminology
University of Alabama
Birmingham, Alabama

CHARLES C THOMAS · PUBLISHER
Springfield · Illinois · U.S.A.

Published and Distributed Throughout the World by
CHARLES C THOMAS • PUBLISHER
Bannerstone House
301-327 East Lawrence Avenue, Springfield, Illinois, U.S.A.

© *1974, by* CHARLES C THOMAS • PUBLISHER
ISBN 0-398-03070-7
Library of Congress Catalog Card Number: 73-20368

Library of Congress Cataloging in Publication Data
Glick, Rush G
    Fraud investigation.
    1. Fraud investigation. I. Newsom, Robert, S., joint author. II. Title.
HV8079.F7G57   364.12   73-20368
ISBN 0-398-03070-7

Printed in the United States of America
K-8

PREFACE

THIS BOOK is based upon a syllabus of specialized courses of instruction presented as an elective in the police science curriculum at San Diego Community Colleges and at the center for Criminal Justice Studies, California State University, Long Beach. The subject is police science, particularly fraud investigation. This is the pole star and all material included is viewed in the light of applicability and direction, whether it points to that star. The question continually posed, is the material included necessarily related to the subject matter or were we adhering to the tendency to transcend the fine line between police science as such, and pure law? Due to the similarities in language, terminology and purpose involved in both areas, this spectre was always present. There was no desire to present, as a finished product, merely another addition to the already ponderous collection of "law" books. With the guidelines established by the reviewers it is believed we were successful in the directing of the text towards the "science."

At the risk of a charge of apostasy, certain areas of study have been included although they have not in the past been a part of the general study of investigation usually presented in the police science course. Their inclusion emanates from the obvious need to understand certain fundamentals before attacking the selected and somewhat unique types of offenses which are a part of the highly specialized field of fraud investigation.

The authors have drawn upon their own experience and that of their colleagues in law and investigation in order to present a wide spectrum of study. The text, because of the resources used, is oriented in some degree to California legal and technical concepts and problems, however, where appropriate, a generalized viewpoint is presented.

ACKNOWLEDGMENTS

T HE AUTHORS are deeply indebted to Brig. Gen. Harold L. Hjelm NGUS (ret) and his Menlo Park group who, with great patience and understanding, reviewed the original (and uncorrected drafts) giving their advice and no little encouragement to the project. Without such guidance, it never would have been complete. The learned counseling of C. Allen Graves, Ph.D., University of Alabama (formerly of California State University, Long Beach) relating to the mysteries of publication and subject matter had great influence upon the final product.

Appreciation is expressed here to the memory of the late Lieut. Ralph Bradford, Long Beach Police Department (ret) who permitted a resume of his check classification system to be included within the text and gave some sage advice regarding the topic of forgery.

Special acknowledgment is given to Harvey M. French, Special Agent, American Insurance Association (ret), for his guidance in relation to insurance frauds and to Lieut. William Hull (ret), Sgt. John Di Betta (ret) and Sgt. Ray Mercer of the Frauds Division, Los Angeles Police Department, San Diego County Deputy District Attorney, Frank R. Costa, for their knowledgeable contributions over a long period of time which proved invaluable. The writers are indebted to Grant Leake of the California Department of Public Health for his contributions to the chapter on medical frauds and his investigative assistance for many years.

Last, but not least, the authors salute their wives, who put up with seemingly endless hours of domestic double duty while the scriveners labored in their dens.

INTRODUCTION

"Crime is rampant in the United States!" This quote appeared in the *New York Times* describing the deplorable conditions of violence in our society today. Yet, to be complete in the assumation of crime, one must explore the more sophisticated criminal actions.

Historically, gifted journalists and criminologists have "reinvented the wheel" with methods of crime detection and causation. These literary pieces have explored and re-explored the realm of reported crime. Seldom, if ever, does any work delve into the mystique of such offenses as fraud. The common response to a "swindle" report given by a majority of law enforcement agencies is that this is a civil matter and that the victim should "see his attorney." Nothing is further from the truth or more frustrating to the victim. All too often, the inability to recognize fraud as a crime results in the "kiss-off" of a case by the responding officer.

Why does this situation exist? The answer is relatively simple. First, the lack of criminal recognition by law enforcement and the failure to correlate the "trilogy" with plain theft. Second is the lack of adequate procedures or personnel for investigations, and third is due to a chronic lack of texts covering fraud and its proof.

The topic of fraud has been neglected by almost all in the literary field. Only specific instances have surfaced in the sea of texts. For the first time, a manual type text has been created, not only defining the aspects of fraud but also delineating the required items of proof.

The authors of this book have successfully combined a legalistic interpretation with a "tool and technique" approach to the problem. Both have bonafide law degrees and Captain Newsom's expertise is second to none in the field of fraud investigation. He has been instrumental in the establishment of P.O.S.T. schools in consumer fraud investigation as well as instruction in California institutions of higher learning. Mr. Glick has had many years of successful legal experience dealing with fraud cases—both defense and prosecution.

The primary purpose of this text is to create a bridge between the pragmatic approach of field officers and the academic theory of causation. This book integrates behavioral research with a well recognized format for the teaching of police investigation without an unnecessary amount of "academic jazz."

To fill this need, this text concentrates on the technique-oriented approach and minimizes the theoretical concepts. No attempt, however, has been made to define in detail the duties and responsibilities of the ideal fraud investigator or to describe a set of guaranteed techniques which will lead to the successful apprehension of the con man. What has been done is the creation of an effective operating manual of guideline procedures required to understand, apprehend and successfully prosecute the fraud perpetrator.

The basic failure of a good many texts is the lack of continuity. This book is a pleasant exception. The authors have developed a credible flow of both ideas and procedures that involves the reader in a logical pattern of thought. All texts should start with a basic conceptual picture of the problem. Newsom and Glick have succeeded admirably in this approach.

As the book progresses, each topic is defined, exemplified and discussed in a concise manner. When dealing with basic intangibles, this could create undue problems. Again, the various frauds are explained in such a manner that the reader can feel comfortable with his conclusions.

C. ALLEN GRAVES
Birmingham, Alabama

CONTENTS

FRAUD
INVESTIGATION

CHAPTER I

BASIC CONCEPTS

The Purpose

THE PURPOSE OF this book is to develop an understanding and appreciation of the basic elements of theft oriented offenses. There are numerous fine articles and books on the topic of fraud in general written and published by knowledgeable people, but there seems to be a dearth of texts that can be implemented in the police science curriculum in which the student has, under one cover, the related law and investigative techniques outlined. It should be kept in mind, however, that a formalized course of instruction or a topical book does not an investigator make. All that these two can actually achieve is the opening of the student's eyes, widen his perspective to some degree and create some guidelines within which he can adequately function. The experience he gains by actual field work, either limited or enhanced by his own natural acumen, will in the final analysis be the determining factor as to his competency. All that is done in this book or any other text is to establish a well tested foundation upon which the student will build his own professional or technical future.

The Problem

In the terms of hard cash outlay all of the men with the guns in their hands or the ones with the prybars to open doors and windows do less harm to the economy of the country collectively than the smoothies of both sexes who rig company books, offer unfunded securities, forge or kite checks, organize credit card schemes, bribe a little here and there, induce the unfortunate

3

and helpless to forego proper medical aid for quackery and numerous other cute tricks to separate the unsuspecting and trusting citizen from his property. The total losses experienced each year from fraud operations can never really be determined. This class of crime from the police position is detectable rather than preventable; an increase of large numbers in a patrol or detective division would be of negligible effect. The prevention of loss is encumbent upon the victim. As one noted writer in the commercial security field said very succinctly, "losses aren't rising because there is too much theft; rather they are rising because there is too little prevention; let us not mistake the symptoms for the disease." Rising theft losses he avers were only the symptoms, the disease being "preventive malnutrition." In this he is right. However, his treatise was directed primarily towards large and highly organized firms with their own security units and not towards the usual business operation of a somewhat smaller size with which the average police fraud investigator would be more often concerned. The latter companies frequently do have the structure to establish really good and proper internal control methods, albeit the concept is one which should be implemented to the degree possible limited only by the organizational size and practicability. Empirical studies have disclosed many operational weaknesses in the smaller companies which can and should be overcome by proper methodology. They have also shown there are other reasons (infra) of a much more subtle nature which regardless of what preventive measures are taken will still result in losses.

Most fraudulent acts are never reported to a police agency because of the integrity of the firm, the reputation of the institution, the honor of the family, embarrassment, the old school tie, lodge brother affinity, personal obligations, or some other weighty factor on the social scale might be the first consideration and would take precedence over legal, moral, ethical and community duties. Also there is not infrequently found the spectre of joint culpability, moral if not legal. The presence of any one of these regardless of degree does not enhance the probability of official denunciation.

There are other problems too that beset the one who would

try to enforce the law in the area of fraud. It is the incongruous attitude sometimes taken by courts, prosecutors and even company directors towards the "sordid profit motive" which tempts someone to stray from the path of honesty and trust, equating this with some sort of unnatural, irresistible, immoral urge that is believed by them to be the driving force behind business operations, thus, the thief should not be unduly persecuted by holding him to answer. When does the "profit motive" cease to be a praiseworthy and acceptable purpose of business as conceived in our social order, and become some degenerated, foul and obnoxious reason? It would seem that this question has not, and can never be adequately answered, there being too many diverse and conflicting sociological viewpoints and theories to consider. Apparently the apologists fail to include in their rationale the very human instincts of avarice and greed. Robert Ardrey in his "African Genesis" * theorizes that man and all creatures desire dominance and acquisition. Another author has stated "honesty is an intellectual concept" and is much weaker than our instinctive drives and impulses, consequently the eternal battle between the two, base instinct and intellect, will always continue; the effort of reason to overcome that which is socially destructive.

Limited Perspective

Police efforts have almost traditionally focused upon the burglar, robber, murderer, rapist, car thief and public drunk. For reasons unknown there has been almost a complete disregard for that area of crime which has such a deleterious effect on our economy, financial security and morale; theft by fraud, and we are all affected by it. Napolean once said of England that it was nothing but a nation of shopkeepers. Americans, due to our heritage and our country's origin similarly attach a great deal of importance to "business papers." The protective machinery of audited accounts and other internal control methods over merchandise, funds, fixtures and equipment of a business firm still leave innumerable loopholes for fraud and error. Trade and com-

---

* See note 1.

merce are swamped with documentation of every conceivable
kind, but no amount of paper security can really outwit or
thwart the thief all of the time if he has the intelligence, patience
and usually the unknowing help of his victim. This is true
whether the scam is the short or street con or up into the ethereal
plane of involved high finance. This is true because the basic
motives of the con-artists are the same as are the responses of
the victims.

Jonathan Swift, the Irish born English satirist, in 1726
wrote his famous "Gullivers's Travels" in which he observed "The
Lilliputians look upon fraud as a greater crime than theft, and
seldom fail to punish it with death; for they allege that care and
vigilance with a very common understanding may preserve a
man's goods from theft, but honesty has no defense against superior cunning." What was true in Swift's (Gulliver's) day is
no less true today notwithstanding electronic data processing
and other phenomenal technical and social advances of our
times. However, our attitudes towards crimes and punishments
have altered appreciably. In 1939 Lord Maughm in the House
of Lords, stated in connection with proposed legislation concerning trade and business practices, "Nothing is harder in cases of
this kind than to catch all the ruffians and let through the honest
man." The measure which was under consideration was of course
viewed as too restrictive and summarily defeated.

It might be interesting to point out here that there has developed a change in the English attitude towards the "ruffians." In
late 1968 the doctrine of "caveat emptor" (let the buyer beware)
was converted to "caveat venditor" (let the seller beware) by
the House of Commons. The new concept now permits the British police to initiate criminal action for violations of the "Trade
Description Act" which is comparable to the false advertising
statutes under California law and that of some other states. The
law specifically covers oral as well as written claims so that any
salesman who waxes overenthusiastically can be prosecuted, as
well as his superiors or anyone else who has aided and abetted
him.

In this unique area of theft which we shall explore it must be
kept in mind that the bulky briefcase may contain nothing more

harmful than a book to read or a bag of sandwiches, but the techniques which can go with it can more easily pry open cash boxes and business accounts than any manner of instrument, blunt, sharp or otherwise. The corruptions and permissiveness of our times should be closely studied, "a little deal around the corner multiplied a thousand times becomes the rot in the core of the community."

The "Con-man," "BTO," "White Collar Criminal" or the "Bandit with the briefcase" as he is referred to in England, or whatever name is used to describe him has always been with us. There were sharp operators in prebiblical times and they have never ceased their attempts to relieve the gullible and trusting of their properties. Fraud activities have increased concurrently with the development of the national economy and commerce; as business and financial affairs became more complex so did the related frauds. The private rationalizations that are resorted to in effort to justify unethical and outright dishonest acts are astounding. It has become difficult to delineate between right and wrong, acceptable and unacceptable. Too often acceptance seems to be the difference in the size of the fraud; if it is large, daring and successful, the perpetrator is more likely than not to be viewed with envy and admiration; if it is small and not achieving the desired goal, the public viewpoint will be one of disapprobation.

Changing Social Attitudes

The philosophy and attitude created by our embracing the new liberalized morality has permeated the framework of our society at every level. The thief, and there is no more accurate description of him, can be the construction worker who steals the contractor's wheelbarrel or shovel, on up the scale to the bookkeeper or office manager who alters a few payroll checks, makes spurious entries into the company books or on into the realm of higher finance where securities are issued to the public without proper funding. The activities are not limited to any particular social strata, ethnic group, cultural or educational level.

Investigation dating back to 1967 has disclosed some interesting figures in the offender's age groups as equated with recidivism. In the area of "fraud" (excluding the more generalized forms of theft) persons under twenty years of age were arrested for subsequent offenses 75 percent of the time; the twenty to twenty-four years old group repeated 55 percent; the twenty-five to twenty-nine years old group repeated 43 percent; the thirty to thirty-nine years old segment again repeated the same or similar crimes 46 percent; the forty to forty-nine years old category reflected a repeat performance of 40 percent; the fifty years and older types repeated over 18 percent; the overall average being approximately 42 percent. This seems to bear out a theory discussed in 1962 at a meeting of the California Check Investigators' Association in which it was stated that there is an inordinate degree of recidivism among embezzlers and check writers to the point that it confounded psychotherapy. Regardless of the treatment, guidance and the resolve of the offender, he will always fall back into the same reasoning and pattern of action when he is confronted with the same life's problems and opportunities; thus the old adage, "Once an embezzler, always an embezzler" seems to have some validity.

A number of Federal agencies concerned with fraudulent practices such as the Securities and Exchange Commission, Post Office Department and the Federal Trades Commission all have consistently reported rises in offenses within their respective jurisdictions. The FTC contends there is an inordinate rise in consent orders and other actions against companies in all industries and these are not just the so-called "fly-by-night" firms, but include the better known companies. One merely has to read daily newspaper to see the validity of this comment. The SEC consistently reports a comparable increase in offenses concerned with the issuance, funding and purchase of stocks and bonds. Here again, major brokerages have been involved, not just "boiler-room" hacks. The gigantic losses in this area have not even been computed other than to assert they are in the hundreds of millions of dollars. This situation, of course, has been aided by the size and complexity of the operations.

The Post Office Department reports constant increases each year in mail thefts and the use of the mails to defraud. This last, and the type which is of basic interest to this text, encompasses a variety of scams such as savings and loan swindles, medical frauds, travel agencies, real estate schemes, lonely-hearts clubs, insurance frauds, etc. Again the figures for the losses are in the millions of dollars with the attendant heartbreak and ruin for the victims. Perhaps the basic cause for reported increases here lies not so much with the mails being the genesis of the frauds but with the fact that hardly any business, legitimate or otherwise can operate without written contact with clients or customers. They must perforce resort to the use of the mails to conduct their business. In other words, it may be more of an ancillary development than the actual means of a fraud.

Judicial Attitude

There is another element which epitomizes the prevailing climate of our mores and customs, this being the attitudes of the courts (and juries for that matter) towards the prosecution of such offenders. Most judges and juries do not become greatly indignant or overly excited when assessing the non-violent type of crime. The accused usually makes a far better appearance in the courtroom than does the narcotic addict or peddler, the prostitute, the hippie appearing murderer, the armed robber and burglar. Consequently his sentence, if in fact he is convicted of anything, is usually much lighter, even though the losses incurred by his victim are always much greater. Then there are the varied and circuitous processes of appeal, review and attendant measures which are not designed or employed with any idea of benefiting the prosecution. Fraud cases being what they are, often involve very complicated questions of law and procedure which invite the filing of appeals.

Furthermore, the con-artist is usually not lacking in intelligence and ability. He is more often than not a shrewd and sagacious person and has the best in legal, technical and business advice. They are tough and well-equipped adversaries. There is adequate legislation to preclude the reincarnation of the robber barons of the last century and similar characters, but with the new types operating today, with their revised and highly skilled methods, education and new exciting ideas, it sometimes appears that law enforcement will always be frustrated in its attempts to control or stop them.

The Prototype

A natural question is "How do you identify the embezzler or con-artist?" There is no way. They do not fit into the prototype of the criminal as we usually visualize him. They live and behave, at least on the surface, like normal people; they usually are very likeable, sincere and sociable (how else would they be able to inspire confidence?); and they are at all levels of intelligence. There is no way in which an accusing finger of suspicion or guilt can be pointed at one unless his methods and mannerisms are so crude and inept they invite disclosure. This does not happen very frequently. As pointed out previously, the type of crime we are dealing with here is not something which can be controlled or eradicated by a large increase of manpower in the patrol division or a police department. In the case of the embezzler, the only effective devices known so far are (1) the implementation of good internal accounting control systems and (2) education. Even these can be circumvented. An audit by an independent outside accountant can in no assured way prevent fraud from happening and it does not of itself necessarily detect it. The auditor's engagement often of necessity includes a great deal of random testing or spot checking, not a detailed entry by entry examination, consequently frauds, especially small peculations (which can mount tremendously), very often will evade his expert gaze regardless of the new exotic and sophisticated machine accounting methods which are almost uniformly employed today. In the case of the con-artist sales, real estate, investment, automobile, securities and manufacturing fields in which involved processes are concerned, the problem is still greater. The doctrine of "caveat emptor" is so well settled, in spite of statutory and common law provisions concerning warranties and full disclosures, the buyer has only one protection, investigate before investing. And here, as with the potential embezzler, there is no sure way to determine before-hand the true situation. The victim is reduced to the position of assuming a calculated risk every time he moves. The old cliche, "You can't tell a player without a program" is applicable here; but where do you get the program?

The con-artist is a high pressure salesman. His whole effort is put forth to create a certain state of mind in his victim and upon reaching this objective, relieve him of his property. Invariably the question is posed, "How can anyone fall for such a scheme?" To those who have yet to be victimized, that small group of the superintellectuals who seldom get caught short, it is difficult to appreciate and understand the psychology involved. They have not been confronted by the radiant and sometimes almost mesmerizing personality of the con-artist with the finely drawn nuances, the emotionalism, the skilled application of rhetoric that can and does become overwhelming. The con-artist possesses tremendous understanding of human weaknesses, idiosyncracies, faults and even strengths which he uses subtly with the unconscious help of the victim, analogous to the judo expert in making his opponent fight himself.

The Police Attitude

"All that appears civil is not necessarily civil;" this parody of a better known metaphor is a truism in and of itself. The archaic attitude in police work that if a problem seems confusing and cannot be immediately classified as a violation of the Penal Code, the Vehicle Code or some local ordinance, "tell them it's civil and see their lawyer," is fast losing its acceptance in the more enlightened and progressive departments. This attitude was born out of ignorance, nurtured on laziness and brought to full growth by a combination of the two. We in this work can no longer evade our obligations by hiding behind a facade of psuedo legal knowledge. We must learn to accept our responsibilities, enlarge our operational spheres and realize that as law enforcement professionals we are not limited to a few finely defined sections of the Penal Code but should and must perform our duties in all areas which by legislation has been determined to be criminal in nature.

The victim in a fraud case admittedly often has recourse in

a civil suit for damages and recovery. But, he also has this concomitant right when he is injured in any manner in other criminal acts against him (assault, burglary, robbery, etc.). This, however, is very often at great expense and personal cost, notwithstanding some new legislation in this area. To deny the right of criminal prosecution for a fraudulent act, either to the individual complainant or to the state, is just as much a deprivation of basic rights as is malicious prosecution. The con-artist is fully aware of the reluctance displayed in the past by police agencies and many prosecutors to take forthright action and has used this to his advantage, tantamount to a cloak of implied immunity. This condition, however, is slowly but gratifyingly changing and the newly manifested attitude being exemplified in modern and forward-looking police agencies, aided by capable prosecutors, is to take the long hard analytical view of situations which come to their attention under circumstances that can be construed to be in the area of probable fraud. At least take the time to look and study; don't come to hasty and baseless conclusions on a minimum of facts and then discard the case out of hand.

The Needed Adjustment

Much has been written and said in recent years concerning the professionalization of the police. Many learned persons both within and without the legal profession, sociologists, law enforcement, lay persons, political philosophers and just plain politicians with some idea of expediency, have vocalized at length about what is right and what is wrong with the present concept of police action. It must be admitted in all candor by us, who make up this much maligned body, that some of the criticisms leveled and theories advanced are not entirely without merit, however much we would like to deny some of our apparent weaknesses. Whether or not we achieve in the future the desired recognition as a profession or respected trade (depending, of course, upon what construction is put to the term "professional"), it must be accepted that we are a worthy and necessary adjunct to the legal profession analogous to the relationship existing between the physician and the nurse or technician (both of the latter presently appear to be attaining such recognition).

To enhance our position and to assure a proper degree of competence within our sphere of activity we must develop an understanding of the basis of our work, the law. This does not limit itself to knowledge of a few frequently enforced sections of the Penal Code, Vehicle Code and local ordinances, but requires examination and assimilation of case law. Our position is much like that of a technician trying to implement the ideas of an engineer. He cannot perform unless he has some basic knowledge of engineering principles and can read a blueprint. We cannot perform unless we can read and understand our blueprint, the law. There must be developed within ourselves an appreciation, respect, understanding and acceptance of judicial decisions and the ability to operate within their framework. This does not mean that we must become attorneys (although it might help), but we must be able to apply the concepts which are established for us during the course of our action.

Law and Techniques

The reading of case law is not a "one-shot deal," but is a continuing thing. It demands our attention constantly due to the ever-changing philosophy as enunciated by the courts. What is true today may not be in vogue tomorrow, and there is always the concomitant spectre of criminal and civil liability confronting each of us as individuals when we transcend those limitations within which we must function. And, we have this individual responsibility for our transgressions, however innocently committed. So, regardless of our personal viewpoints, read, analyze, absorb and implement the prevailing legal concepts as they are set forth however transitory they may be.

In the course of study here we are primarily concerned with only one small segment of the criminal law; theft in it's varied forms, it's legal points and investigative techniques. In the ancient times, the thief, when caught, usually regardless of how minimal the offense, lost "the offending hand" by fire, axe, sword or some other such cruel but effective method. The message, to use the vernacular, was loud and clear. Of course other acts, some of which are no longer viewed as criminal offenses, were handled in similar summary fashion. As the years passed into eons and civilization, with all its refinements of thought and action developed, man adopted a more charitable attitude towards miscreants, rationalizing their acts with their purported needs and motivations, all ascribed to their heredity, usually with some pseudopsychological equation involved and invariably related to some act or condition to which can be attached, rightly or wrongly (depending upon one's viewpoint) some social significance. As a consequence there has evolved a somewhat watered down emasculated set of ideals and principles in the legal and technical approach to offenders of society's rules for self-preservation of which theft is still considered a violation of the commandments, legislative or divine. Paradoxically, there has at the same time developed unusual and far-reaching laws equated with theft, the type and nature of which the early law-givers and arbiters never intended or even possibly dreamed. To appreciate this, one merely has to review the multiple codification of our laws and briefly examine the purpose or the myriad of commissions, committees, special agencies and similar bodies out of which has even evolved a third branch of the law; administrative. The scope can become ridiculously wide; too wide for the student of police science, and even for the law student to some degree. This mainly resulted from the more complex socio-economic structuring which always accompanies the growth of society's industrial, financial and scientific achievements. With this there is collateral growth of varied and different groups which demand legislative protection for their particular vested interests. The end result, as far as concerns law enforcement is obvious; the techniques are becoming as complex as the law which they are being used to support. The demands then upon the modern fraud investigator are becoming more pronounced. He cannot abrogate his responsibilities; neither can his organization if public service is a true commitment. He must prepare for the continuous neverending struggle by availing himself to every tool, and implement any legitimate means to assure he will not lose headway in fighting the encroachments of today's commercial Machiavellians.

---

* Note 1—"African Genesis," R. Ardrey, Dell Pub. Co., New York (1967).

CHAPTER II

TRILOGY OF THEFT

DIVISION A

FALSE PRETENSES

Basis of Statutory Provisions

THEFT BY FALSE PRETENSES (misrepresentation) is a statutory crime of fairly recent vintage when viewed against the backdrop of the common law. That body of legal precepts in its nascency considered larceny by trespass only, or the taking of property without the possessor's consent. Despite the rigid viewpoint it became apparent this was inadequate to cover frequent losses in which trust became the wrongdoer's weapon and he obtained the victim's property and the title thereto by fraud. To fill this vacuum there evolved the theory of the consent element being vitiated when it has been given as the result of misrepresentation or deceit. This concept became formalized through legislation and is what is today the law with varying refinements.

There are as many different forms of false pretenses as there are people to conceive them. Many are unchanging and static, countless more unique and different. Notwithstanding novelty and individual jurisdictional legal limitations the elements of the crime are uniform and are present in one form or other in any scheme which falls within that classification of theft. Such crimes can include the impersonation of another in their private or official capacity, receiving money or property in false character, fraudulent conveyances to defeat the rights of creditors, presenting false statements of financial character or conditions, false or misleading statements in charitable solicitations, removal of mort-

15

gaged property, or any act, pretense or misrepresentation performed or made knowingly and from which the wrongdoer obtains the victim's money, labor, services or property.

The Elements

The first requisite is the intent to defraud; the crime is that type usually categorized as "specific intent." The statutes almost uniformly state "knowingly and designedly, by any false or fraudulent representations or pretense" or similar wording with the same effect.

However, if the defendant can show clearly that he honestly and with his level of intelligence could have reasonably believed his own statements or representations this is a bar to prosecution. There is some similarity to the misrepresentation by a tort-feasor which is actionable if he has made it negligently or recklessly. But the criminal law normally is more stringent and carelessness is not sufficient basis for prosecution. There are some exceptions to this rule, more notably California courts which have held that statements by the accused made recklessly and without sufficient information for a justifiable belief will satisfy the required "intent."

The second element is the misrepresentation. It is the falsification of past or present facts in written and spoken form. It also can be in the form of conduct on the part of the accused or in his concealment or non-disclosure of pertinent information. In other words it can be expressed or implied and in any form of communication. Some jurisdictions have included within the meaning of the element, false promises, or those made with no present intention to perform in the future. A celebrated California case (*Peo vs Ashley*, 42 Cal 2nd 246) in 1954 accepted this precept saying "if false promises were not viewed as false pretenses the legally sophisticated, without fear of punishment, could perpetrate on the unwary fraudulent schemes."

The third element is the reliance placed upon the representations by the victim. There must be a relationship or causal connection between the misrepresentation and the wrongdoer obtaining the victim's property. The victim's release of the property must have been induced in some degree by his reliance on the representation. It is not necessary the representation be the single cause of inducing the victim to part with his property; it is required only that it be of some material effect upon his reasoning. Conversely, if the victim was aware the representations were false or put no credence in them, there is no basis for criminal action. Further, if there has been an inquiry by the victim or he has sought expert advice or opinion rather than accepted totally the word of the wrongdoer the requisite element of reliance is not met. Of course the ultimate limitation is based upon the wrongdoer's representation even if in fact they can be proved as false and misleading.

Sometimes there is what appears to be an inordinate span of time between the representation and the victim handing over his property. This has some relationship to the reliance factor. It is normally held that the representation is a continuing thing and if it can be clearly shown it operated on the victim's mind during the period, the element of reliance is met. It is a subjective thing and the intellectual level of the victim would have to be considered.

The fourth element is the requirement that the victim was actually defrauded. This is not always construed as a literal loss. It is satisfied if he did not in fact get what he bargained for, with or without actual loss. It has also been consistently held that if the victim and the wrongdoer were jointly engaged in some questionable transaction this did not constitute a defense. The fact that the wrongdoer received no personal benefit is not a defense as one case held "the thief is as guilty when he takes it for the benefit of a church as when he takes it for himself" (Peo vs Cheely, 106 Cal App 2nd 748).

The Proof

Theft by false pretenses is differentiated from theft by trick and device by the intent of the victim in each situation and the degree of corroboration required. In false pretenses the victim intends that title should accompany the transfer of the property. In trick and device it is intended that title remain with the

owner and only the use and possession of the property is transferred (*see* Chapter on Bunco-Trick and Device). The corroboration requirement in false pretenses, when invoked in some
jurisdictions, generally calls for the presence of a "false token"
or writing, or some writing subscribed to by the accused, or the
testimony of two witnesses, or that of one witness (the victim)
and corroborating circumstances. The last more often than not
being the method most used and most successful. A false token
or writing refers to "something real, visible, and substantial, or
some writing purporting to be the act of some person, and so
framed as to have more weight and influence in effecting the
fraud than the mere verbal assertions of the accused" (*Lanier vs
Alaska,* 448 P2nd 587 and *State vs Whittaker,* 64 Oregon 297).
The rule of corroboration, where invoked, is based upon the pre-
caution against perjury on the part of an ostensible victim.

Frequently an allegation of theft by false pretenses is based
upon contractual arrangements between the parties. This brings
into play the hard and fast rule concerning parol evidence which
excludes any evidence of prior or contemporaneous verbal agreements which would vary the provisions of a written contract.
However, in a criminal action based upon the same facts the
parol evidence rule has been generally held to be operative between the original parties to the contract only and the state may
go outside its provisions to prove the falsity or the true intentions
of the representations made.

Corroborative evidence need only tend to connect the accused with the offenses and all circumstances related to the
transactions and his entire conduct can be considered to furnish
the corroboration. This includes those activities before, during
and after the alleged predescribed act.

Evidence of similar acts or transactions are admissable to establish corroboration. Evidence of use by the accused of a clearly
defined uniform plan, scheme, pattern and design and similar
misrepresentations at another time and place meets the requirement. Acts in this context are criminal in nature, transactions not
necessarily so. They can be entirely legal and innocuous, merely
being a method or manner in which to achieve some purpose

such as a bookkeeping process utilized which can be implemented both for legitimate and/or criminal means.

Single or Multiple Offenses?

The question of whether a series of wrongful acts constitutes a single or multiple offenses must be determined by the facts and situation of each case. Where property of a different value or character is taken at various times though upon the same misrepresentation a separate crime is consummated upon each distinct appropriation. However if it is established there was a general intent or overall plan, there is only one offense. This is of special importance when a single felony count can be charged from a series of acts, the amounts of which are less than the statutory amounts needed. They can be combined into a single count if there can be shown the general overall intent to steal the total amount which for this purpose exceeds the statutory requirement.

As can be seen from the elements and nature of the crime the specific intent to defraud is a question of fact which can and must be determined from all the facts and circumstances. Also from its nature we have the theory of a continuing offense. By this is meant the crime can be committed and is chargeable in more than one county or state. The scheme to take the property may have developed in one area with certain acts performed but was finally consummated in another area. It is prosecutable and punishable as if all the acts and transactions had taken place in one area. A continuous crime consists of a series of acts set in motion by a single design and operated by an uninterrupted force or concept, regardless of the time it may take to accomplish the ultimate objective.

Classic Cases

Cases reviewed by the courts are not the private interests of lawyers but are an excellent way for the student investigator to gain an understanding of the varied and many issues, both real and imagined, which can be the basis of appeal. When examined they can graphically present the issue and the processes resorted to by the investigators and whether there was success, or failure because of mistakes or sheer ineptitude. They clearly emphasize the need for a knowledgeable, perceptive and cautious approach. There are far more "good" cases lost because of some tactical or strategic error committed during the inquiry stage than during the trial. Most investigators dislike to admit this but nevertheless, the problems at trial began as problems in the field and remained unresolved. Also, the cases present literally the elements of the crime and the manner in which they were established. There is not a better way to study the step by step relation of facts to legal principles.

One such case involved the sale of fraudulent trust indentures.* "L," the defendant, operated as the manager and co-trustee of an organization purported to create trusts in the form of "living trusts" whereby the trustors would have control over the future of their estates; would be able to avoid probate and similar legal/court costs; negate entirely estate and inheritance tax; and eliminate any personal inabilities that may attach to the estate operation. There were promotional publications to that effect coupled with verbal representations. "L" had two co-defendants, one "O" who was a co-trustee and functioned as a secretary-treasurer, and one "D" who was hired as an accountant. All three ultimately were charged with a series of grand theft and conspiracy counts.**

The group disseminated their brochures in an area of southern California and one of them came to the attention of a businessman, one "W" who became interested in the concept being promoted. He contacted "L" who met with him repeating orally essentially the same things printed. The man, relying upon the representations by "L," concerning the avoidance of personal liability and estate and inheritance taxes, purchased the trust plan for $1,800. There was departure here, in degree not kind, in that "L" induced the man to engage in a referral sales scam at a 20 percent commission. As a result, being furnished with written materials and an incalcuable and incredulous belief in "L" and

* ** See Note 1.

his plans, he went to work on his friends. They, believing in him, were induced to purchase the trust plans at somewhat higher prices. "W" is, in this situation, an agent of "L," however, not in the sense of a co-conspirator as there was no criminal intent on his part. He made all of his representations in good faith, total candor and with an ingenuous lack of research or knowledge. The total sales were approximately $20,000 from five married couples.

An embarrassing situation developed for "L" through the prodigious work done on his behalf by "W." "L" and "O" were jockeyed into contacting a local attorney who happened to be a highly respected expert in estate planning and administration. "L" attempted to bluff his way by stating authoritatively that the representations in his brochures concerning tax advantages and trust tenure were accurate and supported by case law. The attorney refuted his contentions and later, after contact by investigators, appeared as a prosecution witness. His testimony established that the trusts as such were revocable and the estate and inheritance taxes were not avoidable as represented by "L."

An examination of "L's" background, which is a routine function imperatively performed if the investigator is properly carrying out his responsibilities, disclosed "L" two years previously had been a defendant in a similar situation (selling "pure trusts" by false or misleading advertising) which resulted in a permanent injunction enjoining him and others from representing the "pure trusts" would avoid estate and inheritance taxes. This by itself destroyed "L's" contention of belief in the representations he made in instant case. It clearly established the basis of the prosecution's assertion "L" et al had knowledge, intent and the state of mind to misrepresent. "L" brought his co-defendant "D" into the picture by stating the accountant had received an oral opinion from the Internal Revenue Service supporting his representations there would be no taxes because the trust would own the assets not the trustor. "D," however, testified it was all a mistake or misunderstanding as no opinion had been obtained. Whether this was an attempt by "L" to create a defense based upon his ostensible but mistaken belief in an IRS opinion or merely a mealy-mouth maneuver by the co-defendant to protect himself is conjecture. "O" attempted to cover herself with a cloak of immunity by stating she believed "L's" representations to purchasers. She also acknowledged the earlier injunction but said she did not think it applicable to the present situation. Her motives also were unclear.

The issue which more than anything else upheld the lower court conviction in this case was the earlier injunctive process. Notwithstanding the falsity of the representations, the reliance upon them by the victims, the elements of the conspiracy clearly established the fact of "L's" *et al* irrefutable knowledge of their falsity via the injunction could not be denied. This was more than sufficient to impute plan, scheme, pattern and design. This was the requisite specific intent to defraud.

I

Investigation

A criminal inquiry is much the same as a battle. The investigator should create a battle plan. He must develop an estimate of the situation, from that determine the mission. In consideration of this last, its manner of execution (the tactical aspect) must then be decided. Logistics, militarily, is the next consideration followed by the euphemism of Command and Signal. In the investigative analogy the first element meaning support, and the last, coordination and direction.

A Situation

The first information brought to the attention of an agency is usually via a complaint by the victim. The other ways are through informants/sources of information and the active seeking out of violations. This last is most often used by regulatory agencies although not unknown to police departments. Its implementation usually results from an exercise of the second, informants, or general information available in the community.

Frauds, like most crimes, are an after-the-fact reporting situation by the victims. They are aware they have suffered a loss, however, the manner and degree is usually hazy and unclear. This is the result of many factors, not the least of which being embarrassment, lack of knowledge and frequently a high degree of emotionalism. The investigator must be adept at soothing hostile feelings in people he interviews and be able to get them to relate information in step-by-step sequential and logical order. Above all, don't "lead" the victim. Too frequently things said or asked by the investigator can be suggestive to an irritated victim from which he can form rationales and theories that are in no way even remotely related to the actual situation.

During the interview of the victim keep constantly in mind the elements of the crime of false pretenses: (1) the representation, (2) that it is false, (3) that there was the specific intent to defraud, (4) that there was reliance upon the representation, (5) that there was suffered a loss; and relate everything said to this frame of reference.

There are additional factors which also lend themselves to the framework and create one of their own: (a) corroboration, (b) documentation (c) jurisdiction, (d) statute of limitations, (e) witnesses both for direct and circumstantial support, (f) availability of witnesses, (g) suspect's identity and detailed background, (h) suspect's availability (will extradition be a consideration?), (i) similar acts and transactions, (j) the conspiratorial concept with that type of proof peculiar to its nature, (k) technical advice and support, and last but no less important, (l) the possible defenses open to the suspect.

The representations which the case is to be built upon must be very definitively set out; if possible verbatim. Who is the suspect? How was contact made between the parties? In what manner was the representation made; in person, by telephone, by mail, by telegraph or through some other means of communication? What fair import can be put to the words and phrases uttered by the suspect? Is the purported representation in such form as to merely imply a condition or situation which could easily be misconstrued by the victim or is it an unequivocal and definite statement of fact? Is it such that a reasonable person could hear and judiciously act upon in an affirmative manner? Did the representation relate to the issue or some ancillary item with no direct bearing? Were the suspect's statements voluntarily made or were they in response to questions by the victim? Is it a situation in which it is not so much a matter of what was said but in what was not said; a failure to make full disclosures of material facts? Was there anything apart from the actual statements such as conduct by the suspect which could be construed reasonably to infer a valid fact? Was there more than one suspect making representations? If there was, each statement made must be related to the proper individual involved. Was there any conflict in things said between the multiple suspects, and how was it resolved?

Companion questions which must be considered are the day and date, the times and places the representations were made. These too often are presented vaguely by investigators in their reports. They must be covered in the same detail as any other material item. The places or situs must be determined as this has a bearing on jurisdictions and the agencies involved. Is the Statute of Limitations a factor to consider? Has it expired (run) or if not, what time is left for investigation and indictment?

The day of the week, not only the calender date, is important as a way of relating, in pin-point fashion by parties involved, certain incidents associated with the issue. In the same manner, the hour of the day is significant (bank/business operational hours, time and distance factors, etc.). What period of time was covered from inception to termination of the transactions?

Who was present at the contacts between the parties besides the victim and the suspect(s)? What did they hear or observe? In what proximity were they to the negotiations; did they take or have an active part or interest in the proceedings or were they merely disinterested onlookers?

Were the representations in fact false? In what manner can this be established; is it one of degree or unequivocal and complete? Is there a remote possibility of good faith on the part of the suspect? From the falsity of the statements standing alone, can the requisite preconceived specific intent to defraud be established?

The victim must clearly define the degree of reliance he placed in the suspect's statements, not only in the collective representations, but also in each individual purported statement of fact. What was the lapse of time between the offer and actual acceptance? If it were inordinately long the reasons must be clearly set out. The victim's personality, emotional stability and mental alertness are material factors, as is his access to funds; whether or not he availed himself to consultation with others and independent investigation; whether there were any mental reservations held by the victim being overcome by the urgings of unconnected third parties, thus mitigating true reliance. Those with whom he discussed the matter must be identified and what was said determined accurately.

Determine in what manner the money or property was transferred from the victim to the suspect. What was the total amount involved? In what installments if exchanged through more than one contact? In what form; cash, check, draft or other? What was the source of the funds; bank, savings and loan institutions, loan from private parties, private savings? If it involved a loan, what was hypothecated as security and the interest rate? Obtain from the victim all documentation in his possession and that to which he can authorize access.

All of the above questions should be covered as fully as possible. The most prudent act of the investigator is to have it reduced to writing in statement form and attested to by the victim. This lessens, although of course not totally, the possibility of the victim recanting at a later and much more embarrassing time. Make an assessment, tacitly, of the victim's character, personality and reliability. Don't forget, your case is founded upon his reliability. Even when corroboration in the form of documentation and witness testimony is extant, if he falters or fails so does the case.

B   The Mission

At this point you have developed, from the interview of the victim, an overview of what transpired as it appeared to him with all the inborn limitations inherent in a reconstruction by one who was involved. What is your next move? What are you going to do? Obviously you cannot predicate a case upon the unsupported assertions of the victim, notwithstanding the documentation you may have obtained from or through him without further exploration and examinations. Tactically then, to meet the legal requirements of this crime, such as corroboration, you move in that direction. You then develop those things which are included within the definition of the term such as witness testimony, instruments and further documentation. In other words your mission is to prove or disprove that a crime was in fact committed.

C *The Execution*

What is to be done to carry out the mission? What witnesses are to be developed? Naturally those who were identified by the victim are primary targets. They must be interviewed in comparable detail to the effort expended upon the victim. Why were they present at the negotiations? Determine the exact dates, places and times; the situation as a whole. Was it pre-arranged or merely coincidental? What exactly was observed and heard? How does this equate with that related by the victim? If they support the victim, why do they? What affinity exists between them, is it social, family, business or otherwise? If they are not supportive, why aren't they; are there underlying motives or is it honest difference of opinions? What documentation is available through them?

The scope of the inquiry should be widened. Look towards circumstantial support. This requires footwork on the part of the investigator. Work in the inverse order from the initial contact between the victim and the suspect. Trace the latter's paths and activity. What possible and probable witnesses are there in this area and what information can they furnish? Hotel/motel clerks, chamber-maids and house records; car rental agencies, parking lot attendants; airline, bars (bartenders and cocktail waitresses) restaurants (hostesses, waiter and waitresses and their tab books) job printing houses; banks, finance houses, stocks and securities brokers/salesmen; department stores, shopping centers; public records centers; financial and real estate editors and staffs; wholesale and retail outlets related to that which was the subject of the negotiations if appropriate; all of these, although not a totally conclusive list can afford a vast source of information and evidence of probative value concerning the suspect and his operations, his associates, his location at specific times and acts of preparation many of which obviously are unknown to the victim and his "eye-witnesses" to the culminating act. The weight of circumstantial evidence is the same as that of direct. It is pointed to attending circumstances which by inference prove the principal issue in showing a condition, the existence of which is the basis from which the main fact can logically be concluded. Don't ignore this area; a multitude of successfully concluded cases were based almost solely upon circumstantial evidence in the support of a lone witness.

The suspect as an entity must be thoroughly researched. The unmerited reliance upon "rap sheets" or other forms of criminal records as a total source of information is inadequate for effective investigative purposes. The inquiries conducted have to transcend his physical description, place and date of arrest accompanied by an infrequent comment regarding disposition. Develop this individual. Who and what is he? Elsewhere in this text ("Investigative Sources") are listed a number of repositories of information which are invaluable for this purpose. The suspect is your enemy; know him. This is axiomatic. The more you know of him as a person the better prepared you are for the "battle." The affinity which exists between the investigator and the suspect is the same as between two opposing military forces, both attempting to defeat the other. You are trying to prove a crime and bring the person responsible before the court to be held accountable. He is endeavoring to thwart your efforts by every means possible. He has the built-in advantage in that he has no particular set of rules to function by, but you do. By knowing him as an individual you can determine fairly accurately his vulnerable points and these are factors to be exploited whenever possible. What are his weaknesses? Are they social, "booze, broads and bookies" or are they tactical, such as previous unsuccessful scams which drew police attention with a group of witnesses available to you? Are they operational in terms of persons, firms or institutions which he must contact, even legitimately, to create the basis for his activity? Remember, in connection with him you are endeavoring to establish (1) his specific intent to defraud, (2) that he made the representations and (3) it was in fact false.

The probability of a conspiracy is usually present in all situations of major fraud. This neither impedes or enhances the case. It does widen the scope of the investigation to some degree making you accountable for the actions of more than one suspect which must be correlated. However, this is not really a burden as it can be a two-edged sword. All acts of co-conspirators when done in furtherance of the plan become the liability of all involved. The actions of all participants even if secondary members of the group, must be examined in depth. The same admonishment of "know your man" is applicable to these persons also. Frequently an injudicious act by one conspirator while not binding upon the others, opens the door to inquiry that may have been disregarded or unobserved previously. Also, the more persons involved in an operation, the more possibilities there are for mistakes. Further, all persons do not have the same strength of character (or more accurately perhaps, disregard of social needs, mores and customs) thus one of the suspects may be weak and vulnerable to the slightest indication of pressure such as police interest. This should be searched for and exploited.

Further consideration, from a very practical standpoint, is that of the suspect's availability. Is he, or are they, within the jurisdiction of the court? If not, will extradition be a factor? Or, as frequently happens, have they disappeared bringing the case to a halt after issuance of a complaint or return of indictment? Many good cases have been virtually destroyed due to an inordinate but unavoidable lapse of time between investigation and trial. If the time period is brief usually the victims and witnesses are psyched or geared up to performance level with their interest running well. They may have even allotted an expected time period in their own schedules for the trial. However, with each succeeding delay their interest weakens and their memory of events dims. This is usually accompanied by a lessening of indignation on the part of the victims and frequently loss of evidence or a lessening of its availability or diminution of its value.

Obviously similar acts and transactions more than any single element establish the requisite specific intent to defraud by disclosing a preconceived general pattern of conduct, scheme, plan and design. In developing this collateral issue don't rely upon the rap-sheet as the sole source. Each known similar act, whether charged or not formally, must be examined in detail the same as the case in chief. Approach each one as a separate but complete inquiry. These are determined by knowing the suspect and his previous areas of operations. If there is an arrest indicated on the rap-sheet obtain the case report, his booking-sheet and if a trial was held, the transcript from the clerk of the court. Analyze it for similarities to your case. Talk with the officers and prosecutors for data that is not indicated in the written reports or trial transcript. This frequently is more informative than the record in the way of investigative leads. Ascertain who else may have been involved with the suspect in past acts. They often turn up again and again. This is supportive of the conspiracy angles. The transactions, ways or manner of performance of functions related to the specific acts, are developed in the same way as the acts themselves and should be related in the same detail. Remember, you are not limited to acts and transactions of prior dates and times, but you can and should develop those which are contemporaneous with, or subsequent to, your case. All are admissable.

D The Support

To follow the military analogy still further you will need sources of support. Logistics is the nominal term. However, for investigation consider it in the light of technical or expert assistance or support. This, for instance, can encompass help from such as a master carpenter if structures are an integral part of the inquiry. Think for a moment of the varied technical trades involved in just building a house. Besides the carpenter, there are electricians, plumbers, lathers, roofers, cement masons, brick masons, glazers to name some of the normal group. The sale of a house, notwithstanding its prosaic nature, can and often is the item involved in a theft by false pretenses. Residential land tracts are not unknown in fraudulent sales schemes. Envision a situation in which a series of new homes have been sold at relatively high prices because of their beauty and strong construction coupled with the purported exclusiveness of the new neighborhood. The next thing to follow is disenchantment of the new owner-occupants, not because of the loss of snob appeal of the location, but upon their finding the beautiful walls are cracked and settling rapidly, doors and windows become jammed, plumbing fixtures fail to function, roofing leaks at the first sign of a cloud and the floors sag. The value of the houses dropped commensurately with every new structural fault observed. This, then is a severe financial loss to the purchaser-owner who gave over his money to the seller based upon the implied and stated warranty of fitness (This set of facts is the basis of a 1971 California case of magnitude which resulted in the conviction for grand theft by false pretenses of the promoters and builders). To establish a valid case of theft, a uniform preconceived plan, scheme and design to willfully misrepresent the value and the fitness of the structures sold will have to be shown. In such a situation the investigator must demonstrate clearly that substandard materials were knowingly used for the purpose of defrauding (ungraded lumber, improper plaster, cement and concrete mixtures, improper wiring and piping, etc.). To do this, unless he has a building contractor's background, he needs specialized support. Anticipate such a situation (Estimate of the Situation -supra) and prepare for it by lining up the needed expertise. What is related here in connection with a simple housing fraud must be considered in any investigation in which there will be a need for specialized support. Don't avoid the issue, act upon it promptly.

E   Coordination and Direction

The military euphemisim, Command and Signal, basically means who commands/directs the operation, his location and related matters and the communication base. For investigative analogy look upon it as who is going to control the investigation, his scope of authority and responsibility. There must be one single individual, in other words the cardinal rule of any operation, unity of command and one boss with the ultimate responsibility. Any time there developes a bifurcated approach, with duplication of direction (more accurately, misdirection) the efforts become confused and coordination becomes a lost dream. Do not allow this to happen. If you value your case and have respect for your purpose, don't permit a self-defeating approach rule you; there can be only one boss in an investigation. There can be delegation of authority and limited responsibility but final accountability has to lie with one person; he who controls. A new concept, relatively speaking, has been developed which is proving a valuable tool for criminal investigation. Its inception was in 1958 with the construction of the Polaris submarine; P.E.R.T., the acronym for Program Evaluation and Review Techniques. It is not an investigation method, but rather an administrative device which facilitates the coordination needed in major cases with multiple and diverse issues to be resolved, large numbers of witnesses and evidentiary matter to be developed and several investigative and support personnel to be controlled and directed. The method has found success within industry and also is used to great advantage in the military. There is no reason it cannot be applied, with modification, to criminal investigation. P.E.R.T. does not make decisions; it only assists in the decision-making process. It is a planning, scheduling, analysis technique using graphic display (a "network") which in effect will disclose "where you were, where you are and where you should be headed and the things done, doing and to be done to get there." As a tool for planning it forces you to plan and cut to a minimum the omissions usually experienced in most planning efforts. A recognized authority on P.E.R.T. and its application to police administrative problems initially and later to major criminal investigations (Sirhan-Kennedy case; Manson Family case) is Sgt. Gilbert J. Burgoyne who retired in 1972 from the Los Angeles Police Department after thirty years service, more than eight of which were with the Detective Bureau. In his assignment in that department's Research and Planning Division he was called upon to study the impact of the P.E.R.T. theory and was later given the opportunity to implement it in major cases such as those indicated.

The advantages of P.E.R.T. are obvious; it shows relationships; it assures more effective planning; it pinpoints problem areas; it improves communication; it permits the proper planning of resource allocation; it discloses alternative courses of action open to the investigator.

The "network" of P.E.R.T. is a diagram of "events" and "activities." A task or job is called an "activity" which in effect consumes time to get from one "event" to another. The "activity" is represented by a line to show the direction it is going. The "activity" line is identified by either letters or numbers. The start and finish of an "activity" is the "event" which is shown on the chart ("network") by a geometric sign. The "events" are numbered in sequence. An "activity" is always completed before moving on to the next one. The length of the line is of no real significance.

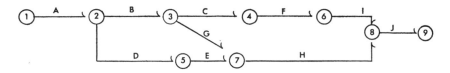

In Sergeant Burgoyne's words lies a simplistic but probably the better description of P.E.R.T.; "– – – – is like a map; once the route is drawn progress can more easily be followed against a check list of keypoints – – – – –. It forces logical thought and compels planning and the recognition of relationships of the parts to the whole. It is management by exception – – –. It serves as a management decision-making guide, it is flexible, it is versatile." Further, "– – – is a tool, a guide, a picture of a project. Applied in its proper perspective, to a proper situation, it can be a great help. P.E.R.T. does not replace good judgment but relies upon good judgment to be an effective tool."

Space and purpose of this book does not permit a complete examination of the P.E.R.T. method. Suffice to say that it is a logical device to use in a complicated case with divers activities being performed. It is not restricted to homicide but can be applicable to any type of criminal investigation. Ample material is available to anyone who wishes to study the theory. The opportunity is there, if it can be useful don't ignore it. Take advantage of anything which is functional and is legal.

DIVISION B

TRICK AND DEVICE (BUNCO)

The Keyword

Fraudulent practices over the years have become so sophisticated and varied with the social and technical developments in commerce and industry that the term "bunco," which was all-inclusive in its original usage, now normally is applied to what is euphemistically called the "short Con" or the "street con;" descriptive of the fast-moving, short-duration, high mobility operation with a commensurately smaller take but with a higher frequency rate. The schemes, when viewed in retrospect, more often than not appear ridiculous and crude, suggesting the victims have less than normal mental development. But, this is not always the situation. People from all levels of society have been, are, and will be taken by the "bunco." In some cases the victim's avarice will play a part, in others naiveté, stupidity or misunderstanding. Whatever the reason, the con-man has developed the groundwork upon which the "confidence" of the victim has been built. This is the key word. The "con-man," "artist," "bunco" or regardless of what term is used, works for one basic thing only, create the feeling of rapport and "confidence" between himself and the victim.

Practical Psychologists

To build the "con," the artist prepares himself by a thorough study of the type of person he intends to work on. This includes

---

* Trust Indenture: An instrument which states the terms and conditions of a trust.

** Peo vs Lynam, 68 Cal Rptr 202.

an understanding of the victim's character, personality, educational level, social and vocational backgrounds. He becomes adept at assimilating all the surface manifestations of these elements enabling him to present an acceptable appearance. He speaks knowingly in the vernacular of the victim or of the person whose characteristics he is assuming, but conversely, can assume a different pose if the expediency of the scam requires such an approach. But, endemic to all frauds, whether "buncos" or major operations, he is a salesman and by autosuggestion he develops in the mind of the victim the desire or impulse to buy. He is a consumate artist in the use of verbiage and even physical props to create an aura of suspense, expectation and desire into which the victim will move, running the gamut of reactions from tranquillity to excitement. The things that are said and done during this period seem to be so logical at the time because of the emotional buildup in the victim which is cleverly (from training and practice) engineered by the artist. It even becomes difficult for many to accept the idea of having been "conned" for a long time after the *fait accompli*. This not infrequently causes victims to be taken more than once by the same trick and device, and even by the same artist.

There are no geographical limitations involved in buncos. There are only variations to fit into the exigency of the moment, place and type of victim. There are as many ideas to "con" as there are people to think of them. For years many scams were ethnically oriented with certain racial overtones present. Thus, till-taps, short-change scams and the "pigeon-drop" was associated with the Negro; "switch-games were attached to the Mexican; "coin-smacks" to the Canadian, Australian or English; "fortune-telling" to the Gypsies, and "charity" scams to the Italians to name but a few. This actually is no longer believed to be correct. Granted, there may be certain racial characteristics which lend themselves to particular schemes, either as victim or con-artist, but our rapidly changing society has, through communication, transportation, education and social contact, broken down many of the older barriers and what was once fairly accurately attributable to a certain group now is practiced by all in variegated forms.

The Structured Approach

The classic bunco has two or more operators and four basic parts. The initial step or part is for the "bird-dog" or "steerer" to select a likely victim or mark and arrange to meet him by some devious means after a period of study. The confidence is developed at this time and information gleaned as to his finances. The next part is the introduction in some manner to the second con-man who continues to build upon this confidence and lay the groundwork for meeting with the third con-man (if one is used) who is the "big-shot," "BTO" or some other such title, from whom all blessings and rewards will flow if the victim will take part in the proposed scheme. The fourth segment or part is the pay-off during which the victim gives over his money or property, followed quickly by the con-men getting rid of him, usually by leaving him standing alone in a very confused frame of mind. If only two con-men are involved, parts two and three are merged. The theft is then concealed through the use of a "cool-off" which can be a promise to return part or all of the funds taken, the inherent fear of exposure to possible prosecution of the victim for having taken part in some questionable activity, embarrassment and even, all to frequently, the futility of reporting the circumstances to a police agency.

Legal Principles

Basically, the legal concept involved in a bunco within the present construction put to the term, is theft by trick and device; the victim did not intend to relinquish title to his property but only possession, giving it over to the con-men to be used for a specific purpose such as a loan, investment, purchases or other similar reason, but the con-men had no intention of putting it to such use, intending from the outset to steal it or divert it to their own use (*People vs Lafka,* 174 Cal App 2nd 312). There is usually no requirement here, as there is with theft by false pretenses, of corroboration. The difference between the two types of theft as covered in earlier chapters is that the trick and device theory can be proved by direct testimony of the victim or by evidence concerning the circumstances under which the money or property was delivered to the con-men (People vs Beilfuss, 59 Cal App 2nd 83). There is, however, still the need to establish a misrepresentation by the con-men, a reliance thereon by the victim and a handing over of the money or property upon this reliance.

The Investigation

The investigative approach to a bunco case is, although the "false token or writing" requirement (or two witnesses or one witness and corroborating circumstance) is absent, essentially the same as with the other forms of theft by fraud. The victim must relate step by step in proper sequence and time intervals, the statements and actions of each person involved. This does not mean just from the moment of first contact with the con-men, but a good resume' of his activities for a logical period of time preceding that act, to determine why, where, when and possibly by whom and how he was settled on as a "mark." This will require good accurate descriptive information of the con-men to be developed from the victim at the outset, thus permitting the investigator to place these individuals through unrelated witnesses at particular locations together prior to their approach to the victim. Such evidence is material in supporting allegations of conspiracy, pattern, scheme and design.

The misrepresentations by the con-men can be in the form of statements or such acts which would lead a reasonable person to put certain definitive connotations that would induce him to take part in a joint venture. These are proved by circumstances and the victim's testimony (supra). Every action by the victim in response to the con-men must be documented wherever possible such as withdrawal of savings from a bank, betting slips, promissory notes, hotel or motel registrations, air or train passage tickets, etc. This should in turn be supported by other witnesses who can place all participants together, regardless of purpose; waitresses, bell-hops, room clerks, taxi drivers, shopkeepers, stewardesses, conductors, car rental agencies, news vendors, bartenders, bar patrons, bank tellers, bank guards; anyone who can place them together or at least in close enough proximity so as to infer logically some type of relationship.

Here again the investigator must establish similar acts or transactions, whether *before or after* the case in chief. Evidence of other activity of a similar nature may be admitted as evidence when *not too remote,* to prove a material fact, or when they tend to show motive, scheme, plan or system (*People vs Darnell,* 97 Cal App 2nd 630). This is done routinely via inquiries with other police agencies, CII and the FBI. If such a record is turned up he must obtain the case report which reflects the *modus operandi* adhered to on other occasions, transportation used and the identities of those involved. Arrest records and booking sheets of themselves can prove useful to show residences, employment, if any, nearest of kin or close associates and areas of operations. The only problem developing in recent years is the influx of amateurs or part-time con-artists into the field, many without prior records. However, they are usually inept and soon have a record which can be used to advantage by the investigator. But, until their initial drop identity becomes a real problem. The "freeways," high speed automobiles and raised speed limits permit mobility which was undreamed of ten, even five, years ago, notwithstanding air travel. It can be safely estimated that for every minute that passes after the victim is finally and irrevocably relieved of his money, the con-men can be one mile away; with a half-hour's time they have gone easily thirty miles. They know this as well as law enforcement agencies know it. The sharper ones do not remain long in an area after the hit. The inquiry then becomes one of gathering material and tracking them down when notification or inquiries from other agencies comes in concerning new scams.

Prevention. An Illusion

Preventive measures, like many other similar concepts in law enforcement, are doomed to failure. Educational programs for the public, formalized or not, seldom achieve their goals. Human nature being what it is, with all the desires and weaknesses, regardless of the other possible strengths, has not changed. There will always be that certain percentage of the group which will succumb to the blandishments of their sharper brethren, either through personal greed, unrequited dreams of success, outsized do-good complexes, overwhelming credulity or just plain stupidity. There is a further complication. The idea of aggressive law enforcement has always appealed to the police and a large segment of the more responsible citizenry; they believed it is better to prevent a crime with its manifold harm than to detect it afterwards. However, the courts and the numerous commissions and committees created by the Federal and State executives and legislatures, and most of which are inordinately sociologically oriented towards the superiority of the individual's rights, as opposed to the group's, have all but eliminated this approach to any police problem. The theories extant with these law and policy making or interpreting bodies have created a need for new approaches and techniques concerning the questions of search and seizure and suspect confrontations. This need is yet to be met satisfactorily. The day is gone when the mere presence or omnipresence of a policeman prevented the commission of a crime. The citizen and the thief is all too familiar with the limitations now imposed upon the investigator. And, it is not possible to keep all the buncos under surveillance until they commit an offense. Besides, this would be a violation of their constitutional right to privacy. They would have no problem in most courts in obtaining an injunctive process to prevent such police activity. This condition, whether a temporary one or perhaps becoming even more restrictive, however, does not do away with the investigator's imperative need to know the individuals operating in the bunco field and the methods they employ. He cannot possibly conduct a proper inquiry without such knowledge and it also necessitates his maintaining reliable sources within that area to keep him informed *before* the fact. Not, as unhappily is the norm, receiving the tip from a so-called informant after the hit is made and the buncos have departed.

The Switches

The "switch" buncos are basically the same although identified and described by a number of names such as the "Jamaican" or the "Mexican" and sometimes by the item or instrumentality of the crime which, in the course of events, is switched. This item can be an envelope filled with money and another identical in appearance filled with play-money or paper cut to billnote size, a handkerchief, package, bundle with exact duplicates, all to be used as substitutes for the real item when the victim's attention is directed elsewhere at the propitious time.

The so-called "Jamaican" switch is normally limited in this context to seaport cities with a large merchant marine activity. It consists of two male Negroes, one playing the part of a Jamaican seaman complete with an "English" or "Spanish" accent and appropriately dressed and "just off a ship docked in the harbor," the other posing as what he is, a local American Negro. The victim can be either Negro or Caucasian. The seaman approaches the victim on the street or some other convenient place (for the con-men) asking for directions to some non-existent hotel or address. The American Negro just happens to be passing by at this time and the seaman asks the victim, who was unable to assist him, to inquire with the American Negro concerning the hotel. The victim normally assents and does call out to the American who then walks over to the first two. At this time the seaman asks the American the location of the hotel saying that he is to meet a girl there for the usual purpose and in which he already invested forty dollars as down payment on an evening of fun and frolic. He then discloses a large "Oklahoma bankroll" and continues his chatter of anticipated erotic enjoyment. The American admonishes the seaman about carrying about with him such a large amount of money advising him to place it in a bank before he is mugged and rolled. This brings out a retort from the seaman to the effect the United States is a bigoted, racist, imperialistic country run by pigs and besides no bank in such a land would do business with a Negro; the bank would allow him to put his money in but it certainly wouldn't allow him to draw it out afterwards. Furthermore, he had all this on good authority from his boatswain and second officer aboard the ship, both of whom had been in this country before.

These statements, as brash as they are, of course puts the victim immediately on the defensive, he rushes into the fray by asserting the error of the seaman's conception of this country and usually before this part of the confrontation is completed has disclosed his own bank and the current balance of his account there. The seaman then wagers him a large amount of money that he cannot make a withdrawal. This bet of course is covered (if the victim is a Negro his reactions are based upon his personal dignity of a black American who enjoys every right of the white; if the victim is Caucasian the reaction is one entirely of defense as the seaman would have alleged that regardless of his being white, the bankers are all crooked and would not honor his right to withdrawal) and all three go to his bank where he makes a sizeable withdrawal and presents it to the seaman who then acknowledges his error.

At this point in the operation the seaman produces an envelope into which he places the amount of his wager, but just before giving it over to the victim he demands to examine the victim's withdrawn funds to make sure they are real. While he examines each bill he places it in the envelope containing his own money which is ostensibly to be given to the victim as his winnings. The American now diverts the victim's attention and the switch is made at this moment, a second envelope of identical appearance containing cut paper is substituted. The victim returns his attention to the seaman who immediately hands him the new envelope. The American then urges the victim to go back into the bank and redeposit his funds and the winnings as it is not safe on the streets. The happy victim responds with alacrity, before he even reaches a teller's cage the seaman and the American are long gone with his funds.

There are endless variations of each facet of this scam but they all evolve into the one basic move; the switch. If the victim happens to be, as indicated above he can be, a Negro he is psychologically forced into showing he is just as good as any white person and can do the same things with no restrictions. Often, if he appears somewhat larcenous himself, the American will tell him the seaman is an ignorant fool and is going to lose his money anyway to either the intended nocturnal companion or someone else equally as unprincipled, so why shouldn't they (the victim and the American) take a cut from the to be lost bankroll before the others by the victim betting he can make withdrawals from his bank.

Although the "Jamaican" caper is of ancient vintage it is still used to take even educated people. The following is a teletype message from the northern California area in late 1968: "Jamaican switch—Suspect "1 MNA, 27, 5'5", 130 Jamaican accent #2 MNA, 50, 6'1", 180, greying hair; Victim, MNA 57 yrs School Teacher; M/O Classic Jamaican Switch. Suspect #1 approached victim in a department store and asked for help to find a place to stay. After conversation Suspect #2 comes up and suggests both he and the victim could help Suspect #1. All three drive in victim's car to a rooming house area. It is suggested victim hold Suspect #1's money and his own which was to be paid to one or the other as a result of a bet concerning bank withdrawals later. It is decided that the money should be tied in a handkerchief and placed in the trunk of the victim's car. The Suspects both go into a large rooming house after placing the item in the car trunk for the Victim. After period of time Victim examines trunk and finds handkerchief containing paper."

The "Latin Charity" switch is practiced throughout the southwest where there are large areas with Mexican and Latin-American population. The Spanish language is invariably used by all participants, thus promoting the kinsmanship between them. The action is again fairly static as with all switch scams. The victim is approached by a Spanish appearing and speaking individual who usually asks directions to some fictitious person. Also at this point in time the second operator happens to be in close proximity and overhears the questions, joins in the conversation with the first operator and the victim ostensibly trying to help in determining the location and identity of the fictitious person being sought.

During the ensuing conversation the first operator reveals to his helpers that he is on a mission of grave importance to his family in Mexico (Panama, Chile, Guatamala, etc.). He says his sainted father is about to pass into the world of lingering darkness from an equally described illness and as a consequence of the family's Catholicity the sacrament of extreme unction was to be given. However, the great tragedy is that his father, during his gasping confession to his parish priest, revealed he had been in "this" city many years before and became involved because of bad companions in the theft of ten thousand dollars, returning to Mexico shortly thereafter escaping arrest. The priest, so the first operator/dutiful son avers, refuses to grant absolution

for the dying man's sins because of the commandment regarding theft, although broken many years ago, had never been
confessed nor penance done, thus all subsequent confessions concerning later sins were rendered false placing him in jeopardy
of mortal sin. He goes on to say the priest called upon the dying
man (who now is very wealthy) to have the same amount of
money returned to "this" city and distributed to charity; once
this being accomplished, absolution for his manifold transgressions would be granted. His failing progenitor then instructed
that he (the operator) come to "this" city in the United States,
seek out the "old friend" (fictitious person) and gain his assistance in making the charitable distribution.

The first operator at this time displays a large amount of
money indicating that it is the ten-thousand dollars he is to distribute. He then asks the victim and the second operator to
assist him in the distribution as time is of the essance and his
search for the illusive fictitious person has proven, after "X" number of days, unfruitful and he must return shortly to his home
to inform the priest of the success of his mission in time enough
to permit the last sacraments be given to his father. The victim
by this time is overcome with emotion at this sad tale of heartbreak and practically insists that he be allowed to help in such
a mission. The first operator then tells the victim and the second
operator that if they can show him they have money of their
own which to him would indicate they are responsible, knowledgeable and honest persons who would not be tempted to take
his ten-thousand dollars, he will turn all of his funds over to
them for the charitable act. The second operator tells both of
them to wait a few minutes for his return. He does shortly and
displays a large amount of authentic appearing bills. This satisfies the first operator. Both operators then turn to the victim ex-
pectantly, asking if he will also obtain some funds to show his
good faith. He agrees, one of the operators accompanying him
to the bank, or whatever place he deposits or hides his money
and returning with him (to assure he will not wander away or
cool-off towards the scam) to the first operator who is waiting
patiently.

Now it is determined that such a venture should receive the
sustenance which can only be obtained from a prayerful session

in a Catholic Church (keeping the victim, of course, away from the rectory or parish house out of reach of a priest although there are cases in which they too have been conned in the same way). Upon going inside and approaching the altar rail in union, the first operator takes the second operator's and the victim's funds and places along with his own in a sack obviously very tightly closed and tied together. All three then assume a position on their knees in a righteous prayerful attitude at the altar rail, or even occasionally a pew. While the victim is communing with God the switch takes place, substituting an identical appearing sack or bag. The victim, after the session is over, is handed the substituted sack by the first operator who effusively thanks him for his kindness and assistance and then turns to the second operator asking him for a ride to the airport for his trip home to daddy. They both depart, telling the victim the second operator will contact him for the distribution upon his return from the airport. They leave, the victim opens the bag and there is the cut paper.

The "Latin Charity" bunco, like the previously described "Jamaican" is still used although somewhat hoary with age. The operators can also be female or even a combination of the sexes. A teletype message emanating out of the Los Angeles area in late 1967 disclosed the arrest of a Nicaraguan female and the search for her Latin male accomplice who had attempted to work the scam on a Mexican female who apparently was little too perceiving for their success. The female operator when arrested had in her possession a bankroll of one hundred Nicaraguan "Un Cordoba" bills with a few United States one-hundred dollar bills wrapped around the outside. They attempted to obtain five-thousand dollars from the intended mark if she could produce that amount of cash to establish her "responsibility." An amount of fifteen-hundred dollars was to be given to her to distribute to charity when she satisfied this requirement. Other than this alteration in the approach everything else was the same.

The Drop

The "Pigeon Drop" is another classic. The operators are usually female of Negro, American or Mexican extraction. The victims are normally females, elderly and often Caucasian. The first operator directs the attention of the victim to the second operator nearby who appears to be picking up a package (or wallet etc.) from the sidewalk, street or even a department store aisle, in fact any place convenient for their purpose. The first operator calls out to the second operator that both the victim and her saw the package, and indicating there should be a division of the contents if the owner cannot be found, as they were about to pick it up also. Operator #2 assents, opening it, and there for all to see is about three-thousand dollars in bills of large denomination, a series of pornographic photos and perhaps even some betting markers. A discussion then takes place, the victim more often than not suggesting it should be turned over to the police to find the rightful owner. This idea gently but firmly is discouraged usually by inferences of police corruption and other such remarks. The first operator then states to the others that they can obtain the proper advice from her employer nearby who is a very knowledgeable and trustworthy man. The victim agrees as it is pointed out to her that the person who lost the package is undoubtedly a bad individual because of the illicit items which were with the money and no real consideration should be given to a person of that nature, and even further he probably wouldn't go to the police to reclaim it anyway because of the terribly filthy pictures. The second female then manifests a sudden impulse of trust in the first female operator and gives over to her the package, who in turn requests the victim and operator #2 to accompany her to a nearby office building where she purportedly is employed.

The first operator then goes into the building, after indicating to #2 and the victim that employees only are permitted entrance due to security restrictions or some other logically sounding reason. They dutifully wait outside. Operator #1 returns shortly saying her employer suggested the money should be divided evenly between all three as long as they observed it simultaneously, but each should prove financial responsibility by showing she (each one) could put up one-thousand to cover the individual share. The second operator at this point flashes a roll purporting to be in excess of one-thousand dollars, gives to #1 who takes it into the building. She presently returns and gives to

#2 an envelope purportedly containing her bankroll and one-thousand dollars, her one-third share of the found package money. The first operator also has in her hand a second envelope said to contain another one-thousand dollars, the victim's one-third share.

When seeing this, the victim is easily induced to go and obtain her one-thousand dollars good faith money. Transportation is supplied by the operators. When she makes her withdrawal from the bank or from under a mattress (even a buried can) all return to the vicinity of the first operator's place of employment. #1 then takes the victim's funds for the purpose of examination by her employer. After a period of time the second operator grows restive and leaves the victim to hunt for #1. The victim waits for a longer period and then goes home knowing she has been taken.

The "Pigeon" has its varieties also and has been known to be merged with the "switch." This is accomplished when the victim has given over her funds to the first operator, and it is counted in her presence, then placed in an envelope ostensibly containing her one-third share in the found money. Her attention is momentarily diverted, the envelopes switched, both parties immediately departing after effusive farewells in opposite directions. The victim comes down from her cloud-ride, looks into the envelope for assurance and then lets out a shriek of disbelief. Cut paper is not very reassuring. This scam, as with the "switches," appears frequently. All-points bulletins indicate this all too often.

An interesting case developed in 1968 in a city located in Orange County involving the "Pigeon." In this situation the victim was an elderly female caucasian, operator #1 a female Negro and #2 a female Caucasian. The approach was made in a department store and contemporary situations were used as the framework upon which the scam was built.

Operator #2 approached the victim and asked "Are you Mrs. Dupree?" The victim responded negatively, #2 then saying that was the name of a teacher she had in Kansas while in high school and the victim looked exactly like her. A conversational topic was then created for mutual discussion. Operator #2 then informs the victim that she is a recent widow, her husband having been killed in Viet Nam about seven months previously, and she had just received four-thousand eight-hundred dollars insurance indemnity and was puzzled why she had not received the whole ten-thousand dollars as is normal in such situations. She then reached into her handbag and extracted a large roll of bills, saying "I have the forty-eight hundred dollars here." She went on to tell the victim that she attempted to deposit the money in the bank but that institution wanted a five percent deposit fee. She then asked the victim whether or not she had an account at the bank to which the latter said she did. This was followed by #2 asking the victim to accompany her to the bank and find out why such a fee was demanded. The victim complied and a lively discussion was maintained enroute concerning the indignities women who are alone in the world must suffer.

Enroute they were stopped by operator #1 who asked them what the "Zip Code" number was of the area, saying she had just found an envelope upon which was written the numbers "934." Operator #2 then took the envelope from the other operator, opened it revealing a note and another smaller envelope. The note had the sentences written, "Joe, here is your $20,000. Your share in the horse race. Be careful of the tax men, no tax has been paid." Operator #1 stated she worked across the street for an attorney and said for the victim and #2 to wait for her while she contacted him to see what should or could be done with the money. She returned a short while later telling them her employer would pay the proper tax for them which amounted to two-thousand dollars and deduct it from the total amount leaving eighteen-thousand dollars to be divided between the three women.

Operator #1 asked the victim if she had a safe deposit box with money as her employer, the attorney, wanted the serial numbers of her bills "to cover the twenty-thousand dollar bills serial numbers." The victim and operator #2 then went to the former's bank and opened a safety deposit box containing approximately eleven-thousand dollars removed it and returned to the shopping area where they had left operator #1. The victim handed over to #1 the money to be given to the latter's employer to record the serial numbers. Operator #1 departed and then returned in about ten minutes saying that the attorney was in a conference with a client so the money was placed in his office safe and would be counted and recorded in about an hour or so and the victim should go there and collect her share as should operator #2. This was agreed upon and they parted agreeing to meet at the office at the stated time. Victim did go to the office as arranged (operator #1 having used the name of an actual lawyer occupying offices in the building) and found to her chagrin the attorney was totally unaware of the situation and had no employee such as described by the victim. He gently informed her of the true circumstances.

The "Pigeon" operators ply their trade for all the traffic will bear. Even small amounts, in a comparative sense, are not overlooked if the mark is an easy one. One such scam was worked in a central California city about five months prior to the one described above. In the early afternoon hours an elderly European born naturalized American citizen who spoke broken English was approached on the street by a male Negro who asked directions. While she was trying to help him a female Negro came up to them displaying a large amount of bills which she said was counted out to be twenty-one thousand dollars and which she had just found along with a note that indicated the money was gambling winnings from Nevada. Again there was the usual discussion as to what should be done, it finally being decided that the female Negro should consult her employer, an attorney, nearby who would properly advise them. The female operator departed and entered a building returning in about five minutes saying she was instructed to share the money with the victim and the other operator if both would have sufficient funds to live on for a period of time.

The victim was then driven to her home where she got her bank passbook which reflected a balance of nine-hundred dollars. She was driven to the bank where she made a withdrawal of the entire amount. The two operators remained in the automobile. She returned shortly with her funds which had been placed in a red colored plastic holder. The operators seeing this, demanded she obtain a white envelope for the money as the attorney liked it better that way. She did not have one so the male negro operator furnished one with her handing him the money to place it in the envelope. He returned it to her at that time, the female having diverted her attention momentarily. She was driven then to the "attorney's office" and instructed to take the envelope to him for examination at which time she would receive her share. She alighted from the car and entered the building and after wandering about aimlessly for a period of time she was informed by a real employee of an office she entered that no such attorney was located there. The police were notified and again it was found a person who can least afford such a loss had been taken.

The Dishonest Bank Employee

The "embezzling bank employee" is a scam that has come into its own in recent years on the west coast from Seattle to San Diego. A good example of such a bunco was related in a teletype from a northern California city during the early summer of 1970. An elderly Negro couple were contacted one morning at their home by telephone by a man telling the husband that he was Mr. Williams and an officer at their bank and required their assistance to apprehend an employee of the bank who had embezzled fifty thousand dollars and that there was already another employee who had been arrested for the same crime. Mr. Williams went to say that some of the money stolen had been taken from their account. He informed them of what "had been the correct balance," however it now contained only four-thousand dollars. He asked the victims to go to the bank and withdraw six thousand dollars which would force the dishonest employee to take the extra two thousand dollars from another account at which time he would be caught in the act of stealing to cover the existing shortage.

Mr. Williams further instructed the victims to obtain the money in the largest denomination bills possible, seal them in an envelope and that a detective would contact them later at their home and pick up the money. He cautioned the victims to make the detective upon arrival identify himself before letting him in the house and that his name was Carter. The victims acted upon those official sounding instructions and went to the bank withdrawing six-thousand dollars, in four one-thousand dollar bills and twenty one-hundred dollar bills. They went directly home where they received a second call from Mr. Williams and while engaged in a conversation with him a man came to the front door of the house and identified himself as Detective Carter displaying a gold badge in a leather folder which also contained a card which stated the bearer was a bank investigator. The victim then informed Williams that the detective was just entering the house at that time. Williams told him to place Carter on the telephone as he wanted to talk to him and be sure he was in fact Carter whom he had sent there. The telephone was then handed to Carter and a brief conversation ensued.

Upon the completion of the telephone conversation between the two detectives the victims asked Carter where he had parked his car and he informed them that when on such an assignment he was not allowed to park his vehicle in front of a house because it so often arouses the suspicions of neighbors. The victims then gave over to him the envelope containing the money which he did not bother to open and count or examine in any manner and then bid them goodbye leaving the premises and area on foot. The husband about this time was becoming somewhat questioning in his mind as to the authenticity of the deal and attempted to follow Carter but lost him at the first corner he turned and did not see any automobile. Upon returning home he received another telephone call from the ellusive Mr. Williams who told him that Carter was back in the bank returning the money to his account. Williams then thanked the victims for their valuable assistance and said the bank manager would be at their home the following Friday with their new bank book showing the correct balance plus a two-hundred dollar bonus for the help they rendered in catching the embezzler. Friday came and went and the bank book reflected the same reduced balance it had since their withdrawal. The manager did not show up either even to pay a courtesy call.

The "Shakes"

There is a related group of scams of particular viciousness which has affected many hapless people in different levels of society and based more than not upon their own weakness and personality defects. These are the "fruit shakes," "abortion shakes" and the "phony cop routine." All are variations of the old "badger game" of antiquity. They would seem to fall more in the area of extortion, "– – – obtaining the property from another, *with* his consent – – – – induced by a wrongful use of force or fear, *or* under *color* of official right" (Sec 518 Penal Code). Further, "Any person *other* than one who by law is given the authority of a peace officer, or uses the authorized badge – – – – – – or who willfully wears, exhibits, or uses – – – badge – – – which falsely purports to be authorized – – – as would deceive an ordinary reasonable person – – – is guilty of a misdemeanor" (Sec 538d Penal Code).

In the early part of the 1960s decade there developed some startling refinements to the mundane old "fruit" or homosexual shakedown by bogus policemen. The con-men, or phony policemen, looked, talked, acted and dressed like the prototype "police detective" so dear to the hearts of writers and readers of pulp fiction. They were conversant with the terminology and vernacular of police work and had a tremendous working knowledge of police procedures and policies. They were equipped with legitimate appearing identification in the form of badges and credentials complete with their photographs (see exemplar). They were thoroughly familiar with the geography of the area in which they operated even unto the layout and floor plan of the police station and courthouse buildings. There was another element in their disguise which is endemic to all good con-men; their prepossessing self-confidence. They were so competent from practice and study of their roles that even police officers had been duped on occasions when talking with them. They were consumate actors with the social instincts of alley-cats. The scams proved so successful that they proliferated and were found to be implemented by a number of groups all over the country, all uniformly equipped with the necessary props and personalities to assure continued success.

In one approach the "cops" used a deviate of their own as bait to work on a selected victim who manifested such inclinations. The victim would be enticed to accompany him to some secluded rendezvous where erotic delights of a new concept of sexual behavior were to be experienced. This of course takes place under the watchful eyes of the two bogus "cops." When the victim is satisfactorily ensconced in a compromising position and from which he can not readily extricate himself, the "cops" appear like magic on the scene and arrest both the passive and active parties. The deviate immediately begins to wail and moan, pleading in his falsetto for his freedom which is peremptorily denied and unceremoniously carted off ostensibly to jail. The victim is told by one of the "cops," the fatherly appearing one, that the deviate is well-known to him and his partner (this being no lie) and has a lengthy record for similar sex offenses; but, the victim, from his demeanor and appearance, obviously is not of this type so he will be released. He is given, at this juncture, a sincere and fitting admonishment concerning such activities. During the course of the confrontation the victim is thoroughly frightened at his own near miss and he reveals much personal information asked for by the arresting officers. He, upon calming down, realizes an arrest on such a charge would bring about his social, professional and financial ruin. He accepts readily, in his embarrassment, the kindly officer's caution and release; an intolerable burden has been lifted from him, a feeling of relief engulfs him and he departs.

Four or five days later when he has shaken off the feelings of remorse, shame and fear and assumed his daily routine he is contacted by the "cops" who tell him in a saddened voice that a problem has developed over his brief detention and the arrest of the deviate. It seems the latter has a high priced attorney who is demanding to know why the other party to a two-party offense was not arrested and that the District Attorney was forced to issue a complaint and warrant for his arrest. But, fortunately, both officers at the insistence of the fatherly one had submitted a fictitious name in the case report in lieu of his. Consequently now, due to their act of kindness, both can be in serious trouble.

Being informed of this development, the victim's nerves reach a breaking point, all the visions of ruinous publicity attendant to such an offense which he had finally banished from his mind, came flooding back over him and he at this moment is ripe for any suggestion of a way out of his dilemma. The "cops" then tell him there is an avenue of escape for all three; he can post a cash bail under the fictitious name without his appearance being made, thus obviating mugging, booking and printing at the jail. This sounds good. He willingly goes to his bank and makes the withdrawal, usually in the medium four figure to the low six figure bracket (some con-men have even been known to add the proper penalty assessment to the amount). He then, in company with one of the "cops," goes to the local police station where another older distinguished appearing con-man meets them in a public hallway and after being addressed and introduced as "Captain," accepts the "posted" cash bail. The victim, upon the assurances of the "Captain" that the matter will cause him no further anguish, departs the police building, sure in his mind that all policemen accept bribes, though he has been very careful throughout the transaction when he has had a moment to reflect and analyze the situation, never to refer to it as such.

The "fruit shake" as discussed above is the classic. But, there have been occasions when the victim who does not have deviate tendencies has been jockied into what appears, at first blush, a compromising position and because of fear has accepted the bunco proposal. This often happens to men who are public figures, professionally or politically, and to whom any allegation, regardless of its baselessness, would spell ruin when viewed in the light of the fickleness of public opinion and adoration, natural political enemies and the idol smashing impulse which seems to be inherent in human beings. Like Caeser's wife, they must avoid the appearance of evil. A case in point happened a few years ago in an older type southern California hotel in which there was being held a political campaign committee meeting. The victim in this situation was a professional man who was also a party officer and very active. He was a family man, happily married and looked upon by his colleagues as accomplished in his field. On the night in question he had spent arduous hours in a meeting coupled with some food intake which had a temporary debilitating but intense, affect on his digestive processes necessitating his rapid withdrawal from the group to the gentlemen's lounge for immediate relief. Unfortunately the accommodations provided by the hotel management were in need of minor repairs. In this instance, the lock on the door of the stall he chose to occupy. Later it was found to have been tampered with for the particular purpose by the con-men to facilitate their operations.

While divested of his coat and seated in the normal fashion, his trousers and shorts were lowered to permit him to achieve his purpose, the door of the stall came open suddenly (the stall was of the older type construction with plenty of leg-room between the knees of a seated person and the opened door edge, having been selected for this purpose by the con-men) and there, going to his knees in front of the victim, was a male of obvious feminine characteristics. The victim was startled out of his reverie and for once was speechless. The intruder immediately leaned forward, putting out his hand in a grasping manner along the victim's upper thighs. Before a protest could be mouthed there appeared directly behind the kneeling homosexual a large, severe looking man of middle age dress in civilian clothing who instructed both parties in a well modulated but heavy and firm voice to readjust themselves and get out of the stall as he and his partner, who was standing nearby, wanted to discuss the action which he had just observed. He identified himself with a proper looking badge as a member of the police vice squad.

With such a situation, the victim albeit a well-educated, worldly person, was beset with doubts and fear. Having been empirically trained in the sub-rosa tactics of political gut-fighting and all too aware of the then disastrous internecine warfare within his own group, quickly realized he was placed in an untenable position, as to himself, to his family, his profession, socially and politically. What followed was essentially the same as in the other described bunco. The one difference, however, was the victim relating the matter to his attorney that evening who recognized the situation for what it was. The victim then displayed a degree of fortitude not usually found amongst politicians by cooperating with the local police agency which set up a trap for the second approach which was not long in coming as he received a telephone call the next day. The effectiveness was destroyed unfortunately by one inept officer who became too eager, prematurely disclosing his and another's position to the arriving "cops" who made a hasty and successful departure.

This type of swindle can be implemented in any situation in which police action is required. Bookmakers, abortionists, prostitutes can all be affected. However, because of the nature of the scam itself and the individuals involved, their susceptibility is based usually upon some act involving moral turpitude rather than upon the commission of a crime such as robbery, burglary and theft. Although even in that area the possibility exists.

The Los Angeles Police Department's Frauds Division experienced a variation of the "shake" which has been written about before, but does bear repeating here because of the uniqueness. The victim having a night on the town, visited a few of the bars in and about Sunset Boulevard (west of Vermont). After a somewhat lengthy period of libation he reached that level of absorption at which things female take on an aura of beauty beyond that which nature endowed or had intended, conjuring up libidinous thoughts. Such palaces of pleasure are infrequently short in supply of feminine companionship, amateur, neophyte, professional or needful. It was not long before the victim sighted in on a delightful bit of fluff appropriately attired in a mini-skirt and deep flowing decolletage disclosing ample development in all areas of interest. This interest was heightened, after the purchase of a drink, by her unsolicited remarks which indicated very clearly she was amongst other necessary things, lonesome, available, capable and completely devoid of commercialized attitudes towards transitory associations.

After a few more drinks during which his intentions and her overpowering desires were acknowledged and accepted, they departed the bistro going to that modern convenience for nocturnal enjoyment, the motel, which abound in that particular sector of the city. It just happened that newly found companion knew of a really well kept and better class hostelry (not of course because she had used herself, but because her dear mother stayed there when she visited the city) nearby where they could discuss and explore their mutual problem. The victim did in fact find it to be a well appointed establishment with a beautiful decor and extremely comfortable conducive to a state of euphoria. After both had exhausted their time and capabilities he drove her to the vicinity of an apartment house where she ostensibly resided and after a few pleasantries departed, both going their separate ways. On his way back to his legal nest, family *et al.*, he was in a jubilant and relaxed frame of mind, satisfied with his foray amongst the less inhibited night people.

The victim was rudely awakened from his somnambulant state about two days later when receiving a telephone call from the manager of the motel which he had occupied informing him there seemed to have developed a problem regarding his brief stay there with his "wife." He is told that apparently either he or his "wife" dropped a lighted cigarette which resulted in a smoldering fire flaring up after their departure in the early morning. The manager went on to say that although the premises are insured for such an incident and indemnification would be made by the carrier, subrogation would necessarily be resorted to for recovery from him and his "wife."

When this little jolt is handed to him he is frantic. He cannot understand how the manager obtained his right name as he had used a fictitious "Mr. and Mrs." registration and didn't pay with check or credit card. He is informed in a little firmer voice that his vehicle license number, which is taken per Municipal ordinance at registration time was the source of that information. He now wonders if the few hours of questionable pleasure was worth the jeopardy to his family and business life. He is told then that the estimated amount of damages (this varies according to who is buncoed) and it is suggested that if this can be handled amicably and privately there would be no need for the insurance company involvement or law suit. He immediately sees the wisdom of this idea and eagerly grasps it as a way out of his dilemma. And, if he would be so bold as to question the amount of purported damages he can be shown the suite he occupied and will find evidence of a fire complete with charred drapery, bedding, carpeting and wall surface damage. This is no problem to the con-man manager to create between the initial telephone call and the later pay-off/examination meeting. Of course if this in fact is what transpires, the victim has two things going for him: (1) normally there has been no report to the fire department and (2) even if there was, the time of the fire can be fairly accurately determined which would show it was subsequent to his occupancy. This is a factor for the investigator to take into consideration if a victim shows more than the usual amount of courage and wants to fight back with police involvement. However, the victim in the normal frame of mind, especially one trying to prevent disclosure of his extra-curricular activities, is not about to raise the issue to such a point and this is exactly what the manager is counting on from the inception of the scam.

There was a brief reference above to the abortionists. This occupation presents double-gaited approach, both with and without the pseudo medical butcher. In the first case the patient becomes the victim of the con. To implement the scheme a phony abortionist (sometimes actual physicians or pure abortionists are involved) sets up shop using the usual channels of information so that soon he is contacted by frightened women who believe there exists some greater reason for aborting the fruit of their mistake rather than assuming their responsibility. The usual approach is the "arrest" of the abortionist, his "nurse" and the patient (and often accompanied by the cause of her condition) at the former's office or mill. Sometimes there is the presence of the fatherly appearing understanding officer who indicates the abortionist is the only one he wants with the apologetic follow-up a few days later for the "bail" much the same as the "fruit shake." Or, there can be the other ploy of an unabashed crude "shakedown" in the form of a "bribe" solicitation at the outset. Normally the patient-victim is so thoroughly frightened that a payoff is made on the spot, the victim sure she is dealing with just a "couple more dishonest cops." After this experience she wends her way to Tia Juana for the usual infectious and dangerous treatment available there.

The other format is the abortionist being the victim. In this situation the "phony cops" use a female as an ostensible patient, sometimes her condition is actual and on other occasions merely an act. The "arrest" of the abortionist is made at about the time the patient is aboard the table and ready for the treatment. There is only one approach here, an outright solicitation of a bribe. They are usually too con-wise to buy the "bail" routine. He sees the handwriting on the wall if he happens to be an actual physician: prison, loss of profession, disgrace and the other related social conditions which would evolve out of an arrest on such a charge. If he is not a bona fide physician but merely a butcher of some type, confinement is his only fear. Regardless, both kinds seems to have adequate reason at the moment for accepting the idea of buying their way out and do so convinced they have been handled by a couple of dishonest policemen. They never complain.

The Marriage Bunco

The marriage bunco is timeless. It has been practiced by both sexes since some formalization of connubial bliss has been required by law; tribal, religious, state or otherwise. It will continue to be practiced as long as there are people whose eagerness to share in the wedded state overshadows their common sense. Of course, when life's juices began to flow, or after having once run their normal course experience a resurgence at a later age, emotions, not reasoning, rules. There are as numerous ways for the con-artist to locate his victims as there are ways for people to meet. At one time "lonely hearts clubs," "old fashioned dances," picnics and even advertisements were used. Now, however, with the emancipation of the female, the embracing of more (not necessarily better) liberal social and moral concepts, improved transportation, creating a more gregarious society, the opportunities for social contact are enhanced.

The type of offense with which we are concerned creates problems for the investigator. The victim is often reluctant to cooperate with the police either from embarrassment or a continuing trust in the con-man. Also during the course of events and prior to any actual loss experience, the family and friends of the victim sometimes become aware of the situation and try to influence her (or him) into breaking off the association. This hardly ever meets with success and frequently destroys the normally happy and amicable relationship between all parties.

The method of enticement used by the con-man is geared to the personality of the victim. But there are two things with which he is concerned; the projection of his "wealth" and the speed with which he can conjure up the idea of marriage in the victim. The first takes care of thoughts about his abilities and achievements, the second with the amount of trust to be given. As the relationship grows more heated the con-man adroitly brings about the subject of a business deal or investment of some type in which he is involved and which must be satisfactorily completed before he and the victim can consumate their intended marriage. By this time the victim thoroughly enamored with this obviously wealthy, traveled and experienced business tycoon, inquires solicituously as to his needs. Having primed her real well, he indicates he needs some funds but cannot use what there is on hand now as they are already committed to a project and his other source is "temporarily" encumbered because of another far ranging deal, both interdependent upon the other. The victim practically begs him to accept funds from her, just as a loan if he wants to view it as such, to clear up his problem, thus they can get on with marriage as planned. He graciously accepts this offer, has the check and cashed it before the sun sets and he goes with it as does her hopes of marriage and bankroll.

Seagoing Scam

The harbor area of Los Angeles furnished the Police Department's Frauds Division a unique scam in 1967 which involved a relatively small amount but nevertheless enough to meet the felony requirement. The victim a young man who was employed as an industrial plant guard, answered an advertisement in one of the city's papers which stated that men were wanted as crewmen and to share expenses for a cruise to the West Indies. The idea of the open sea, travel and adventure which runs in all men asserted itself and he answered the advertisement by writing to a box number given. Three days later he received a telephone call from the first con-man, a man about his own age, and a meeting was arranged for the following day at a yacht landing in the harbor and was taken aboard a beautiful two-masted thirty-four foot ketch. He was introduced to the "Captain," an elderly man who looked the part of an old salt.

The victim was told by the first con-man at that time his share of the expenses would be one-hundred twenty-five dollars per month and he would have to pay three months of it in advance. He agreed to this and was then told that two other crewmen were to be picked at the landing and he should bring money in the form of cash the next day and also arrange right away for his passport.

The victim returned the next day with his money and gave it over to the first operator, the "Captain" being absent. He was then instructed as to what equipment, clothing and personal property he should bring aboard with him. Two days later he returned again to the vessel, this time being met by the "Captain," whom he informed his passport would be ready in three days. He stowed his gear and the "Captain" told him they would be sailing on the morning of the fourth day.

The victim returned to the yacht landing the evening of the third day prepared to ship out to the high seas. He was startled to find the vessel had sailed already. He checked with the yacht landing office and learned his ship and money had departed late at night of the day he had come aboard to stow his gear. He also learned that there was failure by the "Captain" and his partner to pay a dock fee of almost three weeks duration.

A complete book could be written on just the variations of the "switch" alone and an encyclopedia on buncos per se. Obviously all the games and schemes cannot be covered here. But what is presented gives the student an insight into what can be used; and, who can be used. There are classic buncos involving "money-making machines," fortune-tellers (all breeds and types), "hidden treasure maps" for sale, coin matching games and others, all based upon the victim's gullibility and avarice, his hope of something for nothing coupled with the con-man's fast moving, fast talking approach and departure all covered with a haze of confusion and the victim's slow reaction. In all of the scams there exists the basic test for theft by trick and device; the money passed to the con-man but not the title and it was not used for the purpose represented. Even in the "phony cops" game, the victim, it can be alleged, actually thought he was making a "cash bail" to, or bribing bona-fide police officers. There may have been a germ of doubt in his mind, nevertheless at the moment of panic, the unique conditions induced him to believe the representations made and he acted upon them to his loss.

DIVISION C

EMBEZZLEMENT

Part I

Law and Techniques

Embezzlement is not a common law crime. It resulted from legislative action to provide for bridging an unforseen and really unreasonable gap which appeared in the law of larceny as it developed over the years. During this period of legal evolution there were enacted numerous statutes to cover the different circumstances and situations wherein the possession of another's property was acquired without the basic element of trespass and then subsequently misappropriated.

Although there are many statutory provisions which define the varied types or forms of the crime and related punishments, it is the practice in California and some other jurisdictions to charge the accused with the basic crime of theft, since frequently the offense of embezzlement is included within the definition of theft. This does not mean that the elements have changed. The change is one of nomenclature only.

The crime has a uniqueness about it similar to other fraud oriented theft offenses in that it is frequently left unreported. There are two basic reasons for this, the first being that it is not always recognized by the victims and the other, probably the more common, the victim being influenced by other more pressing social reasons.

Sociological Concepts

There are many viewpoints and theories concerning the general character and personality traits of the embezzler. Dr. Donald R. Cressey of the University of California at Santa Barbara and a disciple of the late Edwin H. Sutherland (who probably in his time conducted more in-depth studies of swindlers than any of his contemporaries) published a paper in 1950, the validity of which has yet to be seriously attacked, analyzing the many existing concepts, some found to be acceptable, the majority not. Of course, as a sociologist, he is more interested in causation rather than being concerned with the techniques used both by the embezzler to achieve his purpose and the investigator to prevent and apprehend. Those motivations as examined by the sociologist should not be decried however, as they are essential to the investigator in his efforts to understand his case. The usual explanation given as the root cause is "booze, broads and bookies." This, however, is an over-simplification.

One hypothesis which apparently has been abandoned, is that embezzlers when learning some forms of trust violations are merely "technical violations" and are not really "illegal" or "wrong" per se, this "discovery" becomes a soothing rationalization. Most convicted or proven embezzlers, however, when being candid have said they knew their behavior was illegal and wrong and they merely "kidded themselves" into thinking or believing their conduct was not reprehensible and they were in fact stealing.

There have been other conclusions such as a crime of opportunity because the trust position formed an irresistible temptation sometimes combined with emergency situations, real or fancied. This too, has been rejected as a total theory, although it plays a part. But, empiric studies have presented a new theory and it holds that trusted persons become embezzlers when they conceive of themselves as having a financial problem which is non-shareable. They have knowledge or awareness the problem can be secretly resolved by violation of their trust position, they have the technical capabilities to achieve their purpose, and they can apply any number of rationalizations to their conduct which enables them to adjust the conceptions of themselves and their acts.

The Cressy theory of the non-shareable problem then does not necessarily have to be rooted in some type of misconduct or anti-social behavior. It can be the result of perfectly legitimate conditions, situations or incidents which bring about circumstances which need to be responded to, but, causing the person so confronted to believe it must be done in a completely private manner. The person involved can be, for example, a divorced or widowed woman with one or more children to support on her salary, more often than not without collateral funding in the form of child support. She, like all members of our society, is forced to maintain some outward appearances, if not of affluence, at least to a degree of well-being matched by her peergroup. This all too frequently is achieved by total expenditure of her meager funds. To this then, at an unexpected point in time, add a burden such as a medical bill or some comparable indebtedness which cannot be avoided or circumvented. In other words, a financial problem, and one, which because of social pressures, she conceives as being non-sharable. This is not based in misconduct, but is one which can develop for anyone and her response to it is geared to her social values as dictated by the mores and customs of her group. The classic rationalization resorted to then is the act committed is only one of "borrowing" and not one of theft. Another is that it is a "fringe benefit" and similar concepts. And, those rationalizations become very simple for some people, especially those who already bear a certain amount of malevolence toward companies and other organizations of size. The usual attitude after some irritation from what has become a difficult situation, is that the "great monolith" (the company) won't miss some small sums which "will be repaid." In tax evasions the same rationale is used, the government becoming the overbearing spectre. There is probably no criminal offense other than a crime of violence which begats the number and kind of excuses and rationalizations resorted to by the accused than that of a trust violation. Perhaps a "non-sufficient funds" check offense is an exception. However, there is one factor which appears that the embezzler seems to disregard; recidivism. The rate is probably as high with embezzlers as with check-writers and forgers. It seems inevitable, but each time the embezzler finds himself in comparable positions of stress he is going to revert to kind.

The Elements of the Offense

A FIDUCIARY RELATION. The crime is basically a violation of a trust. There is a fiduciary relationship between the defendant and the victim. The term embraces those who are bound to discharge and express trust. It also means a legal relationship between parties such as principal and agent, master and servant, trustee and beneficiary, and more loosely, as a confidential bond. In other words, a relationship whereby one entrusts property to another.

B CONTROL OF PROPERTY. The property must come into the hands (dominion, control, direction, possession—this last not imperative physically) of the agent/servant as the property of the victim/principal. The property involved belongs to the principal and the agent receives it as such, the ownership remaining with the principal.

C MANNER IN WHICH PROPERTY RECEIVED. The agent must have received the property in the course of his employment. There are exceptions to this element as stated and it should not be too narrowly construed. There is a theory of constructive trusts which is applicable. For example, a person receiving through mistake a large amount of money which he appropriates for his own use and does not return to the owner. He is said to hold the funds in trust for the rightful owner and misappropriation is embezzlement from a constructive trust. In other words there has not been created an express trust, but one by operation of law.

The property must be lawfully in the possession of the agent, eliminating any preconceived intent to acquire it by trespass, false pretenses or trick and device: it is obtained properly within the scope of a particular relationship; then the intent to fraudulently appropriate it is developed.

D PROPERTY MISAPPROPRIATED. The agent must have appropriated the property to his own use or some use not contemplated within the purpose of the trust and with the intent to deprive the owner thereof. This element creates some confusion as it is frequently construed to mean "permanently" deprive the owner of possession as in the general concept of larceny. Most jurisdictions today hold that the intent to deprive the owner of possession *temporarily* is sufficient for the demand of this element.

Other Essentials

(1) The distinct act of taking the property is not a requirement because the gravamen of the offense is a *wrongful use* of the

property entrusted to the servant/agent, employee, bailee, trustee (express and constructive), or in the case of public monies, the public officer.

(2) The owner never intends that the servant-employee shall use the property for any other purpose than specified or agreed upon.

(3) The title to the property remains at all times with the owner.

(4) The possession/control passes to the servant/agent (who is a trustee) but only for a specific purpose of the trust.

(5) The degree of proof does not normally require the corroboration degree as with theft by false pretenses and in some jurisdictions, trick and device (false token, handwriting of accused, documentation, two witnesses, etc.).

(6) There is a general rule that a partner cannot be charged with embezzlement of partnership assets even though the theory of agency between partners does exist. The rule is based upon the idea of joint ownership of the assets and that a man cannot steal from himself.* The exception would be the clear showing that a bonafide partnership did not in fact exist (the innocent partner having been duped into the purported relationship). In such a situation it would be nonexistent from its inception.

In connection with this rule the question of a limited partnership is often raised (the limited partner committing the ostensible theft). For clarification, a limited partnership is one in which certain participating members, known variously as limited or special partners, who are not liable for the firm's obligations *to third parties* beyond the extent or amount of capital they invested. The special partner is also limited in his control of the partnership business. However, in most states it is held that as long as a limited partner along with general partners constitutes a partnership, the general partners are general agents of the limited partners for the purpose of conducting the business, but *all* partners have an interest in the partnership assets. The Uniform Partner-

---

* California Appellate Court recently changed this concept of partner immunity (Peo vs Sobiek, 28 Cal App 3rd 852 and 30 Cal App 3rd 458) by holding such construction put to the law of theft was an error in the interpretation of the legislative intent.

ship Act does not create a new concept of separate legal identities as between limited and general partners. From this then, the rule in issue (stealing from oneself) would seem to prevail regardless of the form of the partnership.

(7) The intent on the part of the employee/agent to return the property after the misappropriation is not a defense. However, if it were appropriated openly and avowedly, coupled with a claim of title in good faith, the basis of a defense is created. But, this type of defense is very limited in that the "taking" must not only be open but clearly in good faith. A surreptitious taking would vitiate the claim. Also a claim of express or implied authority, if in good faith, is a defense.

Statutory Provisions

California, like many other states, has over a period of several years enacted and attempted to enforce a multiplicity of laws concerning the crime of embezzlement. They appear not only in Penal Codes and general laws but also in other codifications such as apply to banking, public officers, insurance, financial, corporations, vehicles and contractors to mention a few. All of these laws were conceived as applying to certain specific situations, many of which were duplications of existing laws. The new Criminal Code of California, which is patterned for a possible uniform codification (other states legislatures indicating similar attempts at simplification and uniformity) places the crime in succinct form in a single section which is applicable to all situations, thereby repealing in excess of ten separate statutes presently appearing in the Penal Code alone. However, there are still in existence a number of sections which apply to the crime in varied ways such as the Corporations Code, but there is no change in the elements; only to whom they are applied under a specific set of circumstances.

Most states, either separately or combined into an encompassing section, proscribe sales of property covered by security agreements, embezzlement by common carriers, misappropriation of funds entrusted for labor and materials, thefts by collectors, falsification of records and embezzlement by public officers, misappropriation by brokers, agents or representatives of insurance companies, offenses by bank officers and commingling of trust funds. They all have the same thing in common; fiduciary relationship and fraudulent intent.

Classic Cases

A ACCOUNTING OFFICE CLERK. In this situation a minor office employee handles the documentation related to vouchers and invoices (a voucher serves as evidence of the disbursement of cash; e.g. a receipted bill; an invoice is a document showing the character, price, terms, nature of delivery and other particulars of goods sold or services rendered). In this case he examines receiving reports relating them to invoices; he then prepares company checks for their payment. He also prepares check requests for salesmen and other company employees who require travel advances, minor cash disbursements and other expense items. The business is appliance sales and leasing, and one of the larger operating expenses is repairs. These are performed by contracting machine shops who submit their drafts for payment on the company's bank. The bank in turn delivers the drafts for payment almost as a daily operation with the account clerk handling the vouchering routine.

The routine itself is not difficult or complicated. A check request is prepared in duplicate form—the payees of the drafts are listed on the request form together with the amounts—these are usually in excess of twenty each day and frequently there is also included an order/request for a cashier's check to cover travel advances needed by the company officers and field representatives. The clerk then attaches supporting repair bills and the office request showing the amount of the cashier's check needed for the travel advances which is then coupled with a company check made payable to the bank covering the *total* amount of the items appearing on the request form. This package then is submitted to a company officer authorized to sign business checks.

The company officer perfunctorily examines the package and if they appear in order approves the check request and signs the attached company check. Frequently there is a second signature required on company checks, such as that of a disbursing officer or someone else of comparable position as this is viewed as being the perfection of internal control. This second officer makes the same type of myopic cursory examination as the first, signs the check and sends the clerk along his way.

The clerk delivers the package to the bank. In return he receives the drafts which are stamped "paid" and the requested cashier's check payable to the company to cover the travel advances. This is cashed and the funds are distributed in cash monies to those requiring them. Occasionally there are cashier's checks payable to a specific person entitled to a travel advance, but generally there is a single instrument which is cashed and the funds handed out to each person prior to his departure on a road trip.

The transaction at this point is completed. The only thing to follow is its recordation. The accountant makes an entry into the cash disbursements record to reflect a reduction of cash in the bank (a credit entry) a charge to the Repairs Expense Account (debit entry) and another charge to the Travel Expense Account. The books, to use a time honored phrase, balance.

This routine, which is normal, continues on daily with little or no alteration. One day, the clerk who is experiencing some outside but unknown pressures, decides to avail himself of a fringe benefit. He has the necessary technical knowledge, and the rationalizations to justify such action as he may take to fulfill his needs. On this occasion when making out the check payable to the bank he makes it for $300 more than the total amount of the supporting bank drafts related to the repair bills. This is not noticeable as the check request does not necessarily show a total of the items listed; and if it did, the forced footing would not usually be observed. If it were he could easily pass it off as a computation error.

The clerk, after the routine approvals are secured, inserts a fictitious name on the original copy of the check request indicating a cashier's check for travel advances is needed. The bank does not question the entry and complies with a cashier's check *to order* in the name of the fictitious person.

The thieving clerk then takes this cashier's check to another bank where he makes the opening deposit on a savings account in the fictitious name. The company records relating to cash disbursements again show a proper reduction of cash in the bank (credit entry) and a charge (debit entry) to the Repairs Expense Account covering the *entire* amount of the check, including the fictitious person's share of the company profits. The books are still in balance, the accountant reaching new heights of ecstasy.

The profit sharing routine continues unabated until the clerk becomes concerned over the burgeoning Repairs Expense Account. He becomes aware of this from two sources; the company operations report, or profit and loss statement, and conversations he has heard within the office. He knows that the Repairs Account is going to be scrutinized closely (as it always is during audits, it being a normal place to bury phony entries covering peculations) which will require his altering in some manner his operations. He might find his next temporary answer by charging the fictitious checks to Accounts Payable. The cash disbursements record will still reflect a reduction in cash for the full amount of the check, but the charge (debit entry) to the Repairs Account is now limited to the actual amounts of the repair bills. Albeit, this new method resorted to in effort to bury his operations creates a new problem for him. To keep the Accounts Payable in balance with the detail of unpaid invoices necessitates a high degree of digital dexterity as he must remove physically an equivalent amount of invoices from the voucher file. Everything will then balance to the satisfaction of the accountant but it requires some adroit foot-work and a good nervous system. The withheld invoices must be replaced very quickly after the accountant's routine working of the records to avoid dunning notices from the vendors and observation by fellow employees. In spite of a cool hand, this can and does become a very nerve-wracking situation especially if his alter-ego (fictitious name bank account) requirements continue. In most cases the clerk suddenly resigns his job and leaves the area. A few weeks later when the normal year-end or accounting period audit is performed it will be found that the Accounts Payable is short an amount which is equal to the forced over-footings of the cash disbursements records.

B   THE PURCHASING AGENT. The purchasing agent, sometimes called the buyer, is normally placed in a position which facilitates his efforts if he is in fact a thief. In the case discussed here the employee is a purchasing agent for a scrap metal reduction plant. Most of its sales are overseas. The scrap metal is purchased from small dealers and wrecking yards across a three-state area in the southwest including a few places in Mexico contiguous to the international border. The agent travels the countryside dealing with yard operators for their metal. For this purpose he uses a special company checking account which has a $25,000.00 balance against which he is permitted to write checks. Since many of the yardmen want cash, the agent has them endorse the check over to him and in return gives them cash from his own pocket which he just happens to have with him. The company doesn't object to this practice. The agent's second endorsements on the instruments are never questioned.

The company, like many other firms, became lax with the seemingly routine functions of long-time employees. It was never deemed really necessary to question in any manner their traveling agent's methods. Thus, the returned checks with their second endorsements were automatically accepted and processed, with no thought given to them. Unknown to the company, however, these instruments didn't always represent scrap metal purchase payments, but in fact were embezzlements. He was resorting to another old ploy of using names of the yardmen as payees on fraudulent checks, forging their first endorsements, then cashing them.

The operation actually required only a simple forgery to implement a likewise simple embezzlement scheme. The fictitious purchases had to be "received" insofar as company records were concerned. This need presented no insurmountable problem as the well embedded daily routine of the accounting office made it quite simple. The clerk handling Accounts Payable never cancelled the railroad or cartage firms' bills of lading which are evidence of receipt of scrap metal shipments; the agent learned in a short time it was very easy to revise them. When he was in the main office between trips no one was ever suspicious enough of his presence at the paid invoice file. This firm like many others had office employees who never questioned the mouthing of some sanctimonious, but otherwise utterly ridiculous statement such as "I'm following up on an order" or "I'm re-examining the pricing I gave on an old order." When this internal condition is coupled with the unmerited attitude on the part of a company towards an "old, valued and experienced employee" the foundation for trouble is all too well established.

The agent's system funneled his embezzlements directly into the Raw Materials Inventory Account. His next move was to have the fictitious inventory charged (debit entry) to operations in some manner with the unwitting help of accounting office personnel. This was not too difficult to achieve. Scrap metal prices in the area covered by the agent varied to some degree, consequently an average cost price was used consistently throughout the year to relieve the Raw Materials Inventory Account for the input to Work in Progress Account. The agent, by his long experience and record of performance was viewed as an "expert" on purchase prices, so he advised the company of the current average cost price to be used. He always, since the start of his peculations, recommended one that was slightly higher than would be considered justified if anyone really took the time to make a close examination of the facts. But this was never done as everyone was satisfied; the agent's prices were considered reasonably accurate because the year-end physical inventory, priced at recent purchase costs, always came close to book value.

The agent's system of fictitious purchases was successful for a long period of time. He then dreamed up a new approach to enlarge his take. He considered the fact that scrap metal was generally purchased during the months of April through October since the hauling was very difficult during the winter, and there were rainy periods in many of the sections of the country where he did much of his buying. The months of November through March saw a stockpiling of materials throughout the area without purchases creating burdens for the yardmen with a commensurate reduction in prices. He then calculatingly advised his company that lower purchase prices could be obtained if he purchased scrap metal during the winter months. To avoid storage problems at the plant and related high cartage expense he would arrange to have the grateful yardmen hold the scrap metal on site for trucking, or with the larger yards, at the railroad sidings until it was needed. He knew that the yards would accept this arrangement as it was a guaranteed sale for them, even if at a lower price, during a slow period. The company, of course, with its eye on the increased profit margin very quickly accepted his suggestion and the agent proceeded to buy scrap metal for future delivery. At the company's fiscal year-end the books reflected an account denominated "Inventory at Outside Locations." It was not really a large dollar amount, and since it was geographically dispersed over a three-state and international border area, the company's auditors really did not consider it practical or necessary to observe and make a physical inventory count.

Now, as with most classic situations, they are brought to an abrupt termination because at long last someone, often to the consternation of fellow employees, actually does his total job. In this case it was an accounting office clerk who for once reacted to the figures he was posting instead of performing his function in the usual rote fashion. At the end of the next fiscal period the clerk observed the account had experienced a startling increase. Very properly, again as a rare exception, the matter was examined by the accountant who referred the matter for further study to the chief auditor. This more discerning company officer directed the examination of the account as it appeared in the books and then did something his subordinates neglected to do previously; he coupled it with a physical on-site testing of the purported locations of the scrap metal. To the surprise of all except the chief auditor, when the sites were visited, no scrap metal was found.

Based upon the findings of a proper internal audit, investigators were called into the matter. The forgeries of the payees (yardmen) signatures as endorsements on the checks the agent used were not difficult to identify by the document examiner. With the inquiries were made into the ostensible "purchases" it became all too clear what the agent had done. When collateral investigation was made of his expenditures as opposed to his income there was little left to do to complete the case for prosecution.

C THE OFFICE MANAGER. The accused in this case was the office manager and bookkeeper of a real estate development corporation. The firm had received nationwide publicity through the medium of a well known "slick" magazine for its number of "low cost" residential tracts constructed throughout southern California and Nevada. It had the normal corporate structure endemic to this type of operation without, however, public sales of its common stock.

The organization's activities, business and extra-curricular, were directed by its president and vice-president, two real mod swinging types. Their secretary resigned (for valid reasons of her own) and they advertised for a replacement. The response they apparently viewed as more amenable to their ideas was a young woman who answered to the name of Polly; she could swing with the best of them, having the social instincts of an alley cat and libido of a guppy. Polly started in at $100.00 per week. Her duties consisted initially of merely routine secretarial/bookkeeping activities. Soon her latent qualities and capabilities became apparent with concomitant increases in responsibilities in the day to day operations of the company's business office, coupled with increases in wages to $140.00 per week.

At first she had no control of the corporate bank accounts, funds or monies, but due to her increasing value to the operation she was eventually given the authority to sign company voucher/checks jointly with the vice-president. A few months later, pursuant to a board of directors decision, she was vested with authority to make and sign voucher/checks within the scope of corporate business, however without any limitations being imposed as to amounts or number other than she was expected to exercise that degree of prudence, honesty and judgment normally anticipated of anyone in such a position.

At the time of her increased responsibilities she was accorded the title of "Executive Secretary" for prestige purposes only. She did not at any time become a corporate officer but remained as a "trusted" employee who had been given a vaguely defined amount of autonomous control over corporate funds placing her in a fiduciary capacity. She was expected to clear with the vice-president generally on any instrument of size. Her functions placed her in control of the cash flow, she arranged loans, made collections, handled a large part of the monetary affairs, and often with a certain amount of supervision and direction, arranged for an unsecured line of credit at a Los Angeles bank and performed practically all the outside "foot work" with local banking houses. In a word, she had arrived.

The vice-president began to question some of the entries he took time to examine in the company expense accounts. He advised the outside auditing firm who ran a cursory check of the items, they also questioning their validity. There seemed to be an inordinate number of instruments with Polly appearing as maker, payee and endorser. These were cashed at local banks. One voucher, however, showed the instrument was for "Xmas presents for the Pres. *et al.*" They never received any presents, but there it was, buried in the President's Drawing Account. It was about this time they decided that all was not well and their trusted and highly efficient office manager was dipping into the till. After giving due consideration to the matter it was given to the local police agency's frauds division to figure out. In the meantime Polly's sixth sense and great experience caused her to terminate her employment. Inquiries disclosed she had a two-page record of arrests and a number of convictions for theft offenses and related crimes.

An examination of the returned instruments, vouchers and ledger accounts by the investigators rapidly disclosed a large number of checks over a year's period having been made by Polly with herself as payee, bearing her endorsements, with the additional stamped endorsements of department stores, tire shops, furniture stores, beauty shops, dentists, pet stores, animal shelters (she was an avid antivivisectionist and animal lover) automobile agency, hardware stores, paint stores, gas stations, hotels, restaurants, bars, liquor stores and nightclubs. All of these were debited to the president's drawing account, auto expense account, purchasing accounts, travel expense account and public relations/ advertising accounts; in other words wherever it seemed appropriate at the time. The only problem that appeared however, was the corporation received no benefit from these expenditures, only good old Polly. It was also found that the company credit cards for gas and oil (including tires, batteries and other necessities), lodging, food and beverages were used to an extent undreamed of even by the swinging twins who ran the firm. The case was finally resolved when Polly was indicted on fifteen counts of grand theft and forgery and later convicted on ten of them.

What should be pointed out here is the foot-work that is required of the investigator in such cases. Each of the persons and companies which could be identified from the checks and other documentation had to be contacted, the transactions discussed with them in detail and any and all ancillary documentation obtained as supporting material. When the prosecutive summary was finally written and submitted to the District Attorney for Grand Jury action there were in excess of sixty basic documents and related instruments, including ledgers and journals from the complainant corporation alone. This was coupled with the comparable amount from witnesses, individuals and companies, who had become involved with her and her machinations.

There was nothing really unique or clever about Polly's operations. She was counting on the fact that her employers were a couple of playboys who cared little or nothing about their business other than the sweet expense accounts they could function with and they would probably never really question the office routines. And, if the auditors did become too inquisitive she had the means to divert their attention to other lines of thought; she was not the least bit reluctant to employ her natural attributes to achieve an advantage. This line of reasoning is often adhered to by female embezzlers when they anticipate finding themselves in an untenable position. Pity is another defensive weapon they will employ. This last, albeit is not limited to women, male thieves frequently resort to the same defense mechanism against prosecution.

D CONSTRUCTIVE TRUSTS. The theft or embezzlement from a constructive trust is one unfortunately not often enough recognized or appreciated by the police investigator. It is a trust created by operation of the law which arises contrary to the intention and against the will; it is declared against one who by fraud, actual or constructive, has obtained property belonging to another and to which he should not by equity, hold and enjoy. This definition or explanation is wide in scope, being applicable to any theft situation in which fraud was a moving force. For purposes here, we limit its application to theft by embezzlement. Another manner of stating the situation is one who gains control of property by fraud, accident or mistake becomes an involuntary trustee of the property for the benefit of the person who would otherwise have it.

(1) A frequent example of such a theft results from a computer error. A woman for a period of about four years had been receiving quite legally $15.00 per week for child support from a former husband. By the divorce arrangement he deposited this sum with the county auditor who in turn forwarded the sum to her. On the occasion in question there developed a computer error causing a check for several thousand dollars to be printed and forwarded. Upon receipt she cashed the county warrant at a local bank and received two cashier's checks for large amounts and the balance of the warrant amount was deposited to her savings account.

The investigation disclosed she then purchased a new car with the smaller of the two checks which more than paid the total cash price, the balance from the car agency being a check that she also deposited in her savings account. She told the salesman the funds were from her winnings at the horse races. The larger of the two cashier's checks she used jointly with her current husband on a trip to a gambling spa located across the border in a neighboring state. Her ineptness at the gaming tables didn't take long to lose about the whole amount. When the computer mistake was found there was a stop payment order put out by the auditor but of course it was too late, at least for its purpose.

Investigation by the police frauds unit disclosed in a short time what had transpired. The results were an indictment for embezzlement of public funds and conspiracy to commit theft. The basis of the theft allegation was the fact when she came into possession of the enlarged check she immediately was deemed as holding it in trust for the county. Her misuse of it was equivalent to theft or unauthorized use of funds she received via her specially created fiduciary relationship to the county.

(2) The kickback form of theft came into its own on a great scale during the World War II period when there was a large degree of free-wheeling purchasing by companies devoted ostensibly to the national defense effort. It is an insidious thing that

invades many levels of management to the detriment of not only the company being victimized by its trusted employee but also to the employee himself. The arrangement becomes a way of life after a little while, especially when it is observed at all levels of industry. It is in essence a form of bribery and it contaminates the employee and vendor both.

What is involved in such a situation and seldom considered by police investigators is that the amounts "kicked back" to a purchasing agent by a vendor actually are held by the agent in trust for his employer. This is a form of a constructive trust. If the monies obtained from a vendor for letting of a favorable contract by the agent is withheld from his employer the act becomes a theft from a constructive trust, a form of embezzlement, and punishable as such.

Some points which can be considered by the investigator in this type of case are those rules most management consultants advocate companies should enforce concerning buyers and purchasing agents. In other words the things that are the subject of admonishment are the things that the investigator perhaps should look for as possible leads.

One of the first things to be proscribed is the situation in which there is clearly a conflict of interest. This phrase is not solely applicable to government personnel but is also a factor in private industry. A purchasing agent must be forbidden to transact company business with any firm in which he has an interest, either directly or indirectly regardless of its form or type. Even if his employer would permit such an arrangement to exist it is fraught with peril.

Most companies, similar to governmental agencies, forbid employees who are involved in company purchases from having private financial transactions with vendors. This same proscription is applicable to the receipt of gifts. Being very candid, a person who is in such a position is going to be approached to any degree he permits by a vendor. If he thinks the gift is a tribute to his intelligence, great capabilities and effervescent personality he is living in a dream world. The only reason gifts or offers of gifts are made is to influence the buyer. He is in the same position of selling his company's purchasing power as the political prostitute who sells his vote.

In an open bidding for contracts most companies will question a situation in which one vendor seems consistently the low bidder. If his product is above average worth when compared to others in the same market and his operational expenses are known to be as high or higher than the others, which would reasonably reflect a lower profit margin for him, there is something wrong; and it is frequently found to be a kickback to the buyer for extended contracts. Conversely, if other companies are competitive in every manner, price and value, but consistently are denied contracts and one or two others seem over a long period to enjoy a favored position, the same situation probably exists.

The Investigation

THE RELATIONSHIP. The first step in an embezzlement case is the same as with any other criminal inquiry; a detailed interview of the complainant/victim. Naturally, based upon the elements of the offense, determine the exact relationship between the two parties:

(a) That with which to establish the existence of a bonafide trust

(b) That with which to establish any other affinity that could merge with, vitiate or destroy the fiduciary relationship

(c) Make sure there are no "special" agreements which would mitigate the allegation such as monies due and owing, back pay, joint venture, or partnership interests in the property. This last must be closely examined to preclude such relationship or interest by estoppel.

OWNERSHIP OF THE PROPERTY. This is an important facet. All parties of interest are vitally concerned and their interests as such must be determined to establish their relative rights.

(a) Is the complainant the owner?

(b) Is the complainant a bailee?

(c) Is the complainant a factor?

(d) Determine who had title or an interest in the title (security interest)

HOW THE ACCUSED ACQUIRED POSSESSION. Determine if the accused or suspect acquired possession lawfully and within the scope of his duties or through some special relationship.

(a) Be certain he did not steal something located outside of his area of responsibility or function

(b) The "lawful" acquisition supports the trust element of the crime

THE INTENT. Determine the point in time the suspect/accused developed the fraudulent intent to appropriate the property.

(a) If after it came into his possession the basic element is satisfied

(b) If it were prior to possession the crime would be either false pretenses or trick and device; there would still be the crime of theft, but committed in a different manner

DUTIES OF THE SUSPECT/ACCUSED. This facet must be examined in depth. It has to cover those both vested and implied.

(a) Determine all authority and how it affected the handling of properties and duties

(b) Determine in detail the methods of accountability and degrees of responsibility

(c) Clarify the manner in which duties, responsibilities, authority and accountability were initially explained to the suspect and by whom, when, where and by what means

(d) There must be outlined a detailed step by step analysis showing every function, movement, decision, purpose, contact (in person or by other means) with other persons, including days, dates, times and frequency patterns if possible

(e) There must be close scrutiny of equipment, monies, machines, documents, books of account, and any other item that passes through or near him

THE LOSS. The investigation must develop at the outset a good general understanding of the total operations and in what manner the functions of the suspect/accused correlate. This of necessity includes a knowledge of the accounting processes and procedures adhered to by the complainant.

DOCUMENTARY EXHIBITS. There is required a development of those items which have probative value—relating to the issue—and take possession of the originals or good clear copies initially.

(a) These would include but not be limited to books and records of account, cancelled checks, invoices, vouchers, requisitions, receipts, payroll records, ledgers, journals, check registers, bank statements, charts of accounts (this is a must for understanding the accounting system), the auditor's working papers, balance sheets, profit and loss statements, sales records, inventory records, trial balances, correspondence, etc: anything of any nature that can assist in determining the manner in which the theft was accomplished

(b) Make charts, diagrams and photographs for the purpose of a graphic presentation and ease of understanding, not only for a jury but for the prosecutor and the investigator himself. All too frequently an embezzlement case presents real problems when trying to follow the twisting winding pattern some transactions take; especially for the person not familiar with even simple bookkeeping methods. Plot out each instrument, each entry and each step of the process you are analyzing and relate them to each other and to the progressions of the inquiry

WITNESSES. Determine the witnesses and interview them in just as much detail as the complainant.

(a) What is their function in the company?

(b) How is their function related to the suspect/accused?

(c) Determine clearly their duties, responsibilities, authority and degree of accountability

(d) Develop the personal information they may have regarding the suspect/accused

(e) Determine the stability of the witnesses and their personal involvement with the suspect/accused both in the business and outside

DEVELOP SIMILAR ACTS AND TRANSACTIONS. This is a basic investigative technique. Any case needs support. Both acts and transactions are admissable if they are relevant to the issue; the similar act meaning a similar offense and similar transaction meaning a similar method or manner employed to achieve some purpose, not necessarily criminal in itself. The test of admissibility is of great concern to the investigator as he must develop the information within the limited framework allowed by law.

(a) The information must tend, logically, naturally and by a reasonable inference, to establish a material fact or to overcome one. If it does it is admissible whether it establishes the commission of another crime or not

(b) Where the evidence of another offense has no connection with the one charged and in no manner tends to prove a current issue, it is irrelevant and inadmissible

(c) Where the theft is in the nature of embezzlement, evidence of other similar acts may be shown to prove intent and a systematic course of conduct, plan, scheme, design or a characteristic behavior pattern

(d) A case that reflects evidence of similar transactions whether criminal or not but which shows comparable methods employed is generally admissable to prove intent, knowledge, familiarity with means and methods of technically achieving a purpose

(e) Evidence of a similar form of offense subsequent to the one alleged is admissible to prove intent, plan, scheme and design

THE SUSPECT. To this point we have related the matter to an identified person, the suspect, whom we hope will become the accused. However, this happy situation doesn't always prevail. All too frequently there can be more than one logical suspect, just as in any other criminal inquiry. This requires, then, a process of elimination to be implemented which can be achieved only by the investigator having a good basic knowledge of general business operations and accounting principles which has been constantly emphasized throughout this book. He must also have a clear understanding of how the complainant's company or firm in particular functions in these areas. Coupled with this is the need to talk with potential witnesses and even with the suspects if the conditions are proper and advantageous to the inquiry.

What are we after? The basic thing to establish is the "source and application of funds" on the part of the suspect. The investigator will ultimately have to determine his "net worth" in some manner or other and go on from there. This brings into play an essential investigative element, albeit not part of the corpus; motive, which is based upon some need, real or fancied, which becomes merged with a person's net worth in some inexplicable way. This is an indirect but effective method of inquiry.

The concern here then is to develop information regarding a potential suspect. In other words; know your man. There are about four basic approaches that can be followed, either individually or combined: (1) the first is information elicited from the suspect's own personal records, if he has any and will make them available, (2) the second is any statements he may make which corroborate to some degree those things you have already developed independently to that point in the inquiry, (3) third, is secondary proof of the contents of his own records which may be obtained from some public records and private sources when he refuses, or cannot furnish, or if it would be a premature move on the investigator's part by disclosing an inquiry is underway, (4) fourth, information obtained from third persons who are in a position to have knowledge concerning the suspect's assets and liabilities such as a co-worker, family, associates, friends and/or enemies.

LOGICAL STEPS OF INQUIRY. From these same basic sources the investigator can develop the suspect's personal history and background with information on his antecedants, school, employment, health, marriages, divorces, annulments, deaths concerning him and his family, income (past and present), property ownership (real and personal), residences, personal activities, vocationally and otherwise.

The following step-by-step approach is a composite of many questions which are timeless in their use and usefulness that have been employed by many investigators to establish basic information concerning net worth, sources of income and application of funds. They are not necessarily in their order of importance but as in any inquiry a logical homogeneous grouping facilitates the investigator's recognition and understanding:

(1) Determine the suspect's salaries and wages for the past five years

(2) Ascertain any and all outside sources of income as to amounts and nature

(3) Find out if his wife, children or any dependents presently

have or did have during the past five years an interest in any business as an owner, partner, stockholder or director

(4) Determine the schools and colleges attended by his children and the costs of tuition, board, lodging, books and "other expenses"

(5) Does he, his wife, his children or relatives own real estate of any description? If so, list the holdings, the purchase price, cash paid, equity, trust deeds, chattel mortgages, the seller, payments and their pattern, tax and assessments and the source of funds used

(6) Detail the amounts paid for water, gas, electricity, telephone, repairs and other costs and expenses related to real estate interests

(7) Determine if there exists any real estate interests which are held in names other than those of his wife, children or relatives such as corporate, partnership or sole proprietorship fictitious names

(8) Ascertain if the suspect or his wife, children or relatives either individually or jointly sold any real estate in the past five years; and if any of them have purchased or contributed towards the purchase of any real estate, the title to which was not taken in their name

(9) Ascertain all of the insurance policies in the name of the suspect and/or family members, the amounts, types, loans against the policies, inception and maturity dates, premiums, claims, proofs of loss filed and indemnification

(10) Locate all bank accounts and other types in his name and members of his family and the balances for the past five years

(11) Determine if he or his wife, children or relatives ever had an interest in any type of monetary account not recorded in their names

(12) Locate all safe deposit boxes in the suspect's name or those in the names of his wife, children and relatives or in the names of fictitious persons

(13) Identify all stocks, bonds and other securities in his name, those of his wife, children and family and any possible alter ego he may have created

(14) List all motor vehicles registered to him, his wife, children, family, or company names in the past five years, the purchase price, payments, operating expense, when sold, to whom sold and for what amount

(15) List all premises rented and the fees for the past five years which were occupied by the suspect and his family and other persons, also the utilities expense

(16) Ascertain all items of personal property purchased by the suspect and his family in excess of $200.00 in the past five years

(17) List all charge accounts, including credit cards types, in his name and those of his family and fictitious names and periodic balances as may correlate to the loss dates under examination

(18) Determine if he, his wife or family have made any purchases of securities or items such as jewelry, furs and clothing in excess of $1,000.00 during the past five years

(19) Find if he, his wife or members of his family have loaned any money to others in excess of $500.00 in the past five years

(20) Determine medical expenses of the suspect and his family for the past five years, including dental and hospital costs

(21) Determine the type of entertainment the suspect enjoys and participates in and the cost

(22) Ascertain the amounts expended by the suspect, his wife, children and others close to him on vacations for the past five years. Include the locations, dates and the method of travel

(23) Find out whether he or his family have been the subjects of prior investigations and the nature of them

(24) List the expenditures over $300.00 by the suspect, his wife, family and/or others close to him for any hobby, charitable contributions, lodges and clubs, sports (events and equipment), collector items and liquor

(25) Determine if he, his wife or family have filed, jointly or individually, income tax returns in any state other than that of residence

(26) Determine if the suspect, his wife, family or anyone else

close to him attends frequently the race tracks, Jai Alai
games, dog races or gaming places and the average amounts
wagered

The steps outlined are not exclusive in kind. There can be variations and combinations introduced to fit a particular circumstance. Further, the reference in each step to family affinities
isn't imperative as the suspect can, and often does, have other
arrangements. The main thing to consider is the strong foundation of information created when these progressive steps can be
and are implemented. Each one developed leads in a chain-
reaction fashion to other logical and frequently rewarding areas
of inquiry.

Part II

Investigative Accounting

An imperative area of knowledge for a competent fraud investigator is accounting. When one considers the type of information which must be developed especially in embezzlements,
real estate, corporate and insurance fraud inquiries to name a
few, it is axiomatic. An accounting system is the very foundation
upon which a business operation is built. If the investigator
doesn't possess, at least in a basic degree, an understanding of
the principles involved and the terminology he will be lost. It
is not the purpose of this book to present an accounting or bookkeeping course of instruction but it is a definite purpose to engender an interest and appreciation for the needs of such knowledge and training. The field is becoming more complex with
the advent of electronic data processing which in itself portends
a wider scope of training for the investigator.

The question is frequently raised by the investigator, "Why
do I have to have this specialized knowledge (chemistry, handwriting, mechanical, biology, accounting, law, physiology etc.)
when I can always get an expert to help me?" The answer to this
query can be "You don't, we'll hire an expert for each problem
that arises and dispense with your services as not needed." However, the better answer is probably based upon the assumption

that no one can have too much knowledge, even in a general way about his job. An analogy can be drawn related to a statement in the first chapter (supra) regarding blueprints or the relationship between the policeman and the lawyer. Just as we need to know and understand the law, this being our blueprint to follow in that ethereal plane, so must we need a blueprint in the technical areas of investigation.

If an investigator doesn't understand what he is working at, the type of inquiries he must conduct to develop the information needed to establish a set of facts, if he doesn't know what to look for, or cannot recognize it when it is there, he is less than useless. There would be no justification for his existence in the area of fraud. The only manner in which he can achieve the degree of competency needed is to learn, at least the basics, of those "specialized" disciplines or areas of knowledge which are integrated with his functional field. For the fraud investigator, accounting is one of these.

The investigator must not only be conversant with practical aspects of his work but also have a familiarity with the theory involved. Frederick the Great of Prussia put emphasis on the idea his military commanders should not rely solely upon their vast "experience" in the field but they should acquire knowledge in depth of the theory of war. He was once asked his opinion of officers who reneged at the theoretical study of their profession, depending only upon their experience. He responded by saying he had in his army two great mules, magnificent beasts, both of which had experienced forty campaigns, performing well, but in the final analysis they were both still mules. The investigator is in a comparable position; he can go so far on experience, perhaps even doing a creditable journeyman-like job, but his value is limited. He can never reach the professional-like level unless he too learns the theory. He has the choice; either the experienced mule or the competent respected professional.

An accounting system records in monetary form all business transactions. It sets forth the buying of raw materials or inventory to their ultimate sale, either for cash or an account (credit), operating expense, manufacturing costs, salaries, wages, value of assets, amounts and types of liabilities, operating profits and losses and net worth. All of these are necessary to the owner/ proprietor from the smallest business up to the level of the gigantic corporations with their multiplicity of transactions and all the tortuous twistings and turnings which are such a large facet of their involved operations. To reflect the information needed there are two basic reports developed by the accountant regardless of the size of the operation or the variations implemented; these are the balance sheet and profit and loss statement. The former tells the financial condition of the business on a particular date, the latter discloses the result of the operations during a specified period of time. The balance sheet, then tells what the business owns, what it owes to others and the difference between the two, its value. The profit and loss statement discloses the action of the business, such as cost of goods sold, the sales, gross profit, the operating expense, and whether or not this resulted in a profit or loss for an accounting period.

The better way perhaps to explain basic bookkeeping principles to the embryo fraud investigator is to present the meaning of the various accounts which appear in the ledger and the report forms listed above. Briefly stated Cash and Petty Cash are separated into two accounts, the first being the monies, either retained on hand or deposited in the bank, the second being a small amount of money kept at the business location and used for minimal purchases and varied payments. Accounts Receivable means what all the various customers owe the business for purchases made on credit. Each individual customer has his own ledger sheet, the total of all these being entered into the control account.

Notes Receivable (promissory notes, secured or unsecured) are those signed by a customer acknowledging a debt. These are *not* entered into Accounts receivable; they are a separate situation. Inventories (Merchandise) discloses the value of goods on hand. The five accounts listed here appear as current assets on the balance sheet (infra). Land accounts disclose the market value of real property held in the name of the business. Building accounts are the value, less depreciation, of structures owned by the business. Machinery, Fixtures and Equipment also appear as separate accounts with their valuation less depreciation. Pre-paid

Expenses include anything paid for in advance such as insurance policies and advertising. These all appear as fixed assets (infra).

Accounts Payable is the total amount owed to all vendors. Notes Payable indicates the total amount of all notes signed by the business proprietor to secure or acknowledge an obligation. Accrued Liabilities accounts are the total of expenses which increase regularly during a period and will be paid later. The Capital account means the amount invested in the business.

The following is a simplified form of a balance sheet, the contents being self-indicative:

3 May 69

Assets		*Liabilities & Net Worth*	
Current:		Current:	
Cash	1,000.00	Accts Pyble.	900.00
Accts Rec.	500	Fixed:	
Merchandise	5,000.00	Notes Pyble.	3,000.00
Fixed:		Accrd. Taxes	500.00
			4,400.00
Prepaid Exp.	200.00	Net Worth:	13,000.00
Fix & Equip.	2,000.00	Capital (4–3–69)	1,300.00
Bldg.	8,000.00	Nt. Prft. (5–3–69)	14,300.00
Land	2,000.00		
	$18,700.00	Capital (5–3–69)	$18,700.00

The comparative balance sheet is of the same format, but reflecting two columns of figures (parallel) to show a comparison of financial condition on different dates.

The term "Assets" means anything of value owned by a business. This includes cash monies, accounts receivable (things owed to the business), notes receivable (written promises to pay), inventory or stock, land, buildings, vehicles, equipment or anything tangible. It should be noted that some companies list the illusive item of "Good Will" as asset, however intangible it may be.

The types of items appearing as "Fixed Assets" are those with a degree of permanency, are affected by depreciation and are not readily convertible to cash. This condition is opposed to those listed as "Current Assets" which of course are convertible at once and fluctuate in value during the accounting period.

Liabilities are the debts of a business, what is owed to others.

They include accounts payable such as merchandise purchases, notes payable which may have been given for various reasons such as loans, purchases, and mortgages or trust deeds that are outstanding. The liabilities are categorized in the same manner as the assets. The "Current" items are those which fluctuate during a period and are to be paid normally within a year's time, while the "Fixed" type are those which payments will extend beyond a year's time.

The "Net Worth" section of the balance sheet, sometimes called "Proprietorship" or "Capital," is the difference between the amount of assets and the amount of liabilities; i.e. assets minus liabilities equals the net worth.

There are four basic elements appearing within the Profit and Loss Statement; sales, cost of goods sold, operating expenses and miscellaneous incomes and expenses. The illustration (infra)

PROFIT & LOSS STATEMENT

For Period Ending 24 April 68

Sales:			
Gross Sales		10,000	
Less; Ret. Sales		200	
Net Sales			9,800.
Cost of Goods Sold:			
Invntry 3–25–68 (Previous)		4,000	
Purchases	500		
Less; Ret. Prchs	100		
Net Purchases		400	
		3,600	
Less; Invntry 4–24–69 (Current)		2,000	
Cost of Goods Sold			1,600
Gross Profit:			8,200
Operating Expense:			
Selling Exp.		1,000	
Administrative Exp.		400	
General Exp.		300	
Total Operating Expenses			1,700
Net Operating Profit:			6,500
Other Income:			
Interest Earned		20	
Rent Received		400	
Purchase Discounts		100	520
			7,020
Other Charges:			
Interest Expense		200	
Sales Discounts		300	
			500
Net Profit:			$6,520

graphically depicts the processes to arrive at the final answer, the net profit or loss. Sales expenses are those items such as salaries, wages, delivery expense, advertising, or any monetary outlay that is directly attributable to the sales activity. Administrative expense are those related to the operation of the office, including salaries, wages, supplies, communication, machinery or anything not connected directly to the sales effort. The general expenses are those which are not related directly either to sales or administration such as heat, water, electricity, rent or lease payments.

There are two items which appear in both the balance sheet and the profit and loss statement; the net profit (or loss) and the current inventory. The "current inventory" appears in the cost of goods sold section of the "P & L Statement" and also in the current assets section of the balance sheet. The "Net Profit" (or "Loss") appears of course as the final item of the "P & L Statement" and is infrequently included as a separate element in the last section of the balance sheet (net worth/capital section), but more often is included within the total amount appearing as net worth.

All of the amounts which appear in both of the foregoing business reports are summarizations of those amounts appearing in the General Ledger of a business. The general ledger is the final repository of all the recordings of business transactions. For every account there is a separate sheet in the ledger, these being set up in the form of a "T" and referred to as a "T account":

Cash Account

Date	Item	Debit	Date	Item	Credit

The words "debit" and "credit" merely mean which side of the ledger the entry in numerical amount is made; the former is the left side and the latter, the right side. The word "charge" is sometimes used in lieu of "debit."

The following are the rules for the debit-credit entries into the ledger accounts:

> All assets, expenses and cost of goods sold accounts are *increased* by a debit entry and *decreased* by a credit entry and have "debit balances" when the books are closed (infra) at the end of an accounting period. All liabilities, capital, sales and income accounts are *decreased* by a debit entry and *increased* by a credit entry and upon closing (infra) have a "credit balance". This is the basis of double-entry accounting process. For every debit entry into an account there must be an off-setting credit entry into another account.

For purposes of clarity a list of transactions is furnished with the appropriate entries in the ledger. It should be pointed out however, this illustration is a very brief representation of a small and basic business operation. Normally the figures appearing in the ledger accounts are "postings" from "general journals" (infra) entries which are footed/totaled at the end of the day (or period) and then entered ("posted") into the ledger, and the ledger has numerous other accounts in which entry will be made.

In larger business firms there will not only be a variety of journals for original entries but there will also be found a number of special or "subsidiary" ledgers. The reason is if all entries during the course of a business day were placed initially in the ledger, and if it were kept in detail, it would become unwieldy and impossible to handle. Thus, it is necessary to create general journals, cash journals, sales journals and purchases journals. This then is expanded into sub-divided ledgers for the same reasons.

The accounting process can be followed fairly easily as each transaction is represented by some memoranda located in a book of original entry which is posted to the general ledger or sometimes into a subsidiary ledger first, the totals then into the general ledger. A form called the "Trial Balance" (infra) is used to prove the accuracy of the postings and resulting balances.

The "Trial Balance" format and the information it discloses is of importance to the investigator. It is a method of testing the

Date	Item	Debit		Credit	
5-1	J. Zilch, invstmnt	Cash	10,000	Cptl	10,000
5-2	Office equipmnt	Equip	2,000	Cash	2,000
5-3	May rent	Expnse	200	Cash	200
5-4	Mdse Prchse.	Invntry	1,000	Acc Py	1,000
5-5	Veh. Prchsd.	Equip	1,200	Cash	200
				Acc Py	1,000
5-6	Off Sppls	Supply	100	Cash	100
5-9	Steno wage	Exp	75	Cash	75
5-10	Ins. Exp.	Pre-pd Exp	100	Cash	100
5-11	Bnk Loan	Cash	1,000	Nts Py	1,000
5-12	Sales, cash	Cst Gds Sld	800	Invntry	800
5-13	Sales, accnt	Accts Rec.	400	Sales	400
5-13	Sales, cash	Cst Gds Sld	200	Invntry	200
5-15	W/Drawal-persnl	Cptl	200	Cash	200
5-17	Utilities	Exp	20	Cash	20
5-20	Paid for mdse	Acct Py	200	Cash	200

Cash

1 Invst	10,000	2 Equip	2,000
11 Loan	1,000	3 Rent	200
	11,000	5 Vehcl	200
	3,095	6 Off Sppl	100
		9 Steno	75
		10 Ins.	100
		15 W/drw	200
		17 Utlty	20
		20 Mdse pd	200
			3,095
	7,905		

Accounts Rec.

13 Sales Acct	400		

Inventory

4 Prchs	1,000	12 Cst Gds Sld	800
	1,000	13 Cash sales	200
	0000		1,000

Equipment

2 Office	2,000	
5 Vehicle	1,200	
	3,200	

Office Supplies

| 6 Purchases | 100 | |

Accounts Payable

20 Paid	200	4 Invntry	1,000
		5 Vehicle	1,000
			2,000
			200
			1,800

Sales

| | | 13 Accnt | 400 |

Expenses

3 Rent	200	
9 Steno	75	
17 Utlty	20	
	295	

Cost of Goods Sold

12 Sales	800	
13 Sales	200	
	1,000	

Notes Payable

		11 Loan	1,000

Capital

15 W/drw	200	1 Invest	10,000
			200
			9,800

Prepaid Expense

10 Insur.	100		

accuracy of the postings to the ledger accounts by ascertaining if the total credits balance with the total debits. The format is a vertical list of accounts with columns for debits and credits. For simplification in constructing financial statements there can be added debit and credit columns for the Profit and Loss Statement accounts and also similar columns for those accounts which appear in the Balance Sheet. This is sometimes referred to as a "worksheet":

			P & L		Bal. Sht.	
Account	*D*	*C*	*D*	*C*	*D*	*C*
Cash	7,905				7,905	
Acct Rec	400				400	
Invntry	—				—	
Equip	3,200				3,200	
Off Sppl	100				100	
Acct Pybl		1,800				1,800
Expense	295		295			
Sales		400		400		
Cst Gds Sld	1,000		1,000			
Prepd Exp	100				100	
Nts Pybl		1,000				1,000
Capital		9,800				9,800
	13,000	13,000				
			1,295	400		
Net Profit or (Loss)				(895)	(895)	
			1,295	1,295	12,600	12,600

Profit and Loss Statement

Gross Sales	400
Cst Gds Sld	1,000
Gross Loss	(600)
Expenses	295
Net (Loss)	$ 985

Balance Sheet

Assets		Liabilities	
Cash	7,905	Acct Pybl	1,800
Acct Rec	400	Nts Pybl	1,000
Invntry	—		
Equip	3,200	Capital	9,800
Prpd Exp	100	Net Loss	(895)
Off Sppl	100	Net Worth	8,905
	$11,705		$11,705

It is apparent from the amounts disclosed in the ledger accounts, proven by a trial balance and then recorded in the profit and loss statement and the balance sheet that the proprietor suffered a net loss for the operating period.

The investigator will often hear the expression "closing" or "closed the books." There is no great mystery attached to the phrase or the activity it describes. It merely means that the operating accounts are balanced out at the end of the accounting period, the time limit of which is selected by the proprietor or sometimes by the Internal Revenue Service and State Franchise Tax Board for particular types of businesses. All that is done is the footing of the columns of figures and entering those amounts on the other side of the ledger "T" accounts. This is normally limited to those accounts appearing in the Profit and Loss Statement. The Balance Sheet accounts are not usually closed because they are not really representative of a particular period but in fact are indicative of total transactions regardless of time of occurrence. The accounts are "closed into" a summary account such as the "Profit and Loss Account" and this in turn is "closed" into the "Capital Account." The "profit and Loss Account is *debited* and the particular operating account is *credited*. If the debit side of the account is smaller than the credit side the balance is placed on the debit side of that account and the Profit and Loss Account is credited. The Profit and Loss

Account is debited in being closed to the Capital Account, the latter being credited with that amount. A post-closing trial balance is usually run to verify the ledger account balances and to determine if any errors had been made by transposition or computing the closing balances.

The books of original entry are of importance to the fraud investigator. These journals vary in number, complexity and format depending upon the size or nature of the business under inquiry. Often the cash and general journals are combined into one with sufficient columns for debiting and crediting a number of ledger accounts. They consist of a General Journal, into which miscellaneous daily entries are made; the Cash Journal, as a separate item, into which all receipts and withdrawals and disbursements normally related to the basic operation of the business are made; the Sales Journal to record daily sales (or services if such is the company business) and the Purchases Journal into which are entered all purchases made. The *totals* of each of these journals are posted to the General Ledger accounts effected, except those from the General Journal which are posted in detail.

The term "Controlling Accounts" are in fact accounts receivable and accounts payable located in the *general* ledger. They will match the totals in both the subsidiary Accounts Receivable Ledger and Accounts Payable Ledger. Their purpose is important to the auditor and investigator as they facilitate the location of errors. If the controlling account balances the subsidiary ledger doesn't have to be analyzed.

Auxiliary records are also of importance to the investigator. They include the petty cash fund, check stubs, cash register tapes, bank statements, deposit slips and the bank book. They are all related to the receipts or disbursement of cash and merchandise the the amounts appearing therein are also entered into the appropriate journals, subsidiary ledgers and accounts in the general ledger. All can and are used for verification.

The finding of errors is the most important part of the investigative accounting function, whether they be clerical, of accounting principles, or technique, and whether they are of omission or commission (willful or not). The trial balance is normally the first thing analyzed for errors. However, if there has been an equal offsetting error in either column nothing is reflected and the error is undetectable by this method alone.

There are a few tests the investigator can make to locate the error. If the trial balance does not foot properly there may be merely an error in computing the columns. This should be checked out first. If the difference between the debit column and the credit column is divisable by two there is usually a posting to the wrong side of an account. If the difference is nine or a multiple thereof, there may be an error in transcription; a difference which is divisible by nine is usually the result of decimal points being misplaced.

If the trial balance fails to foot properly, the accounts appearing thereon will have to be checked back into the ledger for proper balance. If the error cannot be disclosed at this point, the posting from the journals will have to be examined. In other words work backwards from the ledger to the book of original entry, including any auxiliary record which may be available. This is known as "abstracting" the accounts or sometimes called "reverse posting."

The concepts of internal control of a business through an adequate and properly implemented system of internal checks is the most important factor of an accounting system insofar as the security and integrity of the firm itself is concerned and the related path of inquiry which must be followed by the fraud investigator. Primarily, the accounting system must be so structured as to furnish accurate and adequate information. The detailed transactions should be handled in such a manner as to preclude or at least minimize the opportunities for manipulations and falsifications. Also, it must operate in such a way as to diminish errors and at the same time provide a method by which errors, if they do exist, can be located.

An analysis of the accounting system by the investigator will determine the extent of such control features as may be implemented by a particular company. This then, will determine the scope of the verification procedures which he, or his auditor, will be using. It will, of course, largely determine the degree of confidence he can place in the accounting records themselves.

It must be appreciated that the complete elimination of error or dishonesty is not possible in spite of the increased implementation of computerized bookkeeping or the size, large or small, of the business. The larger the business, the greater the opportunities for fraud based upon the necessary delegation of authority and responsibility to subordinates. Similarly, in smaller businesses, equal opportunities are available because of the increased informality.

One of the principles of internal control is the relating of the operating routines of a business to the accounting system. This, in itself, will not prevent errors or dishonesty, but it will assist to some degree in the locating of errors and the persons possibly responsible. If there exists an awkward arrangement of the processes creating unnecessary bottleneck delays, useless non-productive red-tape procedures and antiquated concepts, the possibilities of fraud and error mount commensurately.

The other and most basic principle of internal control and upon which all are founded is that no one person in an organization shall be in complete control of any important part of the business operations. The way in which such a system is created calls for an arrangement of records and procedures in such an order or sequence that no part of the accounts is entirely in the hands or control of a single individual. This permits, in accordance with the prime necessity, every transaction passing through the hands or control of at least two persons. This division of responsibility and authority increases the difficulty for fraudulent acts and errors proportionately with the number of persons assigned. It requires, then, the collusion of persons working in the same area of control, rather than the covert manipulation of the records and cash by a single person. If it is merely an error this can be discovered and located much earlier in the accounting process.

The division of duties in a relatively simplified form could be where one person records the sales and another debits the customer's account; one person will receive collections while another credits customers' accounts; one person handles cash monies and another maintains the cash account in the ledger; one employee makes the sales while another prepares the order for shipment; the purchase of goods are so handled that dif-

ferent persons from those who make the purchase orders and
those who will receive the goods make out the requisitions; one
person will handle the approving of invoices and another will
issue cash or checks in payment; the payroll is handled in similar manner, one employee makes up the roster, another signs
as maker and still another issues the checks.

The small business operation, whether it be a one or two
man professional service firm, or merchandising or manufacturing
unit creates problems for the proprietor when attempting to
establish a competent system with desired divided functions.
The normally small number of employees precludes such an arrangement, in fact forces each employee to double up on duties,
assuming more authority and responsibility rather than less or
divided authority. The problem is magnified today by the ever
increasing federal, state, county and municipal records that a
business concern is required to maintain. This, of course, commensurately increases the opportunities for fraud and incidence
of error. Not a little of this is caused by incompetency and poor
motivation on the part of employees.

The smaller the firm, especially the one-man type which includes the physician, dentist, real estate broker, lawyer, engineer, accountant and similar types, the larger the opportunities
for peculations. They are too often the victims of embezzlements
and gross, costly accounting errors, because they normally resort
to the one-woman office manager/secretary/bookkeeper/cashier
assistant who has complete control of the cash flow, records
and inventory. The factor that is most apparent in this type of
operation is the increased degree of informality in the office
which increases the opportunities for fraudulent practices and
mistakes resulting from a lack of the understanding of basic
bookkeeping procedures. The proprietor or professional man
who practices his business or profession alone has the constant
companionship of his one-girl staff who is often initially employed not just because she a highly efficient worker, but usually because of other and additional attributes, including a good
personality and physical appearance and not a little aggreeable-
ness. The social barriers after an appropriate period become
somewhat weakened and indefinable, finally collapsing. They

both come to know the relative strengths and weaknesses of each other creating unconsciously (sometimes) a new arrangement in their workday lives. The proprietor/principal soon places the complete trust of his every day business personal affairs in her hands. If she does have the instincts and inclinations of a thief, regardless of her other occupational and personal competancies, she encounters little difficulty then in stealing her employer's funds and hiding the fact in the records she maintains. Also, if the relationship has transcended that level which our society, at least for this fleeting moment in the era of social change, normally expects to exist between employer and employee, the probability of fraud is overwhelmingly increased accompanied with an obvious equally strong decrease in incidence of reports, complaints or cooperation with investigators. If the situation is one of error, emperic studies have reflected the employer could care less as other factors apparently more than compensate for any monetary loss he may experience at the hands of his one-girl-friday help-mate.

Why does the investigator concern himself with the examination or auditing of a company's books? The reason is multipurpose. The first is the general verification of the accounts to determine the financial condition which is imperative when he is making inquiries regarding possible corporate frauds, embezzlements or investment scams. The next reason is to determine whether the company's funds and inventories have been properly accounted for. The third, and primary one usually, or else he would not have been concerned initially, is the detection, prevention of fraud or determining the extent of a fraud already reported and the persons responsible. From the practical point of view he, either alone if qualified or in conjunction with his investigative accountant, should ascertain unequivocally the purpose and the extent of the audit. If there is a belief that misappropriations are in fact existent, then a detailed examination of individual accounts will be required. This, an embezzlement, normally is the only reason for an investigator to be concerned with a company's books; he is not in the business of operating a private bookkeeping service. An examination is essentially limited to a definitive purpose or area of interest, being specific in nature. Only in the event of a situation in which the primary effort is the establishing of a corporate securities act violation or investment frauds in the nature of false pretenses and even trick and device when loans for a specific purpose are involved, will justify complete or detailed audits, especially in determining the source and application of funds. The balance sheet audit only reflects the assets, liabilities and resulting net worth for a particular date, although it requires analysis of the respective accounts. It serves no useful purpose to the investigator other than perhaps in a violation in which purported net worth has been published to effect a fraudulent sale or loan. In other words there are two probable paths for the investigator and/or his accountant to follow, an examination of a particular area of the accounts or an extended one of a detailed audit to prove or disprove the accuracy of the whole accounting process.

The sequence of procedures usually adhered to in an audit is the verification of all cash and securities, including all instruments as opposed to the related accounts. This can be followed by a general ledger trial balance. Before any real effort is made at an audit or special examination, however, the investigator must acquaint himself with the company's operations. He should ascertain who the persons are with authority and responsibility for the various segments both in the areas of administration and operations and the scope and limitations of their duties. If a corporate setup is being scrutinized the articles of incorporation, the by-laws and the minutes of the Board of Directors' meetings are not only valuable but imperative to determine specific instructions, obligations, duties, authorities, liabilities, responsibilities, individual interests, policies, operational procedures and other matters which are inherent in the functioning of a so constituted company or firm. If a partnership is the subject of the inquiry the partnership agreement is viewed in a comparable light to determine the same things. And, if it's a sole proprietorship, similar information should be developed from the owner to that degree which is commensurate with a smaller business controlled by a single person. In other words, get to know who and what you are working on before starting.

If, of course, the complainant company can and does have an

independent audit or examination made at its own expense this phase of the investigation is completed. But, this does not relieve the investigator of the obligation and necessity of understanding the findings. He cannot properly perform his function if he does not. He must still review the examination or audit report to determine his own course of action. The accountant's report is not the completed case. It merely discloses a probable crime which must be still tied to a particular person.

The type of inquiry being made by a fraud investigator seldom if ever requires a detailed entry by entry examination of the complete set of accounts. It is only when it has been established that there exists irregularities in a particular area, that the examination in detail is performed searching for repetitious falsificatons. The embezzler is much the same as any other criminal in that once a pattern is established which proves to be successful it is usually adhered to during the course of the peculations. The area of examination can frequently be determined by the type, amount and particular section of interest of the internal control measures. If there is a good cash flow control, perhaps the inventory or sales section may merit closer scrutiny. Do not, however, be misled by assertions of "good" internal control. Often they prove nonexistent. Actually if there are losses, and misappropriations are suspected or known, the controls then evidently are not "good."

Practically every internal fraud with which the investigator will be concerned will involve the theft of cash monies. There are, of course, thefts of merchandise, equipment and supplies, all of which will require some understanding of accounting procedures to disclose the methods used. Normally, however, these usually result with no record being made and will be indicated only upon an inventory. Merchandise thefts can and are often found via records in the sales and shipping sections of a business operation which have been altered to cover the act. An audit in the normal sense will show such a situation. In case of sales ostensibly on credit, these must be supported by records which reflect a charge to a customer and all the charges to accounts receivable are in fact sales. In doing this the invoices must be examined (by serial number if possible), checked as to such record as is maintained and into the ledger. If an invoice is found not to be charged to a customer it probably has been abstracted.

In regard to the inventory count for the period under examination investigators have found it prudent at times to examine the sales invoices at the end of the period to ascertain what goods were actually gone from the stock but still might have been included in the inventory to cover a shortage. Further, if the records reflect inordinate increases in sales towards the end of the accounting period, or a strange decrease during the first part of the subsequent period, which do not seem to conform with the normal business cycle, the shipping records and the order files should come under close scrutiny. Here will be found fictitious charges made to customers with highly active accounts and predated invoices to include the "sale" within the period. Even if the customer is asked for confirmation regarding receipt of shipped goods and he doesn't respond affirmatively, it is often assumed the goods are in transit and his receiving clerk just doesn't acknowledge.

Cash transactions usually receive the larger part of an investigator's attention due to the fact the greater proportion of internal thefts involves spurious entries, the willful mishandling of those records, but more often yet, the calculated failure to make entries or fraudulently handling of related records such as payroll accounts. Properly put, the search or examination is not limited to the accounting for cash receipts or disbursements of record, but also the determination if *all* cash in fact does appear of record. If such a situation does exist and is the alleged basis of the fraud a complete examination is then required which means outside inquiries from all possible sources of cash receipts. Thus, customers would have to be contacted regarding their purchases and the documentation and method of payment.

In the situation where entries have been made in the cash journal special attention should be focused upon the items of discounts, allowances, interest and any other manner of charges which may effect the receipts. A very common method employed by office thieves who have, unfortunately, control of both the cash flow and the related records is *under*footing (diminution) of the cash receipts columns, although having *entered* the *correct* amount at the time and in the proper space for the sale. Joined to this dual action is the third move, the *over*footing (increasing) sales discounts column. For clarification, assume the customer pays *on account* $1,000.00 for a sizeable purchase and for which he is accorded a 10 percent discount in reward for prompt payment. Properly entered, the debit items of $900.00 to the cash account with $100.00 to the sales discounts account will appear and a corresponding credit entry of $1,000.00 to his account under Accounts Receivable. If the office thief decides to steal $100.00 at this time, either from the amount tendered by the customer or from the cash on hand fund, this will alter the footings as indicated in the cash journal columns and they will appear then for ledger entry as $800.00 debited to cash account and $200.00 to the sales discount account column and a credit entry to the accounts receivable. The $100.00 taken must be obscured in some manner, either debited to some other account or *not* entered at all as a credit to the accounts receivable. If it would be entered as a credit the accounts receivable would be out of balance.

When cash received, by company policy, is normally deposited in a bank, verification of such deposits is an integral part of the investigator's function. If this is done temporary "loans" of cash taken by the thief in the forms of "kiting" or "lapping" will be disclosed. These scams are very common, again where the concept of proper internal control is vitiated by permitting the same person to exercise control both over the cash flow and related records. In a "kiting" operation for example (a) $1,000.00 check is received from customer Jones, stolen and cashed by the office thief, but *not* entered in the cash journal as a receipt; (b) when it becomes apparent to the thief that it is advisable to *credit* something to Jones' account, he will take a $1,500.00 check received from customer Smith depositing same but of which he will credit $1,000.00 to Jones and $500.00 to Smith; (c) next a payment of $2,000.00 is received from customer Black by check which is also deposited but from which he will credit to

Smith $1,000.00 and to Black $1,000.00. The remaining deficit of $1,000.00 can often be handled via fraudulent disbursements route such as charging it through an operating expense account. For the alert investigator the first act may not become known unless there is obtained independent information from customer Jones regarding his account such as an inquiry concerning its balance. However, the examination of the bank deposit slip used when Smith's check was included in the total amount deposited, will show the check for $1,500.00 but the corresponding entries in the accounts will indicate only $1,000.00 to Jones and $500.00 to Smith. The next series will reflect on the deposit slip a check for $2,000.00 from Black but related entries to Smith for $1,000.00 and to Black only $1,000.00. About this time the investigator could validly assume that someone is "kiting" the accounts to cover misappropriations.

Fraudulent cash disbursements create comparable accounting problems. The investigator must direct his attention towards the professed "authority" used by the office thief. This means a close look at the vouchers, the numbering sequence of the checks used, the authorized maker's signatures and endorsements appearing on cancelled instruments. Fictitious payees are often used by the thief. Attention should be centered on checks made to company officers and employees and also to "cash." If the degree of frequency appears somewhat out of the ordinary these must be traced all the way, determining all parties and again the purported authorization for issuance.

Fraudulent handling of a company's cash falls generally in two categories, the willful failure to account for cash receipts and unauthorized disbursements. The former includes the act of entering of sales in the record but not appearing in the footings (forced or "underfooted") as debits to the cash account or accounts receivable with the proper corresponding credit to the sales account; sales actually entered and debited to the customer's account but cleared with a corresponding phony credit entry to the merchandise returned account; or sales not even recorded; cash from a customer properly entered in the receipts journal but not included in the footing; an expense account debited to correspond to a credit entry in the customer's account; and various income (other than sales) not being entered into an account.

In regard to unauthorized or falsely contrived disbursements the investigator will often be confronted with situations that include among many others, checks being issued but not recorded, checks with fictitious payees, false payrolls with fictitious employees as payees, "forced" footings, forged signatures on authorizations to make disbursements; second, and even third time use of vouchers which are not examined close enough by some myopic cashier, and the oldest scam of all, the "padding" of expense accounts including false receipts used in support; and acting in concert with vendors to raise the amounts of bills after approval by a company officer and splitting the cash overage. This last is very difficult to ascertain especially in a sizable company which continuously receives large and diverse amounts of raw materials and supplies due to a company officer not being able to recall independently the exact amounts of every check, voucher, purchase invoice and purchase order he may have signed during the course of a business day. The document examiner here is the service aid to the investigator in making the case.

Accounting errors develop from a variety of sources; ignorance, stupidity, carelessness, dishonesty, and poor motivation. All are enhanced by questionable office and bookkeeping methods. However, the basic differences in accounting mistakes is primarily in two areas, unintentional and intentional.

What has been discussed to this point chiefly relates to the embezzling employee. There do exist other reasons for falsification of company records which are just as damaging and costly. In a sole proprietorship, a partnership and especially in a corporate enterprise the net worth can be so falsified to make the assets and net worth of a company appear to be unusually and factually high in order to induce investment by outside persons or conversely so low as to discourage potential worthy investors permitting another collaborating person to gain control. This can be, if discovered by independent audit, the basis of theft by false pretenses. Also if the misrepresentation of the financial worth is used to obtain loans and then the funds are diverted for other purposes not intended, theft by trick and device can be alleged (*see* chapters on False Pretenses and Trick and Device).

Electronic Data

Another spectre on the horizon, and of which the investigator had better take cognizance, is the advent of electronic computing devices. The purpose of this book will not permit a detailed discussion of these new exotic contrivances other than to very briefly look at their impact in the field of accounting and the related frauds. Regardless of the complicated mechanisms involved and the resulting reports, confusing and otherwise, the basic concepts of the bookkeeping processes and principles are not changed. They are merely speeded up beyond that rate which would not have been possible with human manual control and diminishes the number of persons intimately connected with those processes. Concomitantly the separation of people and their duties, the basis of internal control is somewhat vitiated being replaced frequently by the multi-purpose employee who programs the machine and often operates it. The thing to consider is that which is put into the machine by the programmer is going to control completely that which comes out. The machine does not think for itself. It merely stores vast quantities (not necessarily quality) of information that is fed into it and then relates it at a later time in a prearranged style when certain keys are punched by the operator. Unfortunately at the earlier stages of the machines development and use there seemed to grow up about it an aura of mystic omniscience in which mistakes were not considered. Everyone seemed to forget that it was and is an inanimate object with no thought processes of its own and actually only parrots the activized thoughts of the person who put data on the tape or punch cards. It will do exactly what he directs it to do and no more. Especially, it will not correct mistakes.

A good example of programming took place in a New York brokerage firm over a period of about eight years during which an executive who had access to the mystery machine embezzled over a quarter of a million dollars. He programmed the computer to transfer funds from the firm's account into his account. He also programmed it to indicate these funds had been for the purchase of securities. He then sold the securities ostensibly purchased keeping the money. The accounting processes as related by the machine disclosed no imbalance in any of the customers' accounts. No one apparently considered conducting an investigation by such "old fashioned" methods as an internal audit relying instead upon the accuracy of the "scientific" marvel of the age.

Cash is not the only thing that can be effected by the fraudulent programming of a computer. Merchandise and equipment is also vulnerable. A mere changing of one figure will increase the reported normal inventory losses caused by breakage etc. permitting undetected thefts for a period and later the inventory count will be rectified by assuming the original figure amount, the accounts still in balance and the situation remaining undisclosed. Payrolls can be handled in a like manner with fictitious payees much the same as the payroll clerk discussed above in manually operated systems. A related scam to the payroll is the deductions of a few cents extra on each employees' paycheck (who notices 3 to 5 cents extra in the deductions columns on a check voucher?) by the programmer and siphons the amounts off to himself. The Los Angeles District Attorney's Office had a case for prosecution in which a County employee in the payroll processing center merely held down the "repeat" button and permitted his own check to be reprinted several times. As many ways as there are to steal monies and properties as can be conceived by the clerk, bookkeeper, accountant or cashier, so there are ways in which the computer can be adapted for the same purpose and with perhaps greater efficiency; and, unfortunately, concealed better and longer due to the unmerited faith and trust placed in the machine.

The One-Girl Office

The area into which police fraud investigators frequently find themselves projected are the cases of embezzlement in the small office in sales, manufacturing or service firms which employ the single person who performs all duties normally handled

by a collective group of stenographers, bookkeepers, reception-
ists, cashiers, secretaries and file clerks found in the larger organizations. The "Take" may not be as great there as in the
larger firms but the effect can be every bit as devastating to
the proprietor. The relationships which can and do develop
between these "Girl Fridays" and their employers can cause a
number of problems. These affinities too often transcend the
daytime office contact and become very personal. The barriers
are difficult to maintain in close daily contact.

For purposes of discussion let us examine the operation of a
dentist's office in which the receptionist jack-of-all-trades was
dipping into the till and ultimately convicted of grand theft by
embezzlement. One of the first things the investigator determined was the lack of internal controls and the implementation
of faulty accounting procedures. The process was used by the
receptionist in this instance was in the reverse order of proper
bookkeeping, in that the ledger cards were used as the book of
original entry and the Daily Journal as the secondary entry.
She would make out on the patient's initial visit an individual
ledger card (a dental chart on the reverse side) listing their
address, telephone number and other administrative data which
is acceptable procedure. However, when charges were incurred
they would be entered initially into the Daily Journal. When
any payments were made by the patient, again the original credit
entry would be made directly into the ledger card and later
into the Daily Journal.

Bank deposits were supposed to be made daily by the receptionist, consisting of all checks, money orders received and
cash monies as deemed necessary or desirable. She would make
up a bank deposit form, make a total entry of the amount into
the Daily Journal and then take the funds and form to the
nearby bank for deposit in her employer's account. All checks
and money orders received from patients were consistently deposited, never being held and endorsed for outside disbursements.

Another thing the investigator determined at the outset were
the cut-off dates. In other words the dates of the suspect-
receptionist's hiring and termination. Then the dentist's outside

accountant was contacted for his working papers and reports concerning the fiscal period prior to the hiring date. It was found all accounts had been in order and balanced for a period of four years and that the peculations, if any, had come about within the last eleven months under the girl just terminated.

The method employed by our "Girl-Friday" to divert funds followed a fairly classic pattern when such an opportunity was present; little or no supervision coupled with less than adequate accounting procedures and apparent lack of interest on the part of the employer. As payments (receipts) from patients came to the office (mailed or in person) in the form of checks, money orders and cash monies, the appropriate credit entry was dutifully made in the individual ledger cards. All checks and money orders were entered into the Daily Deposit Form by ABA number and amounts, also some funds in cash monies. However, after the Bank Deposit Form was totaled, she would remove cash monies received and then enter into the Daily Journal only those credits which when computed with the starting cash-on-hand for the day, the day's receipts, less the bank deposits and other infrequent minor disbursements, would reflect no overage. Not all cash monies were removed, there being sufficient amounts deposited (appearing on the Deposit Form) each day to eliminate any question that may develop from a cursory inspection of her work. The proper entries into the ledger cards precluded any questions arising from the patients as their statements were computed from these.

The only efforts at internal control were a comparison of the Daily Journal with the Bank Deposit Form, and of course, the amounts reflected balanced, raising no issue unless the figures were compared with the apparent volume of business for the period concerned by someone with the experience to recognize the fact that the receipts did not compare favorably with the activity, in this case, the employer. This is exactly what happened one day when he, without informing his receptionist beforehand, wrote a check on the business account and a few days later the payee telephoned him telling him that it was returned as an "NSF" item. About this time the receptionist quit (she had received the initial call from the payee a few days before during the employer's absence and stalled the payee telling him her employer was out of town for a couple of days and to call again on the following Monday). The dentist then took a closer look at the business/administrative end of his operation and belatedly concluded his faithful employee had gotten to him real good.

The police fraud investigator cannot limit himself in such situations to merely examining the books and seeking a complaint on this information alone. He uses the comparison deficits disclosed (Journal to Ledger to Daily Bank Deposit Forms) for purposes of contacting the individual patients whose credits failed to appear in the Journal. From them he obtains the cancelled checks and all of the information as can be recalled concerning the circumstances at the time of payment. Invariably each instrument had the Dentist's stamped endorsement indicating it had been in fact honored by the maker-patient and dentist-payee's banks, but did not appear in the Journal. From those who had paid their bill in cash, statements were obtained in detail, indicating the receptionist was the acceptor of the monies.

With the supporting information and documentation obtained from the patients analyzed an examination then made of the Daily Journal and Bank Deposit Book (Form) disclosed there had been sufficient cash monies on hand, independent of checks and money orders, on each date of an alleged loss to cover the diverting of cash amounts. The starting balance each day (balance forward) coupled with payments received which were delineated as to form, show an amount available from which is subtracted the cash monies deposited in addition to checks and money orders. On each occasion there was reflected cash monies on hand (received) in the amounts more than adequate to permit removal of sums that were comparable to the checks and money orders deposited but not indicated in the Journal as collected.

This case, although not complex in size or circumstances, presented in somewhat more definitive detail than those analyzed previously in the chapter, a combination of the basic elements; legal, sociological, investigative and technical. These areas of consideration have a tendency to merge into each other. They lose, to some degree, their singularity, but they still should be examined independently. This helps create a structured approach to an investigation which is necessary for continuity and completeness.

CHAPTER III

FORGERY AND RELATED OFFENSES

T HE REASON for inclusion of this topic in the text is that forgery, fictitious checks, the issuance of checks without sufficient funds and related acts are all forms of theft by fraudulent means. Forgers and fraudulent check passers were once viewed with distain by the con-man. But the practice with all its possible variations has become so prevalent and lucrative (and physically safe) that the class-conscious con-man has joined the group. Also gravitating towards the same field are the thugs who initiated their crime careers with acts of violence. They have found the imposition of penalties far less severe and their efforts conversely more remunerating than their experience with robbery, burglary and assault. It is nothing unusual when reviewing the arrest records of known con-artists of stature and experience to see their arrests for embezzlement, use of the mails to defraud etc. interspersed with a number of arrests for check violations. The same is true of their more violently inclined brethren. In fact the field is becoming overcrowded with the amateurs outnumbering the professionals. About 54% of those arrested have had no prior experience or criminal histories. The remaining 46% have usually backgrounds replete with arrests of all kinds; and nearly 25% of all offenders are women.

Lack of Statistics

Accurate statistics are not possible to compute; however, knowledgeable sources estimate that only about 10% of the actual offenses are reported to police agencies. Various estimates by both public and private agencies indicate the probable total loss is in excess of two billion dollars nationally each year and

200 million dollars in the state of California. Hence for every 10,000 cases reported there are probably 100,000 offenses that actually took place. The reasons for failure to report are many and varied both sociological and business. Police agencies in California enjoy approximately 65% "case cleared" record. The check writer probably is the greatest existing operating threat to a businessman's financial stability and security today. He surpasses the burglar, robber and the employee merchandise thief in amounts taken and the frequency of incidents.

The Dilemma

The businessman, storekeeper or merchant is jockeyed into the unenviable position of having to assume calculated risks each time a credit/check transaction is handled. The larger part of this country's business today is done with checks and credit cards. If he doesn't fall in line and take part in the "normal," now accepted, form of business, he loses his customer. The credit card companies and the banks carry on continuous, appealing and evidently successful advertising programs in all forms of the news media urging the public to take part in their attractive well rationalized form of financial transactions. In the face of such, the merchant has no choice but to join the parade. This opens the doors to the con-men, professional and amateur, who can quickly determine the opportunities available.

The insufficient funds check or "NSF Checks" as they are called in California is the major problem. This is the area which has proven so attractive to the amateur. Included in this group are the housewives, alcoholics and playboys short on ready change and others to which it becomes almost a crime of opportunity without a great deal of pre-planning. Because of the frequency of the crime there is developing, valid or not, a sociological viewpoint that it is not really malum per se and the severe penalties which are levied on the usual offense (forgery etc., 1–14 yrs) should be mitigated and perhaps even eliminated because the acceptor probably took the instrument knowing that it was not good, but rather than lose a sale accepted the risk. It is further purported by the same theorists that the "intent to defraud" is merely presumed in such situations and not factual;

that this permits the victim to use a police agency to reduce what, in a sense, are voluntarily assumed business risks, the agency then, in effect, acting as a collection agency. This theory may have validity in some areas, however, a study of the obvious repetitive efforts of the so-called "occasional bad-check writer" that has come to the attention of the authors clearly indicate that the poor maligned forgetful housewives *et al* who over-draw their accounts are actually conniving small-time con-artists with the moral outlook of alleycats. If a police agency follows the rules of proper investigation the "collection agency" concept is eliminated.

There is no reason the merchant should not expect and receive the same degree of honesty and integrity from his customers who purchase on a credit basis as those who still resort to archaic cash monies. The check writer or credit card purchaser, who in effect violates a form of trust, is just as much a thief as the one, who by stealth, takes away the property of his victim. The same intent and philosophy is involved.

Wider Scope

Although we are concerned here with the application of the criminal law and investigative techniques as they relate to fraudulent instruments, it must be appreciated that to have an understanding of the principles, we also of necessity must have a working knowledge of that segment of statutory law usually entitled "Commercial Paper" or "Negotiable Instruments Law." In most jurisdictions it definitively outlines the elements of negotiability, clearly stating the rights, liabilities and obligations of all the parties to a transaction. We will not attempt to go into a detailed summation or analysis of the provisions of the code other than to cover briefly some of the rudiments. But, the student is urged to read and study that part of the law in conjunction with those statutes covering the criminal aspects of the topic.

The term "negotiable instrument" is used with frequency in both the criminal and civil law. What is an instrument as opposed to a document? An instrument is an agreement expressed in writing, signed and delivered by one person to another, transferring title to, or creating a lien on property, or giving the right to a debt or a duty. A document is merely a writing and does not purport to transfer title. An instrument embodying an obligation for the payment of money is called "negotiable" when the title to it and the whole amount of money expressed upon its face, with the right to sue therefore in his own name, may be transferred from one person to another without a formal agreement, but by the mere endorsement and delivery by the holder.

The last-named person also referred to as a "holder in due course" is the one who has acquired the ownership of the negotiable instrument in good faith and for value. He is entitled to overcome all rights incident to ownership and can enforce the instrument, notwithstanding the defenses which the parties liable on the instrument may have had against the person from whom it was purchased. In other words, a thief who might acquire the instrument is not a bonafide holder, this includes one who would take it by force or fraud. Insofar as liability attaches to an instrument, the drawer and endorsers, as between themselves, are liable in the inverse order in which they became parties to the instrument.

There are two basic categories of negotiable instruments, a promissory note and the bill of exchange. All other forms are variations. A bill of exchange is an unconditional order, in writing, addressed by one person to another, signed by the person giving it, requiring the person to whom it is addressed to pay on demand or at a fixed or determinable future time, a certain sum of money, to order or to bearer. There are three parties involved: (1) the drawer/maker, (2) the drawee (bank), (3) the payee. A promissory note is an unconditional promise in writing made by one person to another, signed by the person promising (maker), engaging to pay on demand or at some fixed or determinable future date, a certain sum of money to order or bearer. There are two parties only involved, the maker and the payee. A check, then, is one form of a bill of exchange.

Checks used in present day financial transactions are varied in form. The "personal" check is the most frequently observed due to the ease at which accounts can be opened. When a check is said to be "personalized" it merely means the bank has printed the depositor's name and sometimes his address on the face. However, it is "payroll" or "business checks which are usually involved in the offenses in which large amounts of money are lost and in which a ring of persons are operating. These are normally stolen or counterfeited. Another type of check is the "cashier's" which is purchased, and drawn by the bank upon its own funds. The "certified" check is one for which the bank assumes sole liability by the act of certifying on the face of the instrument that there are sufficient funds on hand or deposit in the maker's account to cover it. The check, then, in effect, becomes the promissory note of the bank. Yet another form is the "counter check." This is merely a blank faced check which the merchant maintains as a convenience and upon which the customer/maker writes the name of his bank (the drawee) and account identifying information and completes it in the same manner as any other check.

Promissory notes include bonds, money orders, traveler's checks and certificates of deposit. They all have only two parties involved, the promissor/maker and the payee.

Classic Proscription

Statutory law in many areas goes into detail in effect to describe the elements of forgery and those things which can be the subject of the crime. One state enacted the following: "Every person who, *with the intent to defraud,* signs the name of another person, or of a fictitious person, *knowing that he has no authority to do so,* or falsely makes, alters, forges, or counterfeits any charter, letters-patent, deed, lease, indenture, writing obligatory, will, testament, codicil, bond, covenant, bank bill or note, postnote, check, draft, bill of exchange, contract, promissory note, due-bill for the payment of money or property, receipt for money or property, passage ticket, power of attorney, or any certificate of any share, right, or interest in the stock of any corporation or association, or any controller's warrant for the payment of money at the treasury, county order or warrant, or request for the payment of money, or the delivery of goods or chattels of any kind, or for the delivery of any instrument of writing, or acquittance, release, or discharge of any debt, account, suit, action, demand or other thing, real or personal, or any transfer or assurance of money, certificate of stock, goods, chattels, or other property whatever, or any letter of attorney, or other power to receive money, or to receive or transfer certificates of shares of stock or annuities, or to let, lease, dispose of, alien, or convey any goods, chattels, lands, or tenements, or other estate, real or personal, or any acceptance or indorsement of any bill or exchange, promissory note, draft, order, or any assignment of any bond, writing obligatory, promissory note, or other contract for money or other property; or counterfeits or forges the seal or handwriting of another; or utters, publishes, passes, or attempts to pass, as true and genuine, any of the above named false, altered, forged, or counterfeited matters, as above specified and described, knowing the same to be false, altered, forged or counterfeited, with the intent to prejudice, damage or defraud any person; or who, with the intent to defraud, alters, corrupts, or falsifies any record of any will, codicil, conveyance or any instrument, the record of which is by law evidence, or any record of any judgment of a court or the return of any officer to any process of any court, is guilty of forgery."

As can be surmised from the wording of the statute the emphasis is on the phrase "with the intent to defraud" and without this element there is no crime. However, it is not imperative that anyone suffer an actual loss. If the accused is charged with the "forgery" segment of the law, independent of "uttering" or "publishing" or "passing," the offense is complete by the mere act of "forging" if coupled with the requisite intent at the time of the act. There is no requirement the instrument be "passed" or "uttered." According to well settled case law the test to be applied is "whether upon its face it will have the effect of defrauding one who acts upon it as genuine" (Peo. vs McKenna, 11 Cal2nd 327). Although this concept goes back a number of years, it has been adhered to by the courts. A separate situation develops when it appears obvious from the instrument itself that it is not genuine or authentic. It can not then be the subject of a forgery.

It should be pointed out that there usually is no legislative intent to unduly limit the things which could become the subject of forgery by the enumerating within the statute those items by name. Neither were there any restrictions imposed by intent relative to the manner in which the forgery, counterfeiting or alteration could be accomplished. This is not an antilogy. The rule that a special statute supersedes a general statute has no logical application here.

Manner of Offense

There are numerous and varied ways in which forgery can be achieved. The classic statute (supra) sets forth "alteration" as one forbidden method. There is no necessity to change or alter the whole instrument. The crime is complete if the change is material; for example, altering the amount appearing on the face of a check or some such act which effects the rights of the parties involved.

A normal type of forgery in business operations is the situation where an employee has been granted the "authority" by a superior to sign instruments, applying the latter's name as maker, and then goes beyond the scope of this "authority." The excessive act, of course, must be accompanied by the specific intent to defraud. The offense is not limited to checks, but includes any manner of instruments which may effect the title and right to the company's or superior's property.

The phrase "utter, publishes, or passes a forged instrument" at times has created some question as to interpretation. "Utter" according to a dictionary definition, amongst other things, can mean "to express or make known in *any* matter;" to "express by written or printed words;" and "to put into circulation, as coins, notes, etc. and especially counterfeited money, forged checks, etc." In our usage it means essentially to declare or assert verbally or by actions that the instrument in question is valid, although the accused knows it is not and he is attempting to "utter" or pass it with the requisite intent to defraud.

The old model statute quoted above is not always the only law concerning forgery in most jurisdiction. Frequently there is a variety of provisions relating to the act. It is incumbent upon the student/fraud investigator to widen the scope of his knowledge of the law relevant to his functional field. He should also have some familiarity with the civil theories which are interwoven with denunciated criminal acts and definitively outline the established rights of the parties.

Specific Violations

Sometimes there are enacted specific laws relating to public officers and public records. One such law states: "Every officer having custody of any record, map or book, or of any paper or proceeding of any court, filed or deposited in any public office or placed in his hands for any purpose, who is guilty of stealing, willfully destroying, mutilating, defacing, altering or falsifying, removing or secreting the whole or any part of such record, map, book, paper or proceeding, or who permits any other person to do so, is punishable by imprisonment in the state prison not less than one nor more than fourteen years." A public record has been determined to be any document, instrument, or record which is properly maintained by the officer in the performance of his duties. This is regardless of form: i.e. computer punch cards, microfilm copies, photostatic reproduction, actual photographs, etc. There are often companion laws relating to persons not public officers who violate public records. These usually have the same element, but neither have the requisite "specific intent," the act being sufficient unto itself.

Most states have legislation relating to the possession of forged instruments. One such law states in essence that anyone who possesses any type of forged or blank/unfinished instrument with the intention of passing same with fraudulent intent (after filling in of course the blanks if such is the situation) violates the law.

A check was viewed by the court as "completed" within the meaning of the statute when the face of the instrument reflected the payee's name had been inserted as had the amount, date, and maker's name. It was held the forged endorsement of the payee would not be required to fulfill the statutory provisions. (*Peo vs Bartsch* (1963) 217 Cal App 2nd 318).

There is in most states a related law concerning the making or passing fictitious checks, commonly called "fictitious prints"

and actually is a form of forgery. It has been held that the
possession of such an instrument if accompanied with the intent
to pass falls within the purview of the statute. Such a law usually sets forth that anyone who makes or passes, *with the intention to defraud* any other person, any fictitious bill, note or
instrument purporting to be drawn on some bank or other repository, when in fact none such exists has committed the offense.
This should not be confused with counterfeiting which is the
printing of facsimile instruments purporting to draw on an *actual*
institution and with existing persons as maker and payee.

Another offense in which the specific intent to defraud is absent concerns the filing for record of false and forged instruments. These laws normally hold that anyone who knowingly
offers any false or forged item to be filed, registered or recorded
in a public office is guilty of a felony.

The statute is limited to "instruments" only (supra) which
have effect upon the title to property or obligations. The fraudulent intent required in most of the forgery or related types of
offenses is not considered here, neither is it necessary to prove
anyone experienced any loss through fraud because of the act
of the accused. The only requirement is to establish he filed, or
offered for recordation a false or forged instrument knowingly
and was aware of its spurious nature.

The Uniform Commercial Code which took effect 1 January, 65 sets forth in Sec. #1201 (43) a definition of the term
"unauthorized" signature or endorsement, stating it to mean "one
made without actual, implied or apparent authority and includes
forgery."

Section #3404 UCC relates to the act itself, providing "(1)
Any unauthorized signature is wholly inoperative as that of the
person whose name is signed unless he ratifies it or is precluded
from denying it; but it operates as the signature of the unauthorized signer in favor of any person who in good faith pays the instrument or takes it for value. (2) Any unauthorized signature
may be ratified for all purposes of this division. Such ratification
does not of itself effect any rights of the persons ratifying against
the actual signer." Subsection (2) above is relatively new law
and there is no clearcut decision as yet whether or not a "forgery"

can be ratified. The question of silence on the part of victim as not amounting to ratification seems fairly well settled.

Section #3405 UCC states "(1) An endorsement by any person in the name of a named payee is effective if (a) An imposter by use of the mails or otherwise has induced the maker or drawer to issue the instrument to him or his confederate in the name of the payee; or (b) A person signing as or on behalf of a maker or drawer intends the payee to have no interest in the instrument; or (c) An agent or employee of the maker or drawer has supplied him with the name of the payee intending the latter to have no such interest. (2) Nothing in this section shall effect the criminal or civil liability of the person so endorsing (1963)." Under earlier decision when another code section was enforced (prior to 1945), it was held a dishonest employee could recover against the drawee bank if his instrument (usually a pay-check) had been endorsed and cashed by someone else even with his being in collusion with the person who forged his signature as the endorsement. With legislative action this inequitable situation for the drawee bank was eliminated by putting the onus on the drawer/maker employer who hired the thief. In other words it was a bearer instrument prior to 1945. Afterwards it was not.

Under the present statute the rule is adhered to but declares such an endorsement is not a forgery, and it will be effective when the person creating the instrument for the drawer intends the payee to have no interest. A classic example are the payroll padding type of cases in which an employee handles the issuing of checks and mails a series of them payable to non-existent workers. He then endorses the fictitious names on the instruments and cashes them. The civil question which then arises is the liability of the bank to the maker/drawer company. Can the checks be paid and then debited to the drawer's account? It would seem that the courts view it in the light of normal business risks and impute the intent of the dishonest employee to his employer, thus the drawee/bank can charge the amount to the drawee's account.

Section #3406 UCC relates to the negligence of the drawer a negotiable instrument. It is quoted here; "Any person who by his negligence substantially contributes to a material alteration of the instrument or to the making of an unauthorized signature is precluded from asserting the alteration or lack of authority against a holder in due course or against a drawee or other payor who pays the instrument in good faith and in accordance with the reasonable commercial standards of the drawee's or payor's business."

This is a new statutory provision and does not, as in the other cases, supersede or replace a pre-existing law. It merely creates a valid defense for the drawee in the event the drawer/maker does something which would mislead the drawee into honoring a forged instrument while acting with the normal acceptable circumspection required in the banking business, otherwise he is still liable.

A number of state vehicle/automobile codes have provisions comparable to their forgery laws relating to registration. These laws, worded similar to general forgery precepts, usually state that anyone who, *with the intent to defraud,* alters, forges counterfeits or falsifies in any manner registration documents, licenses or instruments related thereto, or has in their possession or displays such prohibited items with the same requisite intent has committed a public offense. The punative measures vary widely.

Section #8205 UCC relates to the ineffectiveness of a forged or unauthorized signature appearing on a security. It provides "An unauthorized signature placed on a security prior to or in the course of issue is ineffective except the signature is effective in favor of a purchaser for value and without notice of the lack of authority if the signing has been done by: (a) an authenticating trustee, registrar, transfer agent or other person entrusted by the issuer with the signing of the security or of similar securities or their immediate preparation for signing; or (b) an employee of the issuer or of any of the foregoing entrusted with responsible handling of the security."

The purpose of this new law, in effect, is to enforce the issuer's (corporation's) duty of diligence in the selection of employees who will handle the securities and establishes the particular criteria under which the corporation is estopped from setting up the defense of forgery instead of a general preclusion.

Section #8311 UCC is still another modification relating to the endorsements on securities: "Unless the owner has ratified an unauthorized endorsement or is otherwise precluded from asserting it ineffectiveness (a) He may assert its ineffectiveness against the issuer or any purchaser other than a purchaser for value and without notice of adverse claims who in good faith received a new, reissued or registered security on registration of transfer; and (b) An issuer who registers the transfer of a security upon the unauthorized endorsement is subject to liability for improper registration."

The California Constitution, Article XX Section 11 provides "Laws shall be made to exclude from office, serving on juries, and from the right of suffrage, persons convicted of bribery, perjury, *forgery*, malfeasance in office or other high crimes. The privilege of free suffrage shall be supported by laws regulating elections and prohibiting, under adequate penalties, all undue influence thereon from power, bribery, tumult, or other improper practice." This classic piece of legislation reflects the seriousness with which the crime of forgery was viewed initially by society.

Checks Without Sufficient Funds

Checks without sufficient funds to support them is the basis of the preponderance of reports to any police agency and probably creates more difficulties in developing the elements of an offense and the relationships between the agency and the public. The classic statute provides: "(a) Any person who for himself or as the agent or representative of another or as an officer of a corporation, wilfully, *with the intent to defraud,* makes or draws or utters or delivers any check, or draft or order upon any bank or depository or persons, or firm, or corporation, for the payment of money, *knowing at the time of such making,* drawing, uttering or delivering that the maker or drawer or the corporation has not sufficient funds in, or credit with said bank or depository, or person, or firm, or corporation, for the payment of such check, draft or order and all other checks, or orders upon such funds then outstanding, in full upon its presentation, although no express representation is made with reference thereto, is punishable by imprisonment.

(b) However, if the total amount of all such checks, drafts or orders that the defendant is charged with and convicted of making, drawing or uttering does not exceed a certain amount (varies according to jurisdiction) the offense is punishable as a misdemeanor."

Account Closed Checks

It should be pointed out at this juncture, that "Account Closed" checks are the same as "Non-Sufficient Funds" checks. The only difference being the account is closed instead of merely not having sufficient funds on hand to cover a check. Usually this results when the bank has experienced a series of "NSF" checks and has summarily closed the account itself and notified the depositor of this fact, and in some instances the depositor himself has closed the account and written checks subsequent to that time.

Let us explore the area of "NSF" and "Closed Account" checks. The essential elements are (#1) the intent to defraud, (#2) the making, uttering or delivering of the instrument, (#3) the lack of sufficient funds or absence of an account, (#4) and the knowledge on the part of the accused of such lack of funds or account: The "Intent to Defraud" is the basis of the offense: without such specific intent it amounts to merely an overdraft, but not a criminal act per se. Although all of us look upon the operations of this type of check passer as fraudulent (and from our estimates he constitutes the larger part of all fraud activities) the courts in their omniscience have not expressed themselves as entirely in sympathy with law-enforcement and the businessman's viewpoint. Before any action can be taken on this type of offense, it is imperative that the fraudulent intent be unequivocally established, this means the complete elimination of any possibility of mistake on the part of the passer and that he was informed and had knowledge at the time of making the instrument there were not sufficient funds on hand to cover it. You can see from this the situation is fraught with peril, the spectre of civil liability confronting anyone who would allege a check was fraudulent without first determining all the elements of the offense were present.

The Trap For the Unwary

The situation with which a law enforcement agency is frequently confronted is the question propounded by the victim: "When do I get my money"—and this, unfortunately, when answered according to the precepts of our laws does little in the way of satisfying him. It is necessary to differentiate between civil and criminal liability on the part of the accused, but the merchant, when he has been victimized, isn't too prone to objective analysis. However, under the Anglo-American legal doctrines, the Police Powers of the State cannot be used to implement the collection of a debt without due process of law, meaning that the proper writs and court orders be issued. This is a trap for the unwary officer. It must be remembered that when an offense is reported, the idea of restitution on the part of the accused prior to a complaint being issued, must under no circumstances, be the only or sole motivation. The complainant must be in the position to sign a complaint charging the defendant with a criminal act. Of course, if after the complaint or in most situations, the criminal report, is made, it is decided by the complainant and the accused that there is some proper and logical reason for its withdrawal, this can be done and all further action in the matter will be terminated. It must be remembered however, that the investigator, under no circumstances, can become a party to any agreement or settlement reached by the complainant or the accused. And further, he cannot under any circumstances, advise either party as to what steps should be taken to effect some civil satisfaction of an extra-judicial nature.

Post-dated Checks

Another situation which develops with a degree of frequency is the "Post-dated" check. Where all of the elements of the offense exist the crime is committed regardless of the "Post-dating." However, if the acceptor knows the instrument is "post-dated" at the time he receives it, the circumstances warrant the inference that he was thereby informed that it was not intended to be good until the arrival of the date it bears. Consequently, it is merely considered a promissory note. The recourse then is a civil action for recovery. Related to "Post-dated" checks is the situation which occasionally arises when the maker/drawer informs the payee at the time of making that there is presently not on deposit funds to cover the check. If it is still *accepted* in payment of a lawful existing debt, there can be no allegation of deception or intent to defraud, as the acceptor had notice. Here again, it is merely a promissory note. However, if the accused were to ask the complainant to accept but hold for a period, an instrument before cashing, the latter refusing to comply and so stating at the time, and the accused nevertheless concludes the transaction, this act removes the effect of the prior request and imposes the belief the instrument is good, establishing the intent to defraud. Again, a closely related situation is the custom of the drawee-bank in notifying the customer/maker that he has a series of "NSF" items and then going ahead and honoring them. Now this is a frequent circumstance and often leads to embarrassing moments. It is a common practice by the banks as a favor to a preferred customer/ depositors. If this practice has been adhered to regularly and then on an occasion the bank refuses to continue the practice for some reason, and the accused can show clearly that he has relied upon the bank's previous actions, this will overcome a prima facie case. But, if by other evidence the element of intent can be reflected in regard to a particular check prosecution can be pursued.

Joint Accounts

Joint Accounts and Partnership Accounts create much confusion because two or more persons have authority to deposit and make withdrawals, causing much difficulty in the light of recent judicial decisions when effort is made to establish the specific intent and knowledge of the lack of funds at the time of uttering. The accused always has in these situations the plausible answer that he was not aware the joint depositor had made a withdrawal reducing the funds below that appearing on the instrument. Unless this defense can be overcome with other evidence such as obvious plan, scheme and design, the complainant's recourse here again is only a civil action for the recovery of monies.

It should be remembered here that each offense must be charged on its own merits. There are no two cases alike in all of the basic elements of the offense and practically every case will have some exception to the rule which will have to be considered. Before we leave the somewhat confused area of "NSF" checks we perhaps better cover another typical case. This concerns payroll or "Second-party" checks as they are often called. Of course this name can be attached to any instrument that has a payee different from the endorser. Frequently the payee will cash it at some business establishment, which in turn will endorse it and pass it on in the payment of some obligation. The second acceptor again doing the same thing, until perhaps there will appear three or four endorsers before it reaches the drawee/bank, is protested, and then returned to the last endorser. The liability of holders in due course is in the inverse order of their reendorsing each one looking to the prior holder for recovery. The only criminal liability here lies with the original maker, providing of course, all holders were in good faith and all of the necessary basic elements of the offense were present.

Combination of Offenses

One should remember a salient point of this particular law relating to the combination of offenses. This permits the combining of a series of misdemeanors: those each in amounts less than that meeting the felony requirement, unto an aggregate which would be in excess of the requisite amount. This is one of the reasons fraud investigators sometimes seem to spend an inordinate amount of time and effort on what appears on the surface to be nothing more than a very minor offense, however, one small check of $5.00 can be the deciding point on whether or not an operator will receive a probation sentence based upon a series of misdemeanors or will be charged with a felony. And don't ever think they are not aware of the limitations imposed by law on the police agencies, the complainant, the prosecutor and the courts.

Credit Card Violations

The State of California's original law relating to credit card abuses was repealed in 1967 as a dismal failure. It was succeeded by a newer and much better constructed piece of legislation. The earlier act, according to the belief of knowledgeable people in the fraud investigation came under the heading of "pressure legislation," a type of law-making especially abhorred by the courts.

When imputing to the statute that it is the result of "Pressure," it is only fair to point out the three usual bases for such law: Social, Economic/Financial and Political reasons. In this particular instance, it undoubtedly was economic. It is an accepted fact that today an extremely large amount of financial transactions, formerly handled by check or cash, are now handled through the medium of the "Credit-card." It started with the oil companies, expanded through the hotel-motel circuit and onward into the night-club restaurant area. Now department stores, travel agencies and every conceivable type of business accept their payment through the media. Concurrent with sociological/economic phenomena, there naturally developed our social system's enterprising financial free-thinker who readily saw new fields to conquer. Aided and abetted by the carelessness and questionable philosophies of both the card-holder and the issuing company, coupled with the avarice and inaccurate estimate of the situation on the part of the merchant, it was only a matter of time before the losses experienced would necessitate a very searching appraisal of conditions. This brought about some new law, the efficacy of which was determined in a short time.

The law set out under six separate sub-heads, an all encompassing statement covering the ill-legal use of credit cards. It combined the basic elements of both the theft and forgery statutes and thereby, as will be seen, included some inherent weakness, which were exploited by defense counsels with the approbation of the courts.

To clarify this assertion, it should be said that due to the enactment of this particular statute, the forgery section of the Penal Code had been vitiated. Sub-head #5 stated "Any person, who with the intent to defraud, either forges, materially alters or counterfeits a credit card is guilty of a felony." Subsection 6 which provided for a person who knowingly used or attempted to use illegally held credit card for the purposes of obtaining goods, property, services or anything of value, setting an amount of $50.00, the excess of which was a felony, a lesser amount being a misdemeanor.

Now at first blush, this seemed to add some strength to the law covering forgery, however, the converse was true, permitting the general forgery law to be attacked successfully when applied to credit cards, and one can have no quarrel with the Appellate Court's decision. A typical case is one in which two men were apprehended after they had used a stolen credit card for several purchases at various gas stations in a city and county areas. After the completion of the inquiries the matter was submitted to the District Attorney for a complaint charging one of the defendants with forgery of the true card holder's name covering purchases at approximately $35.00. The Deputy District Attorney handling the case had just completed his forms for a complaint when another one of his colleagues referred him to 213 Adv Cal App 2nd, 477, *The People vs James R. Swann,* decided by 2nd District Court of Appeals on 2–27–63. The Court, in its infinite wisdom, said in part, "The People do not have the power to prosecute under a general felony statute where the facts of the alleged offense parallel the acts prescribed by a specific statute, since the special act is considered an exception to the general statute whether it was passed before or after the general enactment."

The Court further said, "—A cardinal rule of law, section 1858 of the Civil Code of Procedure, statutory interpretation is that the meaning adopted to the law should accord with the ascertained purpose of the law-makers," in other words the legislative intent behind the law determines in a large way the construction put to the law by the Courts.

This is the Courts statement as to this last element: "Legislative intent, to state the Penal Law with respect to misuse of credit cards and to provide appropriate penalties—The People are then precluded from prosecuting under a general forgery statute." In qualifying this last, the Court stated, "The Legislature certainly contemplated false or unauthorized signatures on credit invoices by parties engaged in the misdemeanor use of credit cards under subsection N #6 of subdivision B of the Statute since such signatures are required of credit card users in the customary use of such cards." In view of this decision, in effect, the forgery of a credit card holder's name to a credit card invoice was no longer a criminal offense. In the particular case, referred to, forgery could not and was not charged but there was a felony conviction predicated upon subsection #6 in that the extent of the purchases was in excess of the $50.00 statutory requirement. This, then was a good example of some over-anxious stop-gap legislation. Without this piece of law-making, the accused, in most cases, could have been charged under the existing larceny or forgery statutes. However, the credit card companies being very concerned with the small separate purchases which amounted to less than the $200.00 statutory limit on Grand Theft, which made the majority of offenses a misdemeanor, viewed this as a strong punitive measure, when patterned after the "NSF" check law and the forgery law. You can see the results.

In 1967 the California Legislature, after assessing the results of the initial enactment, created a new law relating to the same subject-matter with greater clarity as to construction. This law in part stated: (1) "Every person who acquires a credit card from another without the cardholder's or issuer's consent or who, with knowledge that it has been so acquired, acquires the credit card, with intent to use it or to sell or transfer it to a person other than the issuer or the cardholder is guilty of petty theft."

(2) "Every person who acquires a credit card that he knows to have been lost, mislaid, or delivered under a mistake as to the identity or address of the cardholder, and who retains possession with intent to use it or sell it or to transfer it to a person other than the issuer or the cardholder is guilty of petty theft."

(3) "Every person who sells, transfers, conveys, or receives a credit card with the intent to defraud is guilty of petty theft."

(4) "Every person other than the issuer, who within any consecutive 12-month period, acquires credit cards issued in the names of four or more persons which he has reason to know were taken or retained under circumstances which constitute a violation of subdivisions (1), (2), or (3) of this section is guilty of grand theft."

Altering credit card or signing the name of another with the intent to defraud. (1) "Every person who, with intent to defraud, makes, alters, or embosses a card or utters such a card is guilty of forgery."

(2) "A person other than the cardholder or a person authorized by him who, with intent to defraud, signs the name of another or of a fictitious person to a credit card, sales slip, sales draft, or instrument for the payment of money which evidences a credit card transaction, is guilty of forgery."

Use of credit card to obtain money, goods or services; Theft, grand theft: Every person, who with intent to defraud (a) uses for the purpose of obtaining money, goods, services or anything else of value a credit card obtained or retained in violation of Section 484e or a credit card which he knows is forged, expired or revoked, or (b) obtains money, goods, services or anything else of value by representing without the consent of the cardholder that he is the holder of a credit card or by representing that he is the holder of a credit card and such card had not in fact been issued, is guilty of theft. If the value of all money, goods, services and other things of value obtained in violation of this section exceeds two hundred dollars ($200) in any consecutive six-month period, then the same shall constitute grand theft.

Merchants who with intent to defraud furnish money, goods, or services on forged, expired or revoked credit cards: Every merchant who, with intent to defraud:

(a) Furnishes money, goods, services or anything else of value upon presentation of a credit card obtained or retained in violation of Section 484e hereof or a credit card which he knows is forged, expired or revoked, and who receives any payment therefore, is guilty of theft. If the payment received by the merchant for all money, goods, services and other things of value furnished in violation of this section exceeds two hundred dollars ($200) in any consecutive six-month period, then the same shall constitute grand theft.

(b) Fails to furnish money, goods, services or anything else of value which he represents in writing to the issuer or a participating party that he has furnished, and who receives any payment therefor, is guilty of theft. If the difference between the value of all money, goods, services and anything else of value actually furnished and the payment or payments received by the merchant therefor upon such representation exceeds two hundred dollars ($200) in any consecutive six-month period, then the same shall constitute grand theft.

Possession of incomplete cards and machinery or plates to complete—prohibited: (a) Every person who possesses an incomplete credit card, with intent to complete them without the consent of the issuer is guilty of a misdemeanor.

(b) Every person who with intent to defraud possesses, with knowledge of its character, machinery, plates or any other contrivance designed for, and made use of in, the reproduction of instruments purporting to be the credit cards of an issuer who has not consented to the preparation of such credit cards, is punishable by imprisonment in the state prison for not less than one, nor more than 14 years, or by imprisonment in the county jail for not more than one year.

The construction to be put to the new law was definitively set forth by the legislature stating "This act shall not be construed to preclude the applicability of any other provision of the criminal law of this (California) state which presently applies or may in the future apply to any transaction which violates this act." In other words, where it is appropriate, a forgery including a credit card can be prosecuted under the forgery section, a general statute regardless of the amount involved.

Since the enactment of the above described credit card law California is in the process of revising its whole criminal (penal) code. Credit card violations will be merged within the statute relating an entirely new and much less complicated law relating to offenses involving written instruments, eliminating the need of specific statutes with the resultant maze and confusion of separate interpretations.

Criminal Groups

Law enforcement agencies records are replete with reports of various scams involving the use of credit cards ever since their inception in the purchase patterns of our society. However, a recently developing and unique operation concerns a gang which has its members "working" between an eastern seaboard state and Hawaii, not missing very many intervening stopovers. There are actually three groups known variously as the "Hawaiian Gang," the "Korean Gang" and the "Canadian Gang" but all involved in the same productive activity; the obtaining of credit cards by theft, burglary, robbery and not a little biological diversion. Their collective take is into the hundreds of thousands of dollars. Their primary base of operation is Honolulu.

The groups are fairly well organized including cocktail waitresses, bartenders, hotel clerks, chamber-maids, bell-hops, post-office and office-type employees who can gain access to company credit cards, and an apparent never-ending coterie of "swinging" girls with the social outlook of Attila the Hun and instinct of tigers. These in addition to outright thugs are the sources of the cards and also the medium through which they can be used illicitly.

One method implemented is the recruiting of the "girls" who are flown to Hawaii where they are ensconced in one of the better hotels. When a guest is checking in a clerk maintains a vigilant watch to determine whether or not he possesses a number of credit cards. The room number is passed on to one of his girls, bell-hops, or chamber-maids who enter the room when the guest is either busy elsewhere (the hotel pool or bar creates the longer periods of absence usually), stealing the card(s) and traveller's checks or money orders which may be present. These are all taken to a local character known by many aliases who in turn reshuffles the item, giving them to another set of girls who use them at shopping centers and airlines. Clothing is usually purchased, all of good quality in excess quantities. The average of these items are re-sold at half or quarter price to receivers or other interested persons. The airline tickets are taken to their "director" who gives the girls thirty to forty dollars. These in turn are sold to others at half-price. A travel agency has also been a knowing purchaser.

When the cards are obtained they are "cleaned up." This was achieved by using a toothpaste which removed the true card-holder's signature. Tape was put around the signature space to prevent the chemical reaction from cutting into any other part of the card. The area was then sprayed with white paint. Upon drying, a girl who was to use it, then signed the card with the embossed name appearing on the face which she was to use for the moment. Sometimes the signature space is very delicately removed and the area replaced with a strip of contact paper or similar material upon which she writes the name she is to use.

Post Office employees are sources of credit cards. They are induced to cooperate for various reasons such as "kickbacks" as are the company salesmen and office employees. The postal employee merely steals any cards from the mails that come to his attention, delivering same to the gang's representative. The salesmen and office employees sometimes report the "loss" of a card to their employer, who usually is slow in reporting it to the credit card company. This lapse of time, only a few days is necessary, creates a sufficient period in which the purchases can be made. They are also known to have just stolen the card, resigned their brief employment, and then turned the card over to the gang contact, everyone concerned going through the same process. One girl is known to have made in excess of 75 airlines ticket purchases with a stolen credit card within a period of eight months.

Another method used is achieved through an employee of a plastic card manufacturing company plant who would steal blank cards already made out for a particular outlet such as a bank. These would be given to the gang who possessed an imprint or embossing machine and a new fictitious print would then be in circulation.

The gang also had a number of restaurants, bars, and night-clubs "wired" i.e. cooperative employees. The cocktail waitresses, headwaiter, bartender or maitre d' would be aware of the stolen cards. If it had not yet made the "hot list" published by the card company or local police agency or merchants' protective group, an added $25.00 in a "tip" would be added to the bill of the "customer." The management, of course, would pay the tip, normally at the end of the evening's shift to the employee, who in turn would turn over the larger percentage of the proceeds to the gang.

The Face of the Instrument

The investigator should have knowledge of the significance of the various items of printing which appear on the face of all checks in present day use. Every bank has a clearinghouse number and the bank number on the face of the check. The usual location is the upper right-hand corner of the instrument, however, there is no actual legal requirement that it be placed as such. Occasionally it is situated in another place on the face if artistic demands justify it so. These numbers in the form of a fraction are referred to as "ABA numbers" for the American Banking Association number. They are a compound of four numbers. The clearinghouse number is always the first on the numerator level and indicates the state or city in which the bank conducts its business. The bank number follows the clearinghouse number on the same level, being separated by a dash. The denominator level of the fraction reflects the Federal Reserve District number and Federal Reserve Branch Bank number in sequence but not separated by the dash:

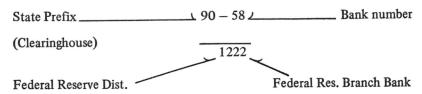

State Prefix _____ 90 – 58 _____ Bank number

(Clearinghouse)   1222

Federal Reserve Dist.   Federal Res. Branch Bank

In California all banks doing business in San Francisco have the state or clearinghouse prefix of 11 followed by the bank number. Banks within Los Angeles use the prefix 16, and all other banks in the state use prefix 90.

Since the advent of sensitized or magnetic numbering the instruments now bear in different form a combination of the same numbers situated near the bottom edge, starting at the left-hand corner. The first line is the Federal Reserve District number and the Federal Reserve Branch Bank number followed by a dash and then the bank number (with space for four digits if needed); then an open space followed by the branch bank number (space for four digits if needed); then followed by a dash and the individual depositor's account number (space for five digits). At the right-hand lower corner at the same level as the preceding numbers appears the amount of the instrument, permitting the writing of eight figure amounts. This last of course is printed thereon by an electronic data processing machine once it is re-

ceived in the bank for collection. The ABA numbers are pre-
printed on the instruments when the depositor receives them from
the bank:

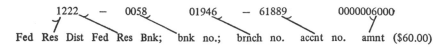

1222   —   0058   01946   —   61889   0000006000

Fed Res Dist Fed Res Bnk;   bnk no.;   brnch no.   accnt no.   amnt ($60.00)

A clearinghouse is a voluntary association acting as a medium
for the daily settlement of transactions between member banks.
It makes possible the exchanging of checks, drafts and notes as
between banks of a designated area, thus eliminating settlements
between individual banks. Representatives of the member banks
come together each banking day handing over checks they have
against other member banks and receiving in return the checks
which the others hold against it, settling any differences in
amounts through clearinghouse association in cash.

The Federal Reserve System was the result of the Federal
Reserve Act on 23 Dec. 13. Its purpose is to provide for the
establishing of Federal Reserve Banks to furnish an elastic currency, to enforce effective supervision of banking. The system is
divided into 12 districts each with a bank and 24 branch banks.
The Federal Reserve Banks are "bankers' banks," the customers
being banks which are members of the Federal Reserve System
in their respective districts. The system's banks can receive deposits *only* from member banks, from the Federal Government
and for exchange purposes solely from other Reserve Banks. They
also issue currency.

District #12 of the system is comprised of California, Idaho,
Utah, Nevada, Oregon, Washington, Alaska and Hawaii. The
District offices are located at San Francisco.

The face of the instrument below, a personalized type, bears
the check number in its proper sequence in the upper right
corner. In the same area is found the drawing date (4–25–73) and
also the printed "ABA number" (however, in this instance not in
the fraction form). The payee of the instrument is the "Chargers"
football team, the written amount, $48.00. The maker's signature
is on the lower right side following the name of the "drawee/
bank," Bank of America. Below the "body" of the instrument is

found the sequence of sensitized-magnetic numbers for the EDP purposes. The reverse or endorsement side discloses the stamped endorsement of the payee's bank (Wells Fargo) and the date (4–30–73) the payee deposited the instrument along with the remainder of the day's operating receipts. Superimposed on this is the Bank of America's perforated dating (small holes punched) reflecting the instrument having gone through the clearinghouse process, being paid on 5–1–73, six days subsequent to the making.

"NSF" Check Investigations Sequence

The normal sequence of events usually present in a forgery or other fraudulent instrument inquiry is fairly static. The victim of an "NSF" offense has received from the drawee/bank notice to the effect that a check he has accepted in payment of some service or goods he provided is not collectible due to the fact there are not sufficient funds on deposit. If he is of the frame of mind to prosecute (and collection is not his only motivation) he usually telephones his local police agency for some action. Depending upon that agency's policy, a patrol unit or a detective will make the initial contact for information and taking into custody the questioned instrument. Some departments request the complainant to bring the instrument and appear in person at the station. Whatever the policy adhered to by the agency, the first thing to take place is a thoroughgoing interview of the actual acceptor. Frequently a clerk is the person who was a party to the action but the proprietor or a superior is the one making the report. The latter can be of little assistance. The actual acceptor of the instrument is the one who was a participant and alone can relate the circumstances attendant to the incident. Anything the owner or superior would relate is hearsay.

From the acceptor develop, in the proper sequence, the actions of the check passer from the moment he was first observed and to his departure. Cover completely as possible the actual words spoken between them, including innocuous remarks that would seemingly appear to have no pertinency to the transaction. Obtain a detailed resumé of the identifying matter proffered by the passer such as driver's license, credit cards, selective service card, lodge or similar organizational membership cards, etc. A description of the passer should go beyond the routine of "WMA, 28, 5'10", 165, blk & brn" and include mannerisms, dress, voice inflections, marks, scars, direction of approach and departure and type of transportation used. Develop comparable data concerning anyone else who may have been with him. Determine the property, monies or services exchanged for the check in detail. Ascertain if there have been prior transactions legitimate or otherwise, and with these develop in some detail comparable information, especially any permissiveness in the past on the complainant's part when accepting an "NSF" check from the same person. Of special importance, because of the effect it has on the transaction, the determination, if any, of agreements or limitations that might have been reached between the parties during their conversation. The "post dated" instrument or some other mitigating circumstance can evolve out of such a situation which can vitiate the position of the complainant.

"Size up" the acceptor and complainant. Be able to determine to some degree their potential and competence as probable witnesses. Often there arises the situation in which the acceptor/victim did not promptly in the course of business take the check to the bank for collection, waiting several days. Upon reaching the bank there were insufficient funds on hand. Actually there is no offense if it is shown there were funds available in sufficient amount on the day and time of the passing by the maker. Diligence is a necessary element of good business practices.

Do not limit the source of information to the acceptor only. Interview other persons who were present during the transaction period such as fellow employees and customers attempting to develop with them identifying data. If the premises in which the action took place is located in a commercial complex such as a shopping center or business area, attempt to develop other witnesses and also of great importance, other victims who may not as yet reported or even have knowledge of their loss.

The next action the part of the investigator is to have the face and endorsement sides of the questioned instrument photographed, xeroxed or copied in some manner. The San Diego Sheriff's Department utilizes the Bradford Classification System in which the instrument is copied, placed upon a $5'' \times 8''$ index card, classified according to the digital system, and maintained in a permanent file. This will be discussed in more detail later in this chapter in regard to technical aids available to the investigator.

The information that can and should be developed at the drawee/bank in a large part will be that upon which the case will hinge. It is here the all important element of fraudulent intent is either going to be substantiated or eliminated. Initially an abstract of the account in question covering a period of at least ten days prior to the date of the questioned instrument and ten days subsequent to it, or if more than one has been passed, ten days subsequent to the date of the last check in series. This will furnish two complete weeks of banking business days before and after the passing of the check(s). The information here will reflect all deposits and withdrawals which will indicate any legitimate attempt by the passer to deposit sufficient funds to cover all instruments made and passed or it will, conversely, disclose a consistent pattern of check writing beyond the reasonable person's knowledge of his account balance.

The rejected items register should also be examined to determine if there are other outstanding instruments not yet posted to the depositor's account. Copies of all instruments, both those in question and others for the same period which may be available in the bank's microfilm, should be obtained; both the face and endorsement sides.

The next step should be the obtaining of copies (both sides) of the signature cards and some details of the account history; the opening and closing dates, if possible, and it can be done if the investigator has developed the close working relationship with the bank operations officer, obtain data concerning the account since the inception such as problems with the depositor, frequent complaints from the others who have accepted instruments, etc. Of special importance is the exact date, time, and method and by whom the depositor was notified as to his overdrafts. If this was not done properly there exists a valid defense. The check passer can always hide behind the facade of ignorance, protesting he had no knowledge of his account deficit balance, eliminating the necessary fraudulent intent. The existence of joint depositors must be determined. If another person has authority to draw upon the account this situation becomes a fairly strong defense, difficult to overcome, unless it can be established in other ways the presence of fraudulent intent. On occasions a whole series of checks could be examined to determine which of the depositors consistently wrote them, the account activity being ascribed to one individual alone, coupled with the fact of bank notification to this same person prior to the date of the instrument(s) in question.

Another item of importance which should be ascertained from the accounting history and signature cards, are the locations of other checking (and savings) accounts, either past or current.

Where these are identified they should be examined in the same manner as the account in question, developing the pattern of the account activity which normally discloses similar check writing problems in the past.

The question often arises concerning the need of notarized or certified letters of protest obtained from the drawee/bank in situations in which an out-of-state or out-of-county instrument is involved. Actually they are a time and money saving device of which most courts will take judicial notice for purposes of a preliminary hearing, obviating the necessity of having a bank representative travel from his area to the court for testifying and return travel at the expense of the county. At the time of trial, however, the bank representative usually has to appear with the appropriate records unless the defense stipulates to their contents based upon disclosures during the preliminary hearings. The suspect's identity and personal history should be developed in some detail. There are infinite sources of information for this purpose. The central repository of all criminal records in the state, of course should be contacted for any prior arrest information. Local police agencies records division are a necessary source because one not only develops an arrest record, such as related by State sources, but the investigator then has available the actual case reports, which contains invaluable information that is never related, other than in exceptional cases, by the state bureau. Of course, based upon the "rap sheet" received from the State the indicated out-of-county or out-of-state agencies can be contacted individually from their information. City prosecutors and District Attorneys offices and the courts, including the county clerk and the county recorders offices are excellent for detailed authenticated information of record.

The Department of Motor Vehicles and the Division of Drivers Licenses can furnish identification of the suspect, sometimes including a photograph and/or thumb-print. This is an especially helpful source if the suspect has no prior criminal record. The motor vehicle registration gives not only the address of the registered owner (suspect) but the legal owner as well. The latter who holds the title to the vehicles and ostensibly receiving payments on the conditional sales contract is often a good source of information as to the suspects back-ground, finances, habits and current location.

The local credit information bureaus are a good source, both retail and wholesale reporting agencies. They maintain fairly accurate files on everyone in their area who has ever applied for a credit account. It includes residences, employment, banking, purchasing habits, education, associates and law suits, both civil and criminal. A later chapter is devoted to sources of information and relates in detail the type and validity of the data coupled with the individual agency policy.

Inter-departmental exchange of information is a priority effort. It makes coordination possible in parallel investigations which often develop, as the check writer seldom stops with the passing of one instrument but usually spreads his cheer indescriminately throughout an area notwithstanding political subdivisions, providing numerous victims in contiguous jurisdictions and related police agencies large size headaches. However, this allows the combination of offenses permitting the filing of a felony count if the amounts involved are in excess of the statutory minimum.

The contacting and interviewing of the suspect is a facet of the investigation which today, because of the limitations imposed by Miranda, Dorado, Escobeda *et al*, is fraught with peril. The construction that can, and is, put to these decisions by some of the lower courts, induces the attitude on the part of the investigator that it is better to completely ignore the suspect, circumventing him entirely, developing the case independent of any information he might furnish. The authors have no quarrel with this concept, in fact endorse it fully wherever practicable. Interrogation, as such, is rapidly becoming a lost art and it is conceivable in the near future police officers under no circumstances will be allowed to interview a suspect. With all this, there is one redeeming feature about the "NSF" check case and that is the nature of the offense permits the establishing, comparatively easily, of the elements through the testimony of the victim and the documentation available from the bank records coupled with the testimony of the bank officer, the specific intent to defraud being apparent in the correlation between the date of the passing and the dates of the overdraft and notification, coupled with a record of additional similar acts. There is also the probability, ever present, the suspect could accuse the investigator not only of violating the usual "civil rights" because of a clearly ennunciated admonition per Miranda and other little niceties were not given, but also he is a "bill collector" and using his vested "power" to enforce a private collection (supra) which in fact is tantamount to extortion. It would seem the better way is to develop the facts via the victim, witnesses and bank documents and records, presenting them, the case rising or falling on its own merits, rather than jeopardize it with the questioned value of facts or fancy elicited from the suspect. Each situation of course has to be judged individually by the investigator.

If and when an arrest is made the suspect upon being booked should be required to complete a handwriting exemplar card, this in turn should be analyzed by a document examiner, even though there is no allegation of forgery. It merely precludes the suspect/accused from raising the issue as a defense. The Bradford or "BCS card" should also be completed which is even more conclusive than the usual alphabetical exemplar form (infra).

Forgery Investigation Sequence

The investigative routine in the crime of forgery is similar to that of the "NSF" check inquiry but with some other avenues to explore. There are a variety of ways in which the forged instrument come into existence, burglary of a residence or business establishment, theft by an employee of a number of blank checks, theft by "friends" or even members of the same household, or the counterfeiting of the instruments to mention a few. The crime of printing fictitious checks demands comparable investigative procedures but with the requisite knowledge of how instruments are created.

A police agency is either notified by the drawee/bank, the depositor or the acceptor when a forged instrument turns up and is being protested. The depositor, when interviewed, should disclose in some detail the normal location of the checkbook and its use. Any deviation in a recent period prior to the date of the forged instrument appearance must be covered extensively developing the reasons, the location, date, time, persons who were present or in proximity who could have acquired even momentary control of the book, such as friends, acquaintances, associates, employees, etc. In addition to obtaining an affidavit of forgery from the depositor, the alphabetical exemplar card and the "BCS card" should also be filled out completely. If the instrument was protectographed an exemplar of the depositors machine should be taken reflecting the same amounts as appearing on the questioned checks, using, if possible, paper of comparable texture and quality as the forged check. This last is best accomplished by obtaining a voided check from the same book. If not, bond paper is acceptable. In situations in which a typewriter has been used, obtain complete examplars from all typewriters on the victim's premises and any others to which he might have access using again voided checks or bond paper. Also obtain a number of cancelled checks passed during the same period for purposes of establishing unequivocally the method employed in the making and for comparisons by the document examiner.

If business or payroll checks are the subject of the inquiry, develop in detail the internal office controls, establishing routines and responsibilities of all concerned. This should be followed up with some background inquiries regarding those persons who have had access to the checkbook. Also all previously reported similar incidents involving the same persons and places should be reviewed, especially keeping alert for any similarities noted on the part of the unknown suspect and the internal situation.

The acceptor of the forged or fictitious instrument should be contacted as early as possible after notice of the incident while the transaction may just possibly be still fresh in his mind. He should be made to relate in detail an account of the transaction and of course whether or not he can identify the passer. The multiple mug-shot routine with a number of similarly appearing persons is quite good if it takes place within a short time after the incident and the acceptor/witness is somewhat perceptive. If not, it can sometimes do more harm than good. Here, again, size up the witness as to his mental and emotional stability and evaluate his potential as a witness on the stand. Determine his length and grade of employment, experience and capabilities.

Technical Aids

There are technical aids available to the investigator that will in a large way determine his case. When the forged or fictitious instrument is received from the bank or the depositor it should be immediately copied, both sides, from the Bradford System files. If there is more than one check involved, one should be retained, if the situation warrants it, for application of the ninhydrin process for latent prints (infra). If it is a case of fictitious prints or forgery by counterfeiting there is always a series of checks available which can be used for laboratory analysis to determine not only the presence of latent prints, but also for paper and ink examinations. In relation to this last, printing houses and wholesale paper outlets are extraordinarily good sources of information. These people have the expertise in the occupational area that is sometimes astounding. Experienced paper people often can tell from the appearance, touch and odor of a piece of paper where it was milled, when, how, by whom, what materials were used and where it can be obtained not only locally but in other areas. Printers have the same capabilities plus the ability to recognize and identify the work of other printers. They can inform the investigator under what conditions the printing was done, probably where, by whom (even amateurs and part-time "woodshed printers"), when, and always how. If the investigator has been applying himself to his work for a period of time, developing all the inter-relationships he should have, the paper suppliers, and printers will often pass on information concerning proposed illegal operations of which they become aware when purchases of supplies and machinery are being made and frequently questionable pre-printing jobs are requested.

Further comment should perhaps be made without, however, transversing too far into the area of chemistry, concerning the ninhydrin process for latent fingerprints. The albumin in the perspiration left by a finger hydrolyzes to amino acids. The amino acids react with the ninhydrin creating a purple color which in turn emphasizes the print pattern. The process has been known for almost 60 years, but it has been only in the last 20 years that it has been applied effectively. There is one drawback, however, in that the use of the chemical turns the document uniformly purple. There are a number of ways in which this condition can be overcome, the better one being the application of the substance via a "ninhydrin bomb" or aeresol spray which be directed at the questioned area of the document leaving the remainder free from the discoloring effects. The greatest achievement of the process in its ability to bring out print patterns that are in excess of 20 years of age, the development being permanent.

The "Identikit" system or composite view is too well known and universally used today to merit additional discussion here, other than to acknowledge its importance to forgery investigations is as well established as it is to robbery, assault and other offenses in which the suspect has been observed but remains unidentified. Its inherent limitations are predicated only upon those of the witness's degree of retentiveness and the ability of the operator who implements the system.

Handwriting and Document Examination

In any fraudulent document or instrument inquiry the time tested and usually conclusive evidence is the determination rendered by the handwriting expert. His testing is essentially the comparison of the questioned writing with the exemplars appearing on a known document. The investigator plays an important ancillary role in this area, however not with the handwriting examination itself. It is incumbent upon him to obtain good exemplars and this of course can, and often does become a tremendous burden requiring tenacity, originality of thought, effort and circumspection. If possible the exemplars should be written on the same type of paper and with the same type of pen, e.g. if a questioned check has been written with a ballpoint pen, the exemplars developed for comparison should also have been written with a ballpoint pen and the paper used should be of the same or near texture of the questioned check. This issue is not often raised by the defense but the spectre is always there and if the prosecution has been well prepared (handwriting examination being part of case preparation) its effect can be minimized. The sources of pre-existing exemplars are numerous, providing the suspect is in custody or at least tentatively identified. Prior arrest records will indicate the location of booking sheets which are always signed, previous motions or applications for probation or parole, the records usually in the suspect's own handwriting, periodic reports to parole and probation officers are usually in the suspect's handwriting, all of which normally have little or no attempts at disguising. Employment applications, bank account signature cards, school records, purchasing contracts, loan applications, driver's licenses, credit card applications and invoices, utility company records, old letters and other checks are all useful and admissable if developed properly within the limitations imposed by Miranda and "poisoned fruit doctrine" envolving out of Mapp vs. Ohio, and being applicable to state level prosecutions.

Related Law

The obtaining of exemplars directly from the suspect no longer presents the problem it once did. The United States Supreme Court in one of its rare moments of omniscience in *Schmerber vs California* (384 U.S. 757) and in *Gilbert vs California* (388 U.S. 263) upheld the validity of handwriting exemplars being taken from an accused, unequivocally stating that it is a proper part of the identification of a suspect, equating it with photography, measurements, fingerprints, blood alcohol, breath alcohol and urinalysis, negating the contention it is testimonial in nature. The courts specifically stated the taking of handwriting exemplars does not violate an accused person's constitutional rights. A California appellate court decision (*Peo vs. Coffinberger*, 254 Cal App 2nd 417) further solidified the position of the investigator, if properly approached and handled, stating, "The defendant was charged with unlawfully using a credit card." At the trial the policewoman (Mrs. Lynn Donnelly, SDPD) testified to the defendant's giving upon request, an exemplar of his handwriting.

The judge sustained the prosecutor's objection to the following question by the defense counsel, "Would you tell me, - - - - - -whether or not you warned him that any writing that he may make at that particular time would be compared and used against him, or could be used against him?'"

The court held that the trial judge's ruling sustaining the prosecutor's objection was proper. Neither Escobeda, Dorado, nor Miranda requires that the police advise the defendant of his constitutional rights before taking from him an exemplar of his handwriting.

Parenthetically it was added that if the defendant refuses to give an exemplar, he should be advised that he has no right to refuse to give such an exemplar and his refusal to do so can be used as evidence against him.

A situation which constantly develops when obtaining exemplars directly from the suspect in custody or in the position of the inquiry focusing directly on him and his being aware of it, is the attempt to disguise his writing. The only practical way in which to overcome this, is having the suspect write numerous exemplars of the same type such as a word, phrase or complete name. Usually, after a fairly short period of time he cannot continue with the altered attempt and will begin to lapse into his normal manner of writing. Never, under any circumstances, furnish the suspect with a check or any other writing to be used as a guide or to copy. This eliminates the originality and true character of his writing. Also, for the same reason, never spell words or names for the suspect. Have him display his own word usage, format (infra) and spelling. The manner in which he adheres to his own writing method and form will often disclose his complicity even in the face of undecipherable and undeterminable disguised exemplars. Another method that the investigator should employ whenever possible, is having the suspect furnish the exemplar under duplicate conditions, as far as possible, of the actual criminal act: e.g. if the suspect wrote the questioned instrument when standing, have him stand in a comparable position when furnishing the exemplar, or if seated when committing the act, have him seated, when writing the exemplar.

The statement is frequently made that a well trained and competent forgery investigator should be a qualified handwriting or document examiner. In theory this sounds good and the authors agree he should have a good understanding of the principles involved. However, from a practical standpoint a forgery investigator actually engaged in the case would not usually be permitted to give expert testimony in court on his own case, (supra). The attitude has developed over the years, rightfully or wrongfully, that his testimony would be viewed as biased and prejudiced. There is developing a concept that all actual expert testimony should come from an independent agency or witness. Whether this is proper or not is not within the purview of this book, but is one of individual thought. There perhaps is some justification for such an approach, but it is still maintained by these authors that an investigator should develop all the specialized knowledge possible, both in theory and practice regarding all facets of his vocation, the law, the scientific and field operations, these are his guidelines. If he does not have a basic understanding of the principles involved he cannot function.

The Bradford Classification System

The discourse on handwriting naturally evolves into the area of the Bradford Classification System. This system of identification of check writers by the methods they employ ("M.O.") is the creation of the late Lieut. Ralph BRADFORD, Document Examiner, Long Beach (California) Police Department. It has proven to be one of the most practical and useful methods which can be implemented by a police agency to expedite the identification of the check writer and the transmittal of the information to other interested departments comparable to the manner in which finger-print classification are used for identification tool and interdepartmental transmission.

The system is one based on the method used in writing the instrument and *not* on the individual handwriting characteristics. This last function is separate and comes into play after the classification or category of the check eliminates all other possibilities by channeling the file search into the proper area. In other words the classification breaks down the search into small groups of similarily written checks and the final identification, there is made by the handwriting characteristics a maximum number of variations have been combined in the classification for two reasons: first, to make the search more complete without additional

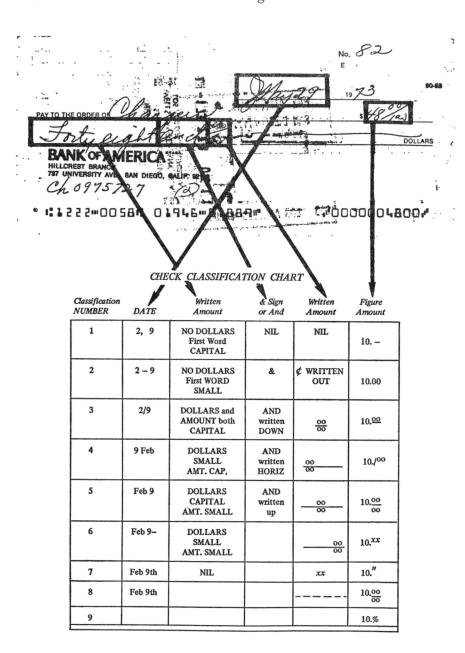

CHECK CLASSIFICATION CHART

Classification NUMBER	DATE	Written Amount	& Sign or And	Written Amount	Figure Amount
1	2, 9	NO DOLLARS First Word CAPITAL	NIL	NIL	10. –
2	2 – 9	NO DOLLARS First WORD SMALL	&	¢ WRITTEN OUT	10.00
3	2/9	DOLLARS and AMOUNT both CAPITAL	AND written DOWN	$\frac{00}{00}$	10.$\frac{00}{}$
4	9 Feb	DOLLARS SMALL AMT. CAP,	AND written HORIZ	$\frac{00}{00}$	10./^{00}
5	Feb 9	DOLLARS CAPITAL AMT. SMALL	AND written up	$\frac{00}{00}$	10.$\frac{00}{00}$
6	Feb 9–	DOLLARS SMALL AMT. SMALL		$\frac{00}{00}$	10.^{xx}
7	Feb 9th	NIL		xx	10."
8	Feb 9th			– – – – –	10.$\frac{00}{00}$
9					10.%

The classification of the above instrument is 51448.

reference searches and second, to make the system easier to learn and use.

The identification of an "unknown writer" of a check is made by the comparisons with "known or previously identified check writers" checks filed in the system or the combining of checks with the previous checks already on hand written by the same "unknown or unidentified check writer."

Over twenty-eight hundred check writer's files were examined to determine the variations in their method of writing checks that would affect or change the classification with each individual; also, what the changes are and where the changes occur in the classification so that they would be caught in the references searches.

The Bradford System was examined and tested for more than ten years prior to its being put into practice by the Forgery Detail of the Long Beach Police Department 20 years ago. At that time there were approximately 40,000 checks on file representing over twenty years of "Known Check Writers." Every check by one writer, with different classification, has been photographed, classified and filed. The names of the writers, if known, with aliases, descriptions, file numbers, etc., were included in the photograph with the check. Finished photographs were enlarged to 5″ × 8″ to make a standard size file. By actual count, covering thousands of checks, it is interesting to note that this system has proved to be better than 98 percent accurate.

The system is divided into five sections, producing a five-digit classification number, which is used to locate the check in the file for comparison and identification.

I—THE PRIMARY CLASSIFICATION is the first section. It is based on the method of writing the *date* on the check and is subdivided into eight sections, the number given to it being the first figure in the five-digit classification number:

1—The date is written, printed, stamped or typewritten in FIGURES only with a space, a period or a comma between the month and the date. And without a dash or diagonal line separating the date and the month. (2.9 1950)

2—The date is written, printed, stamped or typewritten in

FIGURES only with a horizontal line or dash separating the month and the date. One variation is the combined horizontal line and a diagonal line. Whichever is first, is the only one considered. (2—9 1950)

3—The date is written, printed, stamped or typewritten in FIGURES only with a diagonal line separating the month and the date. One variation is the combined diagonal line and a horizontal line. Whichever is first, is the only one considered. (2/9 1950)

4—The date is written, printed, stamped or typewritten in the style used by the United States Military Services, with the date preceeding the month. (9 Feb 1950)

5—The date is written, printed, stamped or typewritten in the most used style, with the month abbreviated or written out in full, and followed by the date, with no dash or diagonal line. (Feb. 9 1950)

6—The date is written, printed, stamped or typewritten similar to #5, except that a DASH or DIAGONAL LINE follows or preceeds the date. (Feb —9, 1950)

7—The date is written, printed, stamped or typewritten similar to #5, except that the contraction of the ORDINAL NUMBER FORM is used for the date. (Feb. 9th 1950)

8—The date is written, printed, stamped or typewritten similar to #7, except that the contraction of the ordinal number form is used for the date WITH A TRADEMARK or characteristic mark underneath it. (Feb 9th 1950).

II—THE SECONDARY CLASSIFICATION is the second division. It is based on the method of writing the WRITTEN AMOUNT OF DOLLARS on the check. It is divided into 7 sub-divisions, and is the second figure in the check classification.

1—The written dollar amount of the check is CAPITALIZED and the word DOLLARS is OMITTED. (Ten)

2—The written dollar amount on the check is NOT CAPITALIZED and the word DOLLARS is OMITTED. (ten)

3—The written dollar amount on the check is CAPITALIZED and the word DOLLARS is USED BUT IT IS CAPITALIZED. (Ten Dollars)

4—The written dollar amount of the check is CAPITALIZED and the word DOLLARS is USED BUT IT IS NOT CAPITALIZED. (Ten dollars)

5—The written dollar amount of the check is NOT CAPITALIZED and the word DOLLARS is USED AND IS CAPITALIZED (ten Dollars)

6—The written dollar amount of the check is NOT CAPITALIZED and the word DOLLARS IS USED but is not CAPITALIZED. (ten dollars)

7—The written dollar amount of the check is BLANK or NIL. No written amount or printed amount is in the normal place for such notation on the check.

III—THE SUB-SECONDARY CLASSIFICATION is the third division. It is based on the method of writing the CONJUNCTION in the written amount of the check, between the written dollar amount and the written cents amount. It is divided into 5 sub-divisions, and is the third figure in the check classification.

1—The conjunction AND or & sign is OMITTED, between the written dollar amount and the written cents amount on the check. (Ten dollars twenty cents)

2—The & sign in any form IS USED, between the written dollar amount and the written cents amount on the check. (Ten dollars & twenty cents.)

3—The word AND is written DOWNWARDS on the check, between the written dollar amount and the written cents amount on the check. (Ten dollars $^{a}n_d$ twenty cents).

4—The word AND is written HORIZONTAL on the check, between, the written dollar amount and the written cents amount. (ten dollars and twenty cents)

5—The word AND is written UPWARD on the check, between the written dollar amount and the written cents amount. (Ten dollars $_an^d$ twenty cents)

IV—The 2nd SUB-SECONDARY CLASSIFICATION is the fourth division. It is based on the method of writing the WRITTEN AMOUNT OF CENTS on the check. It is divided into 8 sub-divisions, and is the fourth figure on the check classification.

1—NIL. No written amount of cents is indicated on the check. (Ten dollars)

2—The written cents amount on the check is written, printed, stamped or typewritten OUT IN FULL. (Ten dollars & five cents)

3—The written cents amount on the check is written as a FRACTION without a line PRECEDING or AFTER the fraction. (Ten & $\frac{14}{00}$)

4—The written cents amount on the check is written as a FRACTION with a straight or wavy line FOLLOWING the fraction. (Ten & $\frac{no}{00}$ . . . .)

5—The written cents amount on the check is written as a FRACTION with a straight or wavy line PRECEDING and FOLLOWING the fraction. (Ten & . . . . $\frac{00}{100}$ . . . . .)

6—The written cents amount on the check is written as a FRACTION with a straight or wavy line PRECEEDING the fraction. (Ten & . . . . $\frac{00}{00}$)

7—The written cents amount on the check is similar to #3 EXCEPT "xx" is used in the numerator or denominator of the fraction. (Ten & . . . . $\frac{xx}{xx}$)

8—The written amount of cents on the check is OMITTED and a STRAIGHT or WAVY line is drawn after the written dollar amount. (Ten . . . .)

V—THE FINAL CLASSIFICATION is the fifth division. It is based on the method of writing the figure cents amount of the check. It is divided into 9 sub-divisions, and is the last digit in the 5 figure check classification number.

1—NIL. No cents or zeros are used ($6.)

2—The cents is written WITHOUT a line UNDERNEATH. ($6.00)

3—The cents is written with a HORIZONTAL line underneath. ($6.00)

4—The cents is written with ANY line except a horizontal line. It is usually a diagonal or flourished line ($6./00)

5—The cents is written with MULTIPLE lines underneath. ($6.00)

6—The cents is written "xx" in the NUMERATOR or DE-NOMINATOR. $\left(\dfrac{\$6.00}{xx}\right)$

7—The cents is written with a TRADEMARK, other than "xx" in the numerator or denominator. ($6.00)

8—The cents is written with "00" or "100" in the DENOMI-NATOR of the fraction. $\left(\dfrac{\$6.00}{100}\right)$

9—The cents is written as a percent or In-account sign. ($4.%)

The checks upon which the written amount (digits 2, 3, and 4) is protectographed can also be categorized. The Bradford system employs the idea of using the "cents." "dollars" and the word "and" as a coding sequence. From a lengthy examination of the types of machines found on the market there evolved a scale of twenty-six ways in which to print the "cents" amount, twenty-six ways in which to print the "dollars" amount and fourteen ways in which to print the word "and." With the "protected" checks letters of the alphabet are used instead of numbers in the secondary, sub-secondary and 2nd sub-secondary classifications, however leaving the primary and final classification points represented by numbers as with the hand-written or typewritten checks.

It is not the purpose here to set forth in its entirety the Bradford system as it comprises a separate book in itself. What has been analyzed here is a small part of the system which can be expanded to meet almost every conceivable demand in the area of classification and category. There is a "Prefix Classification" which is implemented for extending files such as can be used to advantage by the larger agencies. The expanded system includes the (1) Type of check with nine variations, (2) How it was manufactured or printed with five variations, (3) How it was filled out by the maker with seven variations, and (4) Sex and race of the passer with six variations, permitting 1,890 combinations.

The World of Electronics

The advent of the new sophisticated computerized data systems has, with their vast storage and retrieval capabilities, opened the door to coding and classification of worthless checks and other forms of instruments and documentation undreamed of in the past. The Bradford System lends itself to such implementation easily. Due to the wide assortment of sort keys available there can be created several additional encoded items not previously considered such as physical descriptions. If an agency develops a classification system or utilizes "Bradford" its inclusion within the other electronic data processing programs must be considered. In many situations a regional concept is the better approach as a group of agencies could submit the data input and share in the stored information from a wider area and at a much reduced cost. This method permits benefits which would normally be denied if the participants were limited to incidents and related data emanating solely from their individual jurisdictions. In areas of multiple jurisdictions this would be a form of mutual aid based upon reduced shared costs and operating expense.

The Area Alarm Method

The commercial check warning system, another aid to the investigator has been used in its present form for at least fifty years with proven efficacy. There have been of course new innovations at various times, the most recent and effective probably being the "Telecredit" system which was started by a Los Angeles group in 1961. However, for purposes of this study we will examine the system used by the San Diego Sheriff's Department since 1962. The progenitor of such an operation was the late Lieut. "Pat" Slattery of the San Diego Police Department in the early 1920s when he for all intents and purpose created and headed up that agency's Forgery Detail. It has been utilized in various forms by that department since that time. The principle involved is very simple; it is a "fan-out" type method. The first person called by the department's Fraud Detail in turn telephones one other who in turn calls one other participant until the pre-arranged list is completed, the necessary descriptive information is disseminated covering a large area in a number of minutes.

SHERIFF'S CHECK WARNING

PERSONAL ☐   BUSINESS ☐   FICTITIOUS   ☐   Date Warning Issued _____

PAYROLL ☐   STOLEN ☐   MONEY ORDER ☐   Other ☐ _____

Name of Company_____Checks numbered_____thru_____incl.

Drawn on Bank_____Branch_____

Payable To (if known)_____Signed By (if known)_____

                                                            Yes   No

CHECK PROTECTOR USED   ☐   ☐   Color of Check _____

Description of Passer (If known)   Race _____ Sex _____ Age _____ Height _____

Weight_____Hair_____Eyes_____ Clothing_____

FORM R-143 10M 9-62 HILDRETH

IMPORTANT

Anyone attempting to pass the described checks should be delayed and the SHERIFF notified IMMEDIATELY.

San Dego Sheriff	232_3811
Coast Area	753_5711
Vista, Fallbrook	724_2279
Escondido, Ramona	745_5851

TO DELAY THE SUSPECT: Ask him to endorse or re-endorse the check in your presence. **RETAIN THE CHECK.** Ask for Identification Cards or Driver's License and **RETAIN THEM.** DO NOT TIP-OFF THE SUSPECT TO THIS WARNING.

If the suspect cannot be delayed, follow him, note his direction of travel, get his complete description. If he enters a vehicle, note the LICENSE NUMBER and write it down. Note the Make, Model and Color.

The above illustration is a facsimile of both sides of the information pad furnished to the participants. The face is filled in with the data received by telephone and then repeated to the next in line participant. Emergency instructions are on the reverse side.

Each participant is furnished with a "fan-out" call schedule, a brief letter of instruction and a pad of printed information sheets. The establishing of such a system requires initially much personal contact with the merchants within a department's jurisdiction (i.e. "leg-work"). It takes surprisingly little effort to induce them to take part when it is learned they will not have to pay any additional expense over and above their already burdensome tax rate. All that is required is full and knowledgeable participation, immediately relaying the information received to the next person in line. This is the strength and also the greatest weakness of the system. Many merchants are enthusiastic about the idea but often fail to indoctrinate their employees, thus when a message is received it is not passed on immediately for a variety of reasons, someone misplaced the information pad, a sale is in progress, the customer is not to be distracted or disturbed, carelessness, incompetence and other vitiating causes. Consequently the next one in line receives a late message or no message, and often a garbled one.

The genesis of a fraudulent check warning is often Sub-Station Burglary Detail Detectives who may determine a book or several business or payroll checks have been taken; or the theft of personal checks during a residential burglary. They immediately notify the Fraud Detail which initiates the warning system. Another source, of course, is the sudden appearance of a series of fictitious or counterfeited checks, the information here unfortunately not coming to the Department's attention until after they have been passed on a merchant, sent to the bank in the due course of business where they are rejected, this all taking a period of about two days. The banks always do their part by notifying the Department which has jurisdiction, but the lapse of time has mitigated the effectiveness of any warning, although it is still broadcasted. At least when a merchant receives the warning he can often recall such a check and will report the incident even though the bank has not yet returned the rejected item to him. The descriptive information regarding the passer is *sometimes* relatively fresh in his mind proving helpful.

Obviously in a jurisdiction of any size all the merchants or businesses cannot be included in the system. If they were, it would fall of its own weight. The greatest one problem would be oil company credit cards. The preponderance of offenses by this means cannot justify the number of warnings which would have to be promulgated each day. The only thing that should be done in such a situation is to urge all of the service stations in an area to create their own independent warning system. Many of the larger super-market and super-drugstore chains already do this effectively. The private system operating via a mercantile inter-relationship actually parallels and compliments a police agency's system and does not go at cross purposes. The headquarters units of these companies are notified as are the local police agencies when the information is evaluated as proper for broadcast.

It should be pointed out here there is one exception to the type of instrument which can become the subject of a broadcast. This is the "NSF" or "non-sufficient funds" type. Due to the legal niceties involved (supra) in the establishing of the vital element of *specific* intent to defraud, the Department will not usually initiate a warning unless there are such a number of them turning up in an area as to effectively support at least a prima facie case for complaint. Then a warning is broadcast, but limited to only the particular area in which the checks have been, or are being passed.

The warning system which presently numbers in excess of one hundred participants can all receive the necessary information within a forty-five minute period from the time of the initial call from the Fraud Detail. One important thing to remember in the maintenance of such an operation is that there is a need for constant vigilance on the part of the police agency to shore up the weak points. Also businesses open and they close or are sold with new people coming in who must be indoctrinated to the idea of cooperation. The ones who prove uncooperative for one reason or another should be dropped from the system forthwith as they are a liability to the other persons who genuinely want the service and who, in taking their own active and responsible part, rely on others to do the same. It is a neverending circle of effort and the agency which creates or establishes such a system has an obligation to those who want, need and will cooperate with it to maintain constant supervision of its operation.

The system also can be utilized effectively on occasions to pass on descriptive information concerning wanted persons. A burglary ring was apprehended due to the interest and cooperation of the system's participants and there has also been some apprehensions of armed robbers brought about due to the system.

The "Kiter"

The "check-kiter" is a classic scam with the fraudulent check artists and it comes with a number of variations. One James F. Smith visits the main branch of the National Bank and opens a *savings* account with a cash deposit of $20.00. A few days later he goes to one of the National Bank's branches where he presents a check for $1,550.00 drawn on another bank somewhere in the state. He makes a dual transaction in which he deposits $1,500.00 to his account at the main bank and receives the $50.00 remaining balance in cash monies. Then a few days later he goes to a different branch of the National Bank and withdraws $850.00 from his savings account. Within about one or two days the National Bank is informed via the "due course of business" route that the $1,550.00 check has been drawn against a fictitious, nonexistent or closed account, Smith in the meantime has departed the area with $900.00 in cash for his original deposit of $20.00 plus some authentic looking worthless paper.

Another approach to the time-honored scam is that of the same man (or his equivalent) going to a bank and opening a *checking* account for $10.00 cash. The public relations conscious new accounts executive, after informing him of all the fine attributes of that institution, presents him with a "temporary" book containing 20 checks to be used until his "personalized" check book is received from the printers. This is always a nice gesture, making the depositor feel his business is needed and appreciated and he shortly sets about to test this professed rapport.

Usually within a few days the depositor appears at another bank in the area where, using a different name, he opens a new account with a check of $500.00 payable to him and made by the name he used previously and drawn on the original bank where he had made his $10.00 deposit. As is sometimes the situation, the teller in the second bank being somewhat momentarily mesmerized by the con-man's personality, does not immediately contact the other bank for verification or neglects referring the instrument to a bank officer for the same purpose, accepts the new depositor with the same "good spirit of public relations," giving to him (the depositor) his book of checks (always in excess of those needed) as did the first bank. The con-man then decides he wants to withdraw some cash needed for other business, doing so, he receives $250.00, leaving the balance of $250.00 and departs. For the original $10.00 investment at the original bank and the use of the blank checks given to him by the bank officer in an over-eager attempt at implementing the bank's public relations policy, he walks out with a profit of $240.00.

These scam artists will often take a little extra time to build up the confidence of the bank by not abusing or using the account to any extent. They will even make additional deposits of cash to allay any suspicion and to create an acceptable continuing balance and never write a check which causes an overdraft. When the propitious time comes, usually when the account balance is low, they take one of two courses of action. The first is usually a sudden onslaught of several large checks, in which situation the offense is the prosaic "NSF" type or they will go the "kiting" route with a phony deposit by a check and then follow the processes described above.

The "Counterfeit" Check Gangs

The type of offense which creates the greatest problems for the investigator and probably the largest total loss is the counterfeited check, especially when it is the result of a well disciplined, imaginative, intelligent group of makers and passers, well led by a competent planner. They can blanket an area, usually a one or two day operation, so completely (if their workmanship is good) that hardly a merchant or business house is not effected. The amounts of the instruments are always above one-hundred dollars meeting the prevailing criterion of the blue-collar workers' weekly paycheck, and passers all look the part they are playing.

A case in point that was jointly investigated by the San Diego Sheriff's Department and the San Diego Police Department resulted in the indictment of nine men and their conviction after a four weeks trial. Their operations, including the preparation, began in November, 1962 and continued until June, 1963 covering areas in Southern and Northern California and Denver, Colorado. It included the purchases of automobiles, printing equipment, paper and other supplies, the use of photography (which was masterful considering they were all amateurs), air-lines transportation and accompanying acts of burglary.

In November, 1962 an extremely young (23 yrs) and capable building contractor decided to augment his income with a fraudulent check operation and using a few of his construction employees, all of whom were of a larcenous and weak-willed nature, amenable to him, as the burglars, printers, photographers and ultimately the passers. For purposes of this narrative fictitious names will be used as all are now released from prison and, presumably having been thoroughly "rehabilitated," are leading normal productive lives.

The contractor had his offices in one end of a small business office complex in a suburban community's business area. At the other end of the building an electric contractor also had offices, normally occupied during the day by one young female office manager-bookkeeper. The building contractor, Peters, sent one of his more pleasing of appearance workers, one Russ, to get acquainted with the girl, "romance her a little" as it was described in order to develop a good idea of the premises' lay-out, the location of the business and payroll checkbooks, the protectograph which was used, and the locking and keys of the office doors. Russ was apparently effective in his mission (although he disclaimed everything other than the use of personality and small-talk to achieve his purpose) as he brought back to Peters the needed information. One night, after the electrical contractor had closed but still fairly early in the evening, Peters and Russ along with the workcrew foreman, Smith, entered that office, located the payroll checkbook, opened same and taking 10 sheets or pages, each consisting of four blank checks, from the area of the last pages (the book had about 70 pages) then applied the protectograph to the incomplete instruments in amounts near one-hundred twenty dollars and some odd cents figure which had been previously computed, closed the book, returning it and the protectograph to their proper places, departed the premises. The half-filled out instruments were then taken back to Peter's office and completed by a typewriter brought onto the premises for just such purpose. The amounts used were carefully applied reflecting the correct deductions for IRS purposes, bonds, insurance, etc. Each instrument was in the proper amount that a worker would have after all the normal deductions. This was all disclosed in a "box" located on the left side of the instrument in voucher form. The checks were then completed with the exception of the date which was withheld until the proper time for passing and the name of the payee.

A few days later all of those who were to be passers, which included Russ and his close friend Bert (also an employee) Charles, the brother-in-law of Smith the foreman and Ortega, a brick-mason, went to Tia Juana, Mexico separately and for $2.50 purchased authentic appearing California driver's licenses in the names they were to use in the field operations. These documents were complete with fictitious addresses and good photographs, even to the extent of an extremely good seal of California stamped on the reverse side. Upon their return to San Diego and about three days prior to the action Russ, Bert and Ortega purchased in their new fictitious names old junker type second-hand (2nd hand? actually about 10th hand) automobiles, paying cash. The vehicles then were registered by the dealer in their name with the Department of Motor Vehicles, Sacramento (infra). The day was then selected for their foray amongst the innocent and unsuspecting. It was the Friday and Saturday of the Christmas weekend. The instruments were now completed with date and the new fictitious names and given out to the streetmen/passers. With everyone (store managers, salesmen, clerks, cashiers, checkers) all full of Christmas cheer, bottle and otherwise, there was no real difficulty encountered at the supermarkets, liquor stores and drugstores in which they made nominal purchases taking the balance of the "paychecks" in cash monies. Fortunately, as it later turned out, some clerks did record the license numbers of two of the vehicles used, placing them on the face or on the endorsement side of the instrument.

The days between Christmas and New Year then developed into a "king-size" headache for every law enforcement agency in the southern half of the county. The Sheriff's Department, the San Diego Police Department, the police departments of El Cajon, La Mesa, National City and Chula Vista all began getting reports from the drawee/bank about stolen and forged payroll checks. Warnings were broadcast (supra) which developed a few checks being held as not yet returned to the bank for payment. All forty checks turned up disclosing for the merchants a total loss for the first try-out at about $6,000.00. The electric company did not know their premises had been hit until they were contacted by the investigators on December 27th, five weeks later after the checks had been stolen.

Interviews with acceptors in most instances produced merely another facet to the growing composite drawings of the four suspects. One liquor store in San Diego had an 8mm movie camera rigged above the cash register, however the lighting was faulty, the resulting photocut from the film strip and even the film strip itself was not really identifiable until 6 months later when a daughter of the foreman, Smith, inadvertently declared the person as possibly being her uncle Charles (infra). However, little or no information was useful until two separate acceptors and of course the instruments they had taken in revealed license numbers of two separate vehicles. Data received back from the Department of Motor Vehicles led the investigators to the used car agencies which had sold the vehicles to two of the suspects but here again descriptive information was negligible, other than two men came on separate lots and purchased the cars for *cash*. At this time a "stop" on the license numbers was placed at the Department of Motor Vehicles which six months later was the key that opened the door to a successfully concluded investigation.

Time went by with numerous false leads being run out with the usual dearth of factual information. Other cases began taking over the time of the investigators as is normal in a police agency. Then in the latter part of March, 1963 the Mexican police notified the San Diego Sheriff's Department that a California licensed vehicle was found abandoned south of Tiajuana. The car proved to be one of those purchased and used by the check passers. A thorough examination failed to reflect any usable finger-prints or other identifying material.

In May the same areas were again flooded with checks. This time however, they were counterfeited warrants drawn on the account of the Clerk of the Municipal Court. The days selected were from Friday through Monday evening; the places again were liquor stores, supermarkets and drugstores. The amount varied between $110.00 and $165.00 and within a few days there were reported losses in excess of $10,000.00. On each occasion when conversation on the part of the passer seemed expedient he told the acceptor the instrument was a "bail refund" on a traffic ticket he had received some months earlier and had been acquitted by the Municipal Court. The instruments were perfect multilith reproductions, all protectographed and on paper of the same type (pale green basket weave design) with the payee's name typed in with an address (both fictitious), the date and the instrument number. The handwritten item was a name purporting to be the Deputy Court Clerk as maker and of course the passer's endorsement written at the time of the uttering and passing.

What had transpired to create this particular traumatic experience for the merchants was again the product of the fertile mind of Peters. He directed his original people plus three new characters, Jones, Brown and Green to go to Tiajuana again for a new identification, California driver's licenses and on this occasion a new fillip was added, Selective Service Cards, all of course in fictitious names. Charley had departed for Indiana in the meantime and wasn't in on the second local field exercise. They now rented a house in a somewhat secluded section of a rural community and installed their newly purchased multilithing machine, printing supplies, typewriter, a newly purchased protectograph, new photographic equipment and related supplies and the paper they were to use. Jones and Green took up residence there. All of the purchases of equipment and supplies and the rental were in fictitious names and addresses, Peters and Smith picking up from the vendors at the loading docks to obviate the need for any deliveries.

Between the stolen electric company payroll checks and the counterfeited Municipal Court Clerk refund checks/warrants gambits, the Sheriff's Department had received a number of teletype inquiries and telephone calls from the Sacramento Sheriff's Department Forgery Detail regarding methods and possible suspects as they too had a similar situation in which counterfeited checks purporting to be from a local lumber company had been used, again without the bookkeeper becoming aware of any burglary/theft until the checkbook was examined and there was found to be two missing checks from the center. That area had been hit on a weekend by at least three or four passers (the identification and descriptions somewhat vague) who all had in their possession adequate and authentic appearing identification such as driver's licenses for the Sacramento area with fictitious addresses and Selective Service cards. Because of the distance between the two affected areas little credence was put in the possibility of it being one and the same group. How little the investigators knew at the time and how surprised they were to become before the end of the case.

Again leads were run out and again two license numbers had been obtained from the counterfeited instruments plus a small identifiable tattoo noticed on the upper right arm of one of the suspects (it turned out to be Russ). The reason the counterfeits were caught early was that they were perfect in every detail except the "ABA" were not of magnetic ink and of course the computer device in the bank rejected them forthwith. Otherwise, it was extremely difficult to differentiate between the counterfeits and the actual checks.

There was a further lead in the manner in which one of the suspects wrote the numeral "7" on the address he would write into the endorsement and also found on the address he gave on the vehicle sales contract; they again had purchased junker cars the day before the operation in fictitious names. There was an amusing side issue this time, one of the cars had been resold to another used car lot one day after the field work who in turn sold it to another person without his (the dealer's) name appearing on the transfer, thus avoiding sales tax. Again "stops" had been placed immediately with the Department of Motor Vehicles, Sacramento. This particular car then turned up in the transfer files and the Sheriff's Department was notified that a man residing in a central California town now had it, the date of purchase being two days after the last known day a Municipal Court warrant/ check had been passed. He was of course interviewed right away and proved satisfactorily that he had no connection with the counterfeited checks, merely purchasing an old car from the dealer when he was going to central California for a new job. The vehicle transfer had gone directly from Ortega (using his fictitious name) to the new buyer via the dealer but without his appearing of record. Investigators from DMV took a dim view of this and after a hearing his license to sell cars was revoked.

In late June the Department of Motor Vehicles notified the Sheriff's Department that another one of the vehicles had been sold/transferred to Bert (in his actual name) who was residing in a nearby suburban community. Upon arriving at the residence it was found to have been vacated the preceeding day. Permission was obtained from the owner/landlord to examine the premises. The examination proved fruitful. Here were found all the debris normally left behind when tenants move. There were several sales and purchase receipts and other papers in Bert's and his wife's names upon which appeared the uniquely made numeral "7". Also found were discarded payroll check vouchers in Bert's name from the Peters construction company. There were numerous old letters and other items which became excellent exemplars and which also furnished good information as to his family and his background and that of his close friend Russ who it turned out lived one and one-half blocks away. It was learned within a few minutes that Russ and his family also had moved the same day, however, new tenants had already moved in and had placed all of his debris in the furnace. Fortunately neighbors furnished a good description of Russ (and his friend Bert) including a tattoo on his upper right arm and his recent employment with Peters construction company. They also stated that both men and their families were moving to San Bernardino County and both were known for their joint and avid interest in drag racing cars.

As a matter of course Peters and Smith were interviewed as to the employment of Russ and Bert and their possible whereabouts at the time, not however alluding in any way to the fraudulent check operations. Both men were obviously highly tense and nervous which was not lost on the investigators especially in view of the vague and non-committal answers received to questions. Other investigators were immediately assigned to the task of conducting an exhaustive background examination of the construction company, its officers, employees, job sites and not disregarding the fact the office had been located at the other end of the building in which the electric company had its offices, although in March, Peters *et al* had moved to a new location.

During the first week of July the San Bernardino Sheriff's Department relayed information to the effect Russ and Bert were in custody. A complaint had been issued earlier based upon the findings at their old residences in San Diego County. Upon being interviewed both men laid out for the investigators the whole operation and those involved. The electric company stolen checks were discussed as were the counterfeited Municipal Court Clerk's warrants/checks. They stated that the latter had been an actual reproduction of a check given to Peters as a bail refund. Court records confirmed this, he having received it in January, 1963. They also disclosed Ortega and Russ had indeed flown to Sacramento where they burglarized a lumber company office taking only two blank checks from the center of the book as directed by Peters and Smith and which they brought back to San Diego and from which multilith reproductions were made. These in turn were taken back to Sacramento by he, Ortega, Bert, Jones and Green where they drove one rental car, one borrowed car belonging to one of Jones' girlfriends in that area and one car which was driven up to Sacramento by Peters and Smith. They spent two days and one night circulating checks in amounts of $150.00 and $170.00 picking up approximately $16,000.00 all of which, as in previous scams, went to Peters and Smith who returned a small part of the proceeds.

Russ stated that instead of abandoning the car he had used or selling it cheaply to a used car dealer pursuant to the instructions of Peters he transferred it to Bert who needed a car for their proposed move to San Bernardino County. He forgot to take into consideration the records maintained by the Department of Motor Vehicles and their availability to police agencies. He also neglected to inform Peters of the transfer .

Both men further disclosed the operation in Denver, Colorado in late April and which was unknown to the investigators. Russ and Peters had flown to that city, burglarized a machinery company office for one blank check and returned to San Diego. The instrument was taken to the rented house where again it was multilithed perfectly. A further astounding factor was the perfect reproductions of Colorado driver's licenses complete with photographs all of which is colored. This act was performed by Smith who proved extraordinarily capable with both printing and photography. He had no previous training but developed all his techniques on his own by studying instruction manuals. The whole crew then flew to Denver for a three day stay in the last part of May where the area was hit for over $18,000.00, returning then to San Diego. Rented cars and taxis were used for local transportation. A fortunate break for the investigators developed when the airlines company was found not yet to have destroyed the passenger manifest for the flights and all of them were placed on different flights by the fictitious names they had used. Peters had even taken his wife with him, she not knowing she was flying under an assumed name as he had purchased the tickets.

Further interviews elicited the fact the equipment was then in San Bernardino County in a house rented and occupied by Jones and Green under assumed names. During the trip to that area in which Russ had helped them move the items by a trailer they had burglarized a printing-photography shop in Santa Ana next door to the motel in which they stayed, obtaining some needed supplies. This cleared up an unsolved case for the Santa Ana Police Department. Arrests were made of Jones and Green immediately and it was found preparations were underway to hit the Los Angeles sector with counterfeit prints of checks belonging to a machinery company there. New California driver's licenses with yet unused fictitious names had already been printed with the photographs of Russ, Bert, Ortega, Jones, Brown and Green. Test runs had been made on the check reproduction but everything was being held in abeyance until better and more satisfactory prints could be achieved. Peters and Smith had already been taken into custody at the time of the second San Bernardino series of arrests.

All nine men were then indicted by the San Diego County Grand Jury and witnesses from all the effected areas were subpoenaed, including those from Denver pursuant to the Uniform Witness Act. The trial lasted four full weeks with the conviction of the whole crew. The turning point was the innocuous request to the Department of Motor Vehicles to place a "stop" on all known license numbers. If this had not been thought of and carried out the case may never have been cleared.

Credit Card Investigative Sequence

The investigation of the illegal use of a credit card follows a comparable pattern to that of a fraudulent check. The person interviewed must be the actual acceptor, not his employer or supervisor. He should furnish detailed information concerning what was purchased and the manner in which the transaction took place; determine whether the card was used for the entire purchases or if part was paid for in cash or by check; the complete description of the card user, vehicle and other persons with him including any conversation even if unrelated to the activity; whether or not any limitation or mitigating agreements were imposed; determine if he had knowledge, or at least should have, from the credit card company as to the particular card being stolen, lost or overdrawn; and point out very clearly there can be no collections through the exercise of police powers (supra).

The bona-fide cardholder must be contacted to develop a history of card use and especially notification of other indebtedness not yet reported to a police agency by an undisclosed acceptor. He must also furnish information concerning the circumstances attendant to the loss of the card and the date and manner in which he informed the issuing company.

The issuing company should be contacted for verification of the cardholder's and acceptor's information; determination of previous losses by the same holder and acceptor; and a complete resumé of all purchases regardless of jurisdictional areas.

The processes of information dissemination, technical aids such as handwriting, ninhydrin, identikit composites and warning system are all applicable to credit card violations much the same as they are for checks and comparable items. It resolves itself in the final analysis to just plain hard, aggressive and tenacious investigative approach with a concomitant appreciation for the legal technicalities inherent in all criminal inquiries.

CHAPTER IV

INSURANCE FRAUDS

Amateurism and Rationales

THIS IS the area of fraudulent activity which for obvious reasons seems to attract the bulk of the amateurs. People who have never willfully in the past taken part in a scam to cheat or flim-flam anyone, seem to think the "company" is fair game. The range is from the lovely young housewife who is an opportunist with a fender-bender auto accident of minor importance to the businessman who believes he should "sell the business to the insurance company" at an exhorbitant price through the happy medium of an "accidental" fire or large size burglary, theft or robbery. They have one common denominator; they are thieves. But, the rationalizations which are resorted to at both ends of the spectrum will amaze the "square" minded citizen. There seems to be a strong parallel in the reasoning processes between the large company embezzler, the tax evader and the insurance thief; it apparently is based upon their reaction to the monolithic structuring of large firms and organizations, a sort of impersonableness, the attitude that the loss, regardless of magnitude, could have no real effect, merely being absorbed as a tax deduction or routine operating loss of no consequence. The rationale seems to be that insurance premiums are too high anyway; that taxes as assessed are unfair; and that the company does not pay the proper wage level commensurate with the demands upon the employee. Here, then, is the common thread which ties together these apologists for thievery. It is both a crime of opportunity or one of inadvertance and one that can be well planned. The presence of intent, however on the one hand is not a requisite element of the offense (infra), but it is something which has been worked on, thought out to some degree and with action of a planned nature taken towards implementation.

Merger of Offenses

What really exists are two separate offenses. One of theft in its basic form and the other, a technical offense, which in effect proscribes the means used to achieve the theft. Both are separate and triable crimes. It is impossible for investigative purposes to divorce the fraudulent act of a false claim from the act of arson, purported theft or other means employed to bring about the situation. They must be considered together as evidence adduced in one is part of the other. Insurance frauds, more often than not, are brought to fruition by the judicious use of incendiary fires, at least at the level of major losses. These occur more frequently during periods of economic depression or fluctuating business cycles such as inflation or deflation. The classic situations in this type of crime are not unique, they follow the normal behavorial patterns inherent in all crimes involving to a degree, a violation of a trust. The insured businessman might find himself carrying excessive inventory and the anticipated sales do not materialize. Normally he is paying a floor tax in addition to his purchase contract obligation. Of course he has a blanket policy covering not only his structure, fixtures and equipment, but it is also extended to the inventory while it is on the premises. If he is in need of funds to cover operating and other expenses, and their normal source is from sales, it may be decided at this moment to "sell it to the insurance company." Often he will quietly move out his personal possessions, the accurate and true business records, equipment which can be used and not infrequently the inventory if he has a sub-rosa market for it, substituting items of lesser value. The fire is set, the structure goes, including the "inventory," usually with a total involvement, destroying, he hopes all vestiges of arson. His next step is the filing with the insurer a notice of loss which is followed later, after an adjustor's examination, by the proof of loss. This last is the main issue with which we are concerned here. The arson or theft is an important and parallel matter, both issues being inter-related as either are the first of two weapons used by the businessman to cheat and defraud, the other being the proof of loss or false claim. They must be considered together.

The notice of loss to the insurer notifies him that the contingency insured against has occurred. There is no particular format involved but it must be given within a reasonable period of time to permit the insurer to take such action he desires to protect his position and especially not to create problems or conditions which could hamper an investigation. Most policies have a stipulated time period in which this notice must be given, however, circumstances can alter the situation to some degree. But the insured must make every effort at notification within the "reasonable" period.

The proof of loss submitted by the insured, the second in the sequence, must be given over to the insurer within a definite time period unless, again, circumstances permit a delay. This must contain the insured's statement as to his knowledge and belief regarding the cause (and origin of fire involved) of the loss incurred, all parties of interest in the property, the values, the date and time of loss, other insurance coverage and any pertinent information as may be asked for by the insurer. It can usually be completed on a form for that purpose furnished by the insurer. This is the better way as it reduces commensurately the probability of error, definitely placing every element of information requested at a specific place on the form, clearly outlining what data is needed. Further, for the investigator, it reduces the defense that might be raised in which it is purported the insured did not understand what was required of him.

Motivation

The excess inventory is only one of the many reasons for the fire route to insurance indemnification. Sometimes obsolete equipment is a strong factor. There may be lucrative contracts available if the shop can produce sufficient quantities of a product according to specifications and within a certain time limit. If a loan is not feasible, the only source to purchase new equipment or to retool to meet the contract requirements may just be an insurance company again. The inability to obtain raw materials can be a motivation; if there exists a heavy operating expense which includes wages, salaries, repair and maintenance, there must be production to pay the way. If no material is available there is no income, ergo the insurance company is again the fountain of plenty. Partnerships can be problems; one partner wanting to buy out the other but lacks the necessary cash. The sole proprietor may be failing in business because of lack of experience, incompetence or inability to keep up with industrial developments. Poor health has often been a factor. In other words whenever there is an urgent need for ready cash and the proper, ethical and legal ways of obtaining it are temporarily closed some businessmen can and will turn to another source. It should be noticed here, however, the need does not necessarily have to be predicated upon business reasons, it can be a personal crisis far removed from the daily scene such as gambling debts, extra-marital interests and activities or other problems unrelated entirely to business as such. Over-insurance with prohibitive premium expense can be a reason also.

The types of properties involved in an insurance fraud are multiple and varied in nature. It will include commercial categories such as stores and offices (even fruit stands); manufacturing and industrial complexes from the one-man artisan to 1,000 plus employees in size; dwellings; automobiles and other vehicles; and in rural areas it can be haystacks, standing crops, livestock and every mode of structure related to ranch, farm or dairy operations. In other words, anything in which there is an insurable interest.

The three basic avenues followed by the insured in his attempts to defraud the carrier are fairly static: (1) excessive valuation of purported destroyed or stolen property, (2) claim of destruction, damage or theft of non-existent property or property removed prior to the incident, (3) false statements as to cause or knowledge of the cause of the loss of, or damage to the property, all designed to induce the carrier to indemnify the insured for the "loss."

A Legal Concept

The California Legislature in 1935 enacted a unique piece of legislation entitled Section 556 of the Insurance Code which covers the fraudulent claim by a policy holder: "It is unlawful to (a) present or cause to be presented any false or fraudulent claim for the payment of a loss under a contract of insurance; (b) prepare, make or subscribe any writing with intent to present or use the same, or to allow it to be presented or used in support of any such claim."

Every person who violates any provision of this section is punishable by imprisonment in the state prison not exceeding three (3) years, or by fine not exceeding one thousand dollars or both.

There was also passed a companion law, Section 577 of the same code with a lesser punitive measure attached and frequently found in the minor automobile accident (supra): "It is a misdemeanor for any person alone or in concert to prepare or make any bid or other writing which falsely purports to be a bona-fide offer to repair a damaged motor vehicle or any other damaged property, with the intent that the same be used for the purpose of fraudulently leading an automobile liability insurer to believe: (1) That a bid of some other person represents an offer made in open competition, or (2) That the policy provisions of such insurer governing bids for repairs of vehicles or other property insured under the policy have been complied with in good faith."

The California Legislature in codifying the law in 1872 had already provided some measure of punishment for those who attempt to cheat and defraud an insurer with the enactment of a Penal Code provision which was later (1923) amended to its present form: "Every person who willfully burns or in some other manner injures, destroys, secretes, abandons or disposes of any property which at the time is insured against loss or damage by fire, theft or embezzlement, or any casualty with the intent to defraud or prejudice the insurer, whether the same be the property or in the possession of such person or any other person, is punishable by imprisonment in the state prison for not less than one (1) year and not more than ten (10) years."

This particular law provides for practically every conceivable method by which to destroy or hide real or personal property for the purpose of a fraudulent claim. The *specific intent* to defraud is the basic element and it must be shown indemnification under an insurance policy was at least believed possible. It is a physical act of damaging property and if achieved by burning it can still be charged independently as a separate offense from the basic charge of arson per se. Many jurisdictions have comparable sanctions.

There is another similar statutory provision, Section 450a Penal Code: "Any person who willfully and with intent to injure or defraud the insurer sets fire to or burns or causes to be burned, or who aids, counsels or procures the burning of any goods, wares, merchandise or other chattels or personal property of any kind, whether the property of himself or another, which shall at the time be insured by any person or corporation against loss or damage by fire, shall upon conviction thereof, be sentenced to the penitentiary for not less than one nor more than five years." As is obvious from the wording, the acts are limited to the *burning* or *personal* property only and the element of *specific* intent must be present. The offense is often alleged in connection with automobiles burned for insurance in conjunction with Section 449a Penal Code which is the destruction by arson of personal property. As with Section 548 Penal Code (supra) it is a separate offense, not included within the basic act of arson.

Supporting Case Law

At this point our attention is focused upon Section 556 California Insurance Code, its provisions, construction and enforcement. The landmark case most frequently referred to by the courts, because of its cogent interpretation of the legislative intent, is *People vs. Grossman*, 28 Cal App 2nd 193, decided in 1938. This case involved the defendant, an attorney, a co-defendant physician and a beautyshop operator who conspired to defraud an insurance company by having a shop customer agree to file a false claim for a purported burn injury, the latter immediately notifying the District Attorney and the police regarding the situation. Justice Sturtevant in his dicta stated, amongst other pertinent things, that the gravamen of the offense was the *intent* to defraud. The concept has been restated a number of times in *People vs Teitlebaum* (163 Cal App 2nd 184) in 1958, in *People vs. Burham* (184 Cal App 2nd 836) in 1961 and in *People vs Benson* (206 Adv Cal 608) in 1962. In Grossman the defense contended a mere letter was not sufficient to come within the purview of the statute. The court held that it did, and in fact was clear evidence of a claim submitted to the insurer. It was further determined that a written claim and proof of loss are seldom embodied in one document, therefore, *any* writing, regardless of form, in support of a claim was proscribed by the statute. In Teitlebaum, involving a staged fur store robbery, this included an itemized statement purporting to be an inventory delivered to the adjustor, which was *not* part of a sworn proof of loss.

An interesting issue developed in two cases (*People vs Zelver,* 135 Cal App 2nd 226), the first of note in 1955 involving a structural fire and related false inventory and the second in 1962 (*People vs Loomis,* 24 Cal Rptr 281) involving a contrived airplane accident, with the unanticipated fatality of a co-conspirator, in which it was held that a writing need not be false or fraudulent in itself as long as it is intended to be used in support of a false claim. This situation also satisfies the statute.

In Benson (supra) it was held that the person submitting the false claim, although not an actual policy-holder, is not immune from prosecution, the gist of the offense being the intent to defraud. It was also held that an inference of "reckless disregard of the truth" was reasonably drawn when it was shown the defendant, an attorney, had been advised repeatedly his client had not suffered any injury, but yet he forwarded his client's false medical report in support of such claim. Disproportionate valuations used in a claim for property destroyed also can be the basis of a charge under the statute (*People vs Kanan* (1962), 25 Cal Rptr 427).

In Zelver (Supra) the court held, amongst other things, that corroboration was established when it was shown the defendant had taken out a "use and occupancy" insurance policy five days prior to the fire, coupled with the fact it was disclosed he and his company were in financial difficulty. This of course was greatly assisted when the fire was shown to be of incendiary origin.

Insurance, Purpose and History

It is axiomatic to say the fraud investigator if confronted with an insurance case must have some fundamental knowledge of insurance itself. The topic is of such magnitude it is not feasible to present here a study in depth. However, some of the basics will be discussed to give an insight into its operations, nature and areas of interest with which the investigator will have frequent contact.

Insurance is not a phenomenon of the current industrial age but had its genesis in ancient times. The Babylonians 4000 years before the birth of Christ had a form of contract for shifting the risk of loss from the shipper to a third person. The Mediterranean bottom is littered with the rotting hulks of grain ships, galleys and triremes of the ancient Phoenicians which were covered by the "insurance contract" of those times. By usage down through the centuries into the Grecian period 400 years before Christ and later into the Christian era, there developed the concept of "bottomry." This is in the nature of a mortgage by which the owner of a ship or cargo borrows money for various purposes, pledges the ship (keel or bottom of the ship) as a security at an advanced rate of interest (sometimes called maritime interest because of the high risk factor) it being stipulated that if the ship or cargo were lost during the voyage by any of the perils of sea enumerated in the contract, the lender would be the loser, having assumed the risk at the high loan interest rates. That age was not without its sharpies. There have been fraudulent practices since the time of the first contract between two people. Willfully scuttled ships were not unknown and falsely contrived cargo manifests played a large part in the schemes. The contract was called one of "respondentia" if it covered the cargo only. The loan was paid back if the voyage were successful. Maritime ventures then evidently were the basis of the first indemnification contract.

The fifteenth century saw the widened scope of insurance through the commerce activities of Spain and Italy. Wherever these people sought trade their individual business practices of course followed, affecting other trade nations such as England, France and the Netherlands. In fact the word "policy" as used in the modern English language to denote the insurance contract is from the word "polizza" of the Italian language meaning the written evidence of an obligation. That word's a partial derivative from the Greek word "apodeixis," meaning *proof*. As commerce practice and rules became more complex there was a concomitant evolvement in the insurance field. By the time the 16th century had arrived marine insurance principles were fairly uniformly understood and practiced by the maritime nations. In

England there was actually no specialized business of insurance but risks were undertaken (underwritten) by individual merchants. By the 18th century, however, along with other commercial and trade refinements, insurance did emerge as a specialized business. Those engaged were still burdened with the individual liability of the underwriter who not infrequently, when faced with a loss could not handle the situation. There began the system of insuring part of the loss along with other individual underwriters. As is natural these early brokers began to meet together for business discussions. There happened to be a coffeehouse known as "Lloyd's" which ultimately became their focal point, this later became the center of the group known to the world as "Lloyd's of London." The risks to this time appear to have been limited to maritime ventures.

Fire risks, although there is some indication in the 15th century were assumed, were not considered. Apparently the need was not recognized at the time because the loss was not considered as great and the articles lost were something familiar and usually without a recognizable capital investment as opposed to shipping ventures. There was another common factor present, the kindness of friends, neighbors and family who frequently contributed to the restoration of property destroyed by fire and the tendency for people to disregard risks to which they have become accustomed. It was after the London fire in the late 17th century that fire risks were then considered.

The insurance business like all other forms of human commercial enterprise has undergone varied periods of growth and refinement to evolve into what we have today. The first American company came into being at Philadelphia in early 1600s and was limited to maritime coverage. In the 1680s there were policies written by representatives of British companies to cover ships trading with the colonies which ultimately expanded into a formalized group some years later. Benjamin Franklin in 1750 organized a mutual fire insurance company which is still in existence. Fire underwriting finally came into its own because of the industrial development of the country which required construction of buildings, docks, warehouses and other collateral needs to maintain pace with the burgeoning economy. These, then, began to take on the element of risk to investment, something which was not recognized previously other than with shipping ventures. In the 1790s there was the development of other types of companies which started with marine risks, extending then into fire and other types of policies. There was also the concomitant inceptions and growth of life insurance companies, casualty groups and as time went on with the expansion of society's needs, it included fidelity-surety-theft coverage, vehicle, health, endowment, annuity and many other types of risks to the structure we have today with its wide spectrum of coverage. This growth was not without its problems. There were speculators, swindlers and other charlatans both within and without the industry preying upon each other. There were numerous costly and sometimes embarrassing inquiries which resulted in strict governmental controls, but the business has been able to withstand the onslaughts of the unscrupulous and evolve into the recognized stature and importance it has today in our national and international economy.

Modern Structuring

At this point it should be clarified what the differences are between stock companies and mutual companies; terms which are often met during the course of an investigation. A stock company is one organized to sell insurance for profit. It is structured as any other corporation, the capital deriving from the sale of shares and premiums paid by the policy-holders. The surplus is frequently invested in other ventures, adding to the capital. In the mutual company there are no stockholders as such, the policy-holders being members of the company and having a voice in its operation. The source of operating capital is the premiums paid, in advance, by the policy-holders sometimes subjected to special assessments when the total amount is not sufficient to handle policy indemnification. When the total amount is in excess of total payments and operating costs and expenses, the overage on a pro-rated basis is sometimes returned to the policy-holders.

Insurable Interest

"Insurable Interest" is a term meaning that type or degree of interest a person has, either in personal or real property or the physical well-being of another individual, the destruction, injury to which or death, would cause him to suffer a financial loss and which can be indemnified. For example a person who has a beneficial interest in property, a lessee of property, a tenant who improves real or personal property, a seller or buyer in possession of property, a husband or wife interest in the spouse or children.

Moral Hazard

The euphemism "moral hazard" is used in relation to a number of personal characteristics of the insured which could possibly increase the probability of fraud. His personal history and background are examined to determine previous acts or situations which might have an effect on his present reactions to comparable conditions. The term "physical hazard" relates to the physical condition of the property being insured and possible ancillary conditions which could have an effect on its safety and well-being. Both have a bearing on the rating to be applied by the insurer when selling a policy. Of some significance here is the assigned risk pool related to motor vehicle insurers. The insured is carried at a higher premium rate because of his driving record and the insurer undertakes to carry him on the basis of a system similar to a lottery employed by the insurance company agents or brokers of an area.

The Contract

The insurance agreement or policy is a contract and is replete with the same rights, liabilities and obligations inherent in any contract. It is an agreement between the insurer and insured, the former to indemnify the latter upon the happening of some contingency covered within the provisions of the policy/contract and taking place between the inception and termination dates included therein. This arrangement imposes certain obligations upon the insured; the absence of fraud being the main one. He must make a full disclosure of known material facts concerning the property involved when applying for a policy and make no misrepresentation. If, upon the incident insured against, all covenants of the agreement having been adhered to such as permitted inspections, efforts at preservation against further loss, no concealment or misrepresentation as to condition, cause and origin and numerous others, the insurer carries out his obligation of indemnification or replacement. In this connection, the payment is based upon the actual value of the property at the time of loss regardless of the amount ascribed to it at the policy inception date. The elements of depreciation and market/saleable value are considered. The *valued* policy is an exception to this rule. In that situation it is agreed that the amount stipulated in the policy shall prevail. This occurs when the property is unique or is of undeterminable value. Also in relation to property insurance the loss must be the direct result of the contingency insured against and not a remote unconnected thing. The insured normally must, if asked, submit to examination under oath as all phases of his reported loss and its cause.

Subrogation

The right of subrogation frequently enters upon the insurance scene. It merely gives the insurer the right the insured may have against a third party who may have been the cause of the loss or injury. Thus, if the insured suffers a fire loss caused by the third party, the insurer, upon indemnification for loss, then has the right to proceed against the third party for damages in lieu of the insured. In other words, it is a substitution.

Coverage

The insurance policy is fairly uniform in content and format. The provisions can be and are modified frequently by a rider which sets forth any exceptions to be noted, other property to be considered and other risks to be covered. A clause also can alter a policy usually by limiting the coverage and include a third party of interest such as a mortgagee or trust deed beneficiary who are referred to as loss payees. Some policies are for specific coverage, for one type of property at a definite location; floating coverage for items in transit or with changing locations; blanket policies for a variety of items at one location or one type of property at many locations (merchandise in warehouses and on retail premises are covered with this type). A type of contract often involved with the insurance fraud is the so-called business interruption policy. This indemnifies the insured when his business operation is stalled usually after a fire or explosion. It is almost a guaranteed income during the period of business suspension and is based upon computable probable operational income that would have been enjoyed except for the fire or explosion forcing the closing of the business. The insured is actually hedging his operating expenses and losses by such a policy.

Scheduled property, a term often met, means property that is unique such as pairs, sets, parts or singles for which there is no feasible duplication. The policy will list these items usually as to the artisan who made them, a jewelers' or furriers' individual numbering or marking, description, value, basic materials used, date and place made or constructed, repairs or alterations made during the period of ownership and by whom.

Often a question of coverage will hinge on a term called a "binder." In effect it means an insurance company is bound from the date and time its agent has negotiated with and comes to an agreement with a policy-holder. This takes effect without the actual written policy being in existence at that time. The company's liability starts then, with the written formalized document being sent later.

The investigator is usually concerned with two basic types of insurance policies; the first being fire coverage, the other theft coverage. The New York Legislature in 1887 enacted some provisions which standardized the writing of fire insurance policies based upon the obvious need at the time because policy writing had become so involved and ambiguous forcing inequities on both the insurer and the insured. There were periodic changes in the format over the years but these were finally resolved in 1943. Most states adhere to the form with only minor revisions to fit local needs, customs and legal principles. The fundamental concept of fire insurance is a contract which provides for the compensation to the insured for *actual* loss sustained and never beyond that point. It is also a *personal* agreement between the insurer and insured, the latter being indemnified for a *personal* loss and it is limited to him only. Third party interests must be specifically ratified and become part of the contract. Any assignment of the policy, such as upon sale of the property concerned, must be consented to by the insurer. Fraud and misrepresentation are proscribed very definitively in the contract, and which requires the full and honest disclosure of all material facts having a bearing on the issuance of the policy. There are also a number of positive acts the insured must perform to abide by the contract obligations, these include proper care of the property concerned prior to and also after the fire to prevent further loss or damage.

The theft policies fall within two general classifications, employee dishonesty and the burglary-larceny/theft-robbery offenses committed by persons from outside the company premises. Although there is a degree of standardization there are numerous sub-categories of the two basic classifications and the individual policy must be reviewed to determine the limitations and scope of coverage. The alleged offenses are construed according to their common law meanings, however, statutory changes can and do affect them. Thus, in conformance with Section 490a Penal Code, the terms theft and larceny in California are used interchangeably. Here again, as with the standard fire policy, full and honest disclosure of all material facts must be made and certain positive acts must be performed before and after the purported theft by the insured to make the agreement binding upon the insurer. It is suggested the student obtain his own specimen policy for further clarification.

Loss Accounting

The determination of a fire loss or any reportable insured loss is essentially a bookkeeping problem, notwithstanding the physical inventory and other investigative processes involved. This function falls within the purview of the adjustor's duties (infra), but it is proper for the investigator to have some understanding of the principles. The valuation of structures, goods, fixtures and equipment is the replacement value at the date of loss or damage. Attempts will be made by policy-holders to use their book value which is the initial cost less the depreciation. However, this is generally disallowed as an unethical insured could increase falsely these values for settlement purposes. Conversely, sometimes there is an appreciation to property increasing its value which would result in a loss to the insured if the items were quoted at their book value.

In a fire or explosion situation where the records are partially destroyed it is a difficult thing at best to reconstruct the books and other data to determine the actual loss. An interpolative process must be resorted to by the investigative accountant or adjustor if the missing information gaps are to be filled in to disclose the actual situation at the time of the purported loss. This involves several basic accounting sequential steps. The first is the taking of the trial balance at the last closing period. The balances which appear therein are considered with the transactions that have occurred between that date and the date of the loss:

	4-1-69		Adjustment 4-1/7-31		7-31-69	
	Debits	Credits	Dbt	Crdt	Dbt	Crdt
Cash	10,000		34,000 (1)	40,000 (2)	4,000	
Acct Rec	20,000		20,000 (1)	33,500 (1)	6,500	
Uncllct		1,900		500 (4)		2,400
Nts Rec	4,000			500 (1)	3,500	
Invntry	50,000				50,000	
Prepd Exp	900			200 (3)	700	
Frn & Fix	20,000				20,000	
Dprtn		5,000		1,250 (5)		6,250
Accts Pybl		30,000	30,000 (2)	8,000 (6)		8,000
Cptl		68,000				68,000
Oprtng Exp			10,000 (2)			
			200 (2)			
			500 (4)			
			1,250 (5)		11,950	
Prchs			8,000 (6)		8,000	
Sales				20,000 (3)		20,000
	104,900	104,900	103,950	103,950	104,650	104,650

The initial entry made by the investigator is the cash receipts for the questioned period. The amount can be computed by a simple method briefly described here:

The total cash disbursements as disclosed by the check register added to the *current* bank balance (in this case $40,000 plus $4,000.00 equaling $44,000.00). From this total subtract the cash balance at the last closing of 4-1-69 ($44,000.00 less $10,000.00 which is the total cash receipts of $34,000.00 (1). Notes Receivable were $500.00 (1) of this amount, consequently the remaining $33,500.00 (1) came from the Account Receivable which for ease of computing includes Sales (infra).

The next step is recording the Cash Disbursements for the period ($40,000) (2) with $10,000 being earmarked for Operating Expenses (2) and $30,000 to Accounts Payable (2). The categorizing is based upon the information appearing in the Check Register indicating the reason for each payment. The third step is entering the Prepaid Expenses total of $200 (3). This figure includes the insurance policy premiums usually paid quarterly, annually or bi-annually and indicates that part which has already expired during the period. This information is available from the insurer or the adjustor.

The next items are the recording of the Uncollectible Accounts of $500 (4) and the Furniture and Equipment Depreciation of $1,250 (5) (this last based upon a four year life-span at $5,000 each year for a $20,000 initial cost). These are followed by Purchases for $18,000 (6) and Sales at $20,000 (7) for the accounting period. The method of computing these balances will be covered below.

With the adjusted trial balance the entries based upon collateral records (Check Register, invoices either on file or from vendors who can be circularized etc.) a fairly accurate picture is drawn of the various account balances with the exception of the Inventory Account. This is usually the one, in addition to Buildings, Fixtures and Equipment (infra) which is the basis of a purported loss. A simplified manner to compute the estimated inventory at the time of loss is as follows:

From the *4–1–69 Inventory* of $50,000 *add* the *total purchases* learned from the invoices for the period ($8,000) which totals $58,000. From this amount subtract the Cost of Goods Sold (70% of $20,000 Sales) $14,000 which leaves $44,000 as the probable inventory amount on 7–31–69. The method is referred to by accountants as the "Gross Profit Test" and by adjustors as the "Statement of Loss". Both mean the same thing and the findings arrived at by the same manner.

It is usually at this juncture that the insured attempts to defraud by overstating his inventory. If the interpolative accounting method shown here is followed, definitively stating the account balances through the use of ancillary documentation (remember the records ostensibly have been partially destroyed), the inven-

Gross Profit Test:

Inventory	4–1–69	$50,000
Purchases via Invoices		8,000
Total Item Valuation		58,000
Less-Cst Gds Sld (70% Sales)		14,000
Balance, Invntry	7–31–69	$44,000

Statement of Loss

Inventory	4–1–69	$50,000
Later Purchases		8,000
Total Accounted For		58,000
Sales	$20,000	
Less Profit (30%)	6,000	
Cost of Goods Sold		14,000
Value of Stock at Fire 7–31–69		$44,000

tory account can be fairly accurately stated, even if a physical count is not possible.

The items which are useful for reconstruction of the records are Cashbooks, Journals or Daybooks, bank deposit slips, cancelled checks, check stubs, pages from the Check Register, loan ledger cards, payroll records, old financial reports, old tax returns, accountant's Worksheets, inventory cards, sales records and purchase records to name a few. Even if they are only fragmentary they can be useful.

In a situation where fixtures, equipment and structures are the prime loss figures a similar method can be employed insofar as plant interior items are concerned. Most businesses maintain separate accounts for these items disclosing the type, purchase date, cost, condition, depreciation, breakage, repairs, adaptability to the job requirements, and the number on the premises. The descriptive information includes, besides the manufacturer's name, the model number, size and identifying serial numbers which are invaluable in tracing the individual history of the machine. The valuation here is of course determined by the adjustor who employs some of these methods discussed and an appraisal method which takes into consideration the increased reconstruction and replacement costs. In this situation an inventory is usually possible and much easier to perform in contrast to the inventory count due to the destructibility from fire or the ease with which such items can be disposed of or hidden. This is the companion area of fraud; the falsification of equipment accounts by value and number.

The disclosure of a possible fraudulent claim is usually brought to the attention of the investigator by an adjustor who has been assigned the settling of the claim or by the agent of the insurer. Of course, as with many other crimes, the information can come from a variety of sources, such as witnesses to the event which precipitated the claim, associates of the insured, or even be determined by the insured's past record in business and otherwise. The two most frequent situations which are the bases for the false proof are loss and theft, the latter including burglary and robbery (infra), the insured either taking advantage of an actual loss incident for overstatement or formulating and directing the whole scheme. In either circumstance the first things to determine, although not in themselves elements of the offense, are the existence of motive and opportunity; is there a financial reason and did the insured have the opportunity to create the situation or incident which was the proximate cause of the loss or damage? In ascertaining this, the investigator will cover numerous avenues which often disclose the part played by the insured. The guideposts then are apparent. The "claim" as such does exist; it must be proved false. Either the property covered by the policy is lost or destroyed or it is not. If it is, then was the act one that was premeditated for that purpose? If it is not, what was done with it before or after the incident said to cause the loss or damage? Witness information and physical evidence are the basic things needed to prove the case.

Loss Incident

The loss incident, the basis of the claim, must be thoroughly investigated. If it is a fire, the cause and origin must be determined. This requires close cooperation with the arson investigators as their findings will have a tremendous bearing on the fraud inquiry, especially if it develops to be of incendiary origin. And even if not, the conditions prior to, and found to exist immediately at the knock-down and overhaul are material in determining the accuracy of the claim. If the loss is the purported result of theft, either actual or fictitious, the fraud investigator will perform the larger part of the inquiry himself. If it falls within the burglary/robbery sub-category, there exists two paths; it is either a false report engineered by the insured or an actual incident being taken advantage of to embellish an otherwise legitimate claim. Either situation requires close cooperation with those officers normally handling such offenses to ascertain the actual circumstances. In any event there is the basic requirement of the premises or area involved be examined thoroughly. If a fire is the cause, the location of the lost or destroyed items must come under close scrutiny to determine if there has been any movement or alteration in normal conditions before or after the conflagration. All physical evidence related to the event must be taken and recorded in the same manner as in any other crime against property. All remaining items are examined for type, model, serial numbers, condition, operating usefulness, location and value (supra). In the case of theft comparable processes are invoked to develop physical evidence. Copies of all investigative reports covering these facets of the overall inquiry are obtained and become part of the case record. In this connection the reports of regular periodic inspections by the fire department for prevention purposes are invaluable as are the reports by building inspectors concerning sanitation and various structural requirements. Both often reveal the location or non-existence of items purportedly lost or damaged.

The Agent

The insurance agent who handled the policy is contacted at the outset. He can furnish comprehensive data on all aspects of the policy and the policy application, which contains fairly reliable background, reputation and personal history information. Of importance is the nature of the insurance coverage, the inception and termination dates, special clauses, modifications, limitations, provisions, amount of coverage, premiums, other policies (both with his and other carriers), previous claims in detail, any changes that may have been made recently, and the purpose or reason given by the insured. Inspection reports are usually available which can and do disclose the actual conditions of the premises at the inception date and any changes which may have occurred between then and the date of loss. Inspections, however, are normally limited to the commercial type structures and not to private homes or small business houses. A word of caution is appropriate here and it is not in derrogation of insurance agents as a class; however, unless the particular agent concerned is known to the investigator, the questions asked must be discrete to say the least. Too often, the agents, who are actually salesmen, are garrulous by nature. This, coupled with the fact that effective sales operations demand a certain amount of social contact between the parties (service clubs, country clubs, mid-morning coffee klaches, lodges, etc.) thus creating an affinity which sometimes goes beyond normal arms-length dealings. When this condition exists any question which the investigator may raise will frequently find its way to the insured; sometimes willfully to thwart the investigation, more often because of sheer stupidity on the part of the agent who becomes apprehensive about a policy he sold which later, instead of proving profitable to his principle, the insurer, becomes a possible sizable financial loss upon the indemnity. Under such circumstances the agent should be bypassed and all such information developed through the insurance company itself. Also collusion between the insured and the agent is not unknown or unique in the annals of insurance frauds.

The Adjustor

The insurance adjustor plays an important part in the investigation. He is normally an independent contractor although a number of large insurance companies have their own claims adjustors. His purpose is to make an equitable determination of the loss experience and assist both the insured and insurer in settling the claim. He contacts the insured and ascertains the latter's interest in the lost or damaged property; he determines the value at the time of the incident and the amount of physical loss or damage excluding any estimated loss of operational profits. This last, if it is to be considered in the indemnification, must be insured against by a separate policy (supra). He finds out if there is other insurance coverage on the same property and if the loss occurred during the contract period. He also determines whether the items lost are those described in the insurance contract.

The adjustor must determine: if the loss was a result of conditions or perils insured against; whether or not the property was located as described in the policy, if the insured is in fact making a full and fair disclosure of all material facts either before or after the inception date of the policy, during the insured period or after the incident and the cause of the loss or damage if he can; whether the hazard insured against was willfully or negligently increased by the insured; the interest in the property of any beneficiary of a trust deed, mortgagee or seller under a conditional sales contract who may be the loss-payee; the existence of any other hidden third-party interests; and the insurer's right of recovery against other persons who may have caused the loss or damage.

The adjustor also makes inquiries into the insured's background including financial, business (especially other business interests) and character data, loss claim history, and in fact develops any and all information possible that he can within his capabilities and time which may have a bearing on the issue. He takes (or is supposed to) written statements by the insured and signed proofs of loss which are ultimately turned over to the insurer as the basis of the claim. He normally retains all correspondence from the insured and if alert, will have a record of all telephone calls, their content (taped sometimes) and stenographic or taped transcripts of all face to face meetings and interviews.

Examination Under Oath

There is another item which is a potent weapon for the fraud investigator and the insurer; the examination under oath. This can be conducted by special agents of the underwriter, the insurer's legal counsel, and even infrequently, the adjustor. This is provided for by the insurance contract and it is at the option of the insurer. It is normally conducted at the insurer's premises in the presence of a certified shorthand reporter, and allowing the insured to be represented by counsel. This procedure puts the onus on the insured. If he declines to answer or appear, the insurer has sufficient basis for refusing the claim. And if fraud is involved, the insured is the loser. The profit has gone out of the venture. The choice is his. In acquiescing, the information is admissable as evidence at a civil or criminal trial. It can sometimes be a difficult choice. The interrogatories cover a wide spectrum. The insured can be required to furnish all books and records of account, documentation of interest and ownership, records of operation profits and losses, net worth, both of himself as an individual and the company, firm or business suffering the loss. Here then, is the area of diligent search by the fraud investigator. Here is the place to determine motive for fraud. To paraphrase a literary cliché of mystery novels ascribed to French detective geniuses, "Cherchez la femme" (look for the woman) should be changed to "Cherchez l'argent ou le manque de l'argent" (look for the money or the lack of money). This is the reason; all others are subordinate in our society. We can offer desire for power, sex, gambling losses, liquor, poor investments etc. but all are achieved or realized through a single means; money. It's the key which opens the door. If the insured does not have it, and he is inclined to unethical conduct, he is going to acquire it through such means as he can, legitimate or otherwise.

The comparison of statements by the insured both off and on the record to the adjustor and the insurer to those made to the investigator can prove enlightening whether concerning the loss, its cause, personal or background information and his activities before and after the incident and other interests, either business, professional or even hobbies. Sometimes little or insignificant details gained through off-hand chance remarks can lay bare a whole pattern or network of lies which will indicate the avenues of inquiry to follow.

Know Your Man

Background and personal history of the insured are emphasized for the investigator. Know your man. Develop every facet of his character possible. This is not limited to his period of residence or business in the area, but go back to his birthplace and date. Cover his education from the earliest years; his employment; his Armed Forces service if any; his marriages; property ownership, real and personal; hobbies; associates and social contacts; identify other members of his family (covering them in the same degree); domestic problems; extra-marital affairs; criminal activity; gambling or other social problems which can be a drain on funds; vocational and professional training and licensing; business experience and reputation; other insurance coverage and claims; property tax payments; license fees; criminal history; comparative net worth and operational profit or loss over a period of at least five years; business cycle potential for the insured to determine a possible recession; activities just prior and subsequent to the incident causing the loss, looking for the unusual and abnormal.

Signal Flags

A point of interest to the investigator is a part of the dicta in a Federal tax case (Spies vs United States, 317 US 492) in which the court said very succinctly the "badges of fraud" which indicate the intent to defraud were: (1) the keeping of a double set of books, (2) the making of false entries, alterations or false invoices and documents, (3) the destroying of books or records, (4) the concealment of assets, (5) covering up sources of income, (6) handling affairs in such a manner as to avoid record keeping of transactions, (7) any act or statement which could mislead or conceal. Of course the elements set forth here are from a tax case, however, the existence of the same things are sought in an insurance fraud case with the additional element which could be numbered (5A), the application of funds (income), or what has happened to the money.

Documentation Problems

In the area of documentary examination touched on here, there are posed serious questions of legal principles involving the constitutional guarantees against self-incrimination. The fraud investigator is in no position to request the personal and private papers or records of a sole proprietorship or a partnership. There

is some support to the contention that the records of a corporation, due to its existence as a separate entity and at the suffer-
ence of the sovereign state, can be demanded if certain procedural requirements are adhered to. There is a collateral issue
involved here, the need to examine the documents and records
of third persons to the extent the insured is mentioned or involved (e.g. a vendor who has sold the insured some item and
documentation is needed). There is no right here at the investigative stage to secure the item. However, at trial it is subject to a subpoena duce tecum. The United States Treasury
Agents do have subpoena power over taxpayers' books and records, tempered by the reasonableness of the demand, and even
over third party records with the same limitations. This last is
constantly under attack (*US vs 1st Ntl of Frt Smith*, Arkansas,
173 Fed Supp 716; 1959).

Consequently, the usual manner in which the investigator obtains the necessary recorded information is after its disclosure by
the insured when examined under oath. The Constitutional guarantees are upheld here as the insured was represented often by
counsel and all revelations were voluntary (or perhaps more cor-
rectly, "reluctantly" as he is motivated by greed and avarice
which surmounted his normal timidity, caution and fear of exposure).

Another source of the same data can be business credit agencies to whom the insured has submitted financial reports for
various reasons. Banks, escrow companies, transcripts from law
suits, business opportunities brokers, real estate agents, mortgage
companies, building and loan firms, land title companies, to name
a few are similar places the same information can be developed.*
Don't disregard the insured's personal friends or associates of recent vintage. Once there has been a disagreement, even if only of
short duration, they seem impelled to tell all, either for revenge
or merely self-justification of their position. They frequently have
documentation of dealings with the insured which by using the
interpolative process (supra) his financial report can be recon-
structed.

---

* See Note #1, Chapter VIII for Limitations

Ask For Help!

Without digressing too far into the theoretical and philosophic sectors to analyze why an investigator is an investigator (his drives, ambitions and motivations) it suffices to say, perhaps pedantically, that he is more aggressive than the average man which cannotes a certain excessive amount of self-reliance and egoism. This, if offered for purposes of explaining paradoxically what otherwise is a recognized strength and virtue of a good investigator, is also, unfortunately, a glaring weakness on the part of many, causing them to lose good cases. Sometimes it takes years of experience to overcome this attitude, but it must be eliminated. What is needed is an investigator who is not ashamed to ask for specialized help when he needs it. Too often the attitude of "I'd rather do it myself" has destroyed what was otherwise good competent work. If you reach an impasse, a point beyond which you must go but do not have the technical or specialized knowledge or training to handle, *ask for help*. This is why there are experts and specialists in all areas of human enterprise. You are not expected to be completely knowledgeable in every field which may be crossed during the course of an investigation. Suppress the natural ego which is present and accept the fact gracefully there are many things about which many people have little or no knowledge and that there are a few people who have great knowledge about a few things. Develop a wide diversified scope of contacts amongst the experts and specialists. Be able to locate and have the qualified assistance of electricians, electronic engineers, hydraulic specialists, structural people with knowledge of steel, wood, glass, piping, masonry and other building trades, accountants, chemists, biologists, medical and dental practitioners, industrialists, economists, statisticians, photographers, business administrators, psychologists, physiologists, anthropologists, and investment counselors. Take advantage of colleges and universities research and development firms in your area, creating a working rapport. The investigator should perhaps look upon himself as a coordinator of the efforts of others, analogous to the staff general who directs the overall strategy but leaves the tactical approach to the battle in the hands of his field officers.

Closely connected with the preceding concerning expertise and specialization is the fraud investigator's working association with groups or agencies which are comparable to the Special Agents of the now defunct Fraud and Arson Bureau, American Insurance Association (formerly the National Board of Fire Underwriters). Although the new groups are small organizations and spread literally all over the country these agents are the recognized "experts" because of their experience, training and education in the functional fields of insurance frauds and arson investigations. These organizations with their agents and records are veritable founts of knowledge and information. The agents are all former criminal investigators from various Federal, State, County and Municipal agencies and will work with and assist local law enforcement agencies in any manner possible. Avail yourself to this opportunity when handling an insurance fraud. They have their own unique ways of acquiring information which can and does cut through procedural red-tape and requirements, obtaining necessary data in a timely fashion. Their technical advice and assistance has proven invaluable for many years to law enforcement.

Similar Acts and Transactions

The development of similar acts and transactions is an important part of the insurance fraud inquiry. This is one of the better means to establish the intent to defraud. Granted, under Section 556 California Insurance Code, the "specific intent" is said not to be an element of the crime, however, there is no better way to convincingly establish in the jury's mind the criminal operation of the accused then to show unequivocally his *intent* to commit the offense. This is especially true if arson was the means as it is a "specific" intent offense. The term "acts" is construed in its narrowest senses as *criminal* acts of a similar nature. This requires an examination of the insured's personal history to ascertain if he has previously submitted what can be construed as a false or fraudulent claim to an insurance carrier (*People vs Burnett* (1937), 21 Cal App 2nd 613). A later case involving a bunco scam (fraud by trick and device) held that evidence of acts of a similar nature, whether occurring before or after the crime charged may be admitted when not to remote in time and nature, to prove a material fact or when they tend to show motive, plan, scheme and design (People vs Darnell (1950) 97 Cal App 2nd 630).

The construction put to the phrase "similar transactions" does not necessarily impute criminal design, but merely shows a similar or comparable method of doing certain things endemic to a business operation or dealings with other individuals which follow parallel paths to achieve their goal as that of the criminal act alleged, but in itself it may or may not be criminal (*People vs Ferguson* (1962) 209 Cal App 2nd 387). In the case cited here, the court said that evidence of previous fire insurance claims by defendant is admissable, despite the lack of proof the fires were of incendiary origin, as it showed his familiarity with the method of recovery on such claims and his acute consciousness that insurance benefits were a ready source of cash. In re Darnell (supra) is also applicable to this situation. (*See* Chapter II, Div A. False Pretenses)

There seems to be reluctance at times to invoke the theory of similar acts or transactions as not being admissible, following mistakenly the general rule that the charged offense cannot be proven by evidence of the commission of another unconnected crime. The purpose here is not the same. What the investigator is attempting to do is show a predisposition to act in a certain manner under a definite set of circumstances. As long as a similar act or transaction tend "to logically and naturally and by *reasonable* inference" establish any material fact it is admissible regardless if it proves another crime or not, or is merely descriptive of certain actions on the part of the accused which are relevant to the issue.

The Suspect

In approaching the insured for an interview the investigator is confronted with a situation fraught with peril. Due to limitations placed upon such an investigative technique by the courts, the authors have mixed feelings. There must be an individual assessment of the insured and the needs of the case at a given point and, from this, a value judgment made. "Interrogation" as such has become a lost art and once that point is reached in the inquiry that the insured under normal circumstances would be interviewed, the focus of the investigation is on him regardless of how it is disguised. This, then, is the accusatory stage and if the proper admonishment per Miranda is given with all its refinements as required, there is going to be no eliciting of worthwhile information. And, if it is not given there is a violation of constitutional right making anything obtained from that point one or its natural outgrowth worthless as being excluded. Frequently it has been found the better way is to completely circumvent the insured, ignore him. This often has a very salutory effect upon him and even his attorney at times. It is not unusual to have them both request a meeting to "discuss" the situation. Once this point is reached the odds are in favor of the investigator and it is usually best to decline the invitation. There is no requirement that you must talk with them. Besides, the false proof of loss is already an existing item and the investigation is merely developing information which is documentary, testimonial and even sometimes physical form to refute the claim. This evidence is practically always obtained from third parties who can, in varied ways, refute or challenge the claim. All the insured can or would do is make self-serving statements if he spoke at all and receive a free education as to the progress of the investigation. Of course these at times are valuable when they can be proved false, but the spectre of a civil rights violation is so real as to cast grave doubts on the value of such a confrontation. It is not unusual to investigate an insurance fraud, the period of inquiry lasting three or four months, and never coming face to face with the insured until arraignment for preliminary hearing. To say this has a tremendous psychological effect on the insured/accused, is a vast understatement. After all, this is not a game but a serious business with most of the odds in favor of the defendant. There is nothing morally reprehensible or of questionable legality in using such a tactical approach.

Witnesses

Witnesses can pose problems similar to the insured. They are not always cooperative and will avoid interviews. A large percentage of them are reluctant to involve themselves for a variety of reasons, economic, fear, distrust and apathy to name a few. This can be complicated further by those who are kindly disposed towards the insured funneling everything which is discussed right back to him and even, not infrequently, destroying or secreting evidence and furnishing false or misleading information. Under no circumstances pressure a witness in any way to cooperate. A case in point is *Smith vs U.S.* 344 Fed 2nd 545 in which the court held that any information elicited from a reluctant witness was void and that subsequent data regardless of probative value evolving out of the initially declined interview is "tainted" and inadmissable. This is a new application of the "poisoned tree doctrine" from *Mapp vs Ohio* in 1961 (367 US 385). If the investigator finds himself at an impasse, knowing the witness does in fact have accurate information which can be of help in resolving the matter, he can proceed, with the help of the District Attorney, under the "Impelled Testimony Rule" which is adhered to in several jurisdictions. The witness pursuant to this law can be subpoenaed before the Grand Jury to testify and if he refuses, can then be brought before the Superior Court where he can be instructed to answer all questions put to him, with immunity in case there is any personal involvement creating a civil or criminal liability. The witness then has three choices: (1) refuse to testify and be jailed for contempt until purged, (2) testify falsely and be imprisoned for perjury, (3) or testify factually and completely. They usually select the third alternative.

Civil Deterrent

There is no such thing as the perfect case. No one, investigator or attorney, has ever been at trial, even successfully, without being confronted with questions which were not really answered conclusively and frequently not even anticipated. Related to this, the investigator sometimes has what both he and the prosecutor consider a good case, sufficient for an indictment or bind-over from a preliminary hearing but also realizing at trial or upon appeal that it would be lost. The need for proof beyond a reasonable doubt for a criminal conviction may not however really be established to the satisfaction of the court. When this situation develops there is a tactical approach which can be used in an insurance fraud case that will achieve success by a circuitous route. It is commonly called a "civil deterrent." The method is for the insurer to deny indemnification to the insured. The latter then will be forced to initiate a civil action for recovery of his purported loss. He then becomes a plaintiff and must take the stand to support his complaint. The insurer becomes the defendant; the fraud investigator appearing as a defense witness. The rules of evidence in this arena are not the same as in a criminal trial. A fact may be proven by a fair preponderence of evidence. The insured then is also subjected to cross examination, something which seldom is available at a criminal trial. This is a two-pronged attack on the insured; his claim will be denied taking the profit out of his act, especially if he resorted to arson to achieve his goal; and the testimony and evidence of record in the civil case can be used at a criminal trial later if the facts justify further proceedings. There should be no question of constitutionality here as the insured was adequately represented by counsel at all times.

CONSUMER FRAUDS

THE AVERAGE CITIZEN probably has more direct contact with consumer type frauds than any other as they are concerned almost exclusively with his daily purchase patterns. The annual loss experienced defies the imagination. In the early 1960s it was estimated that Los Angeles County, with a population of about six million, was suffering a yearly loss of over $100 million dollars from falsely advertised, fraudulently packaged goods, deceitfully drawn contracts with exhorbitant but cleverly concealed interest and payment rates coupled with submarginal products. The swindles or scams are not limited to any particular segment of the merchandising community but can and do infect it at all levels, from the sale of a hair-pin to the sale of a yacht. The larger old-line companies have proven to be just as culpable as a new "fly-by-night" purveyor of goods and services. Federal Trade Commission records can quickly establish this. The methods employed are varied and at times even unique and are not limited to just the using of a telephone in a boiler-room operation, use of the mails, the door to door sales pitch and blatantly false and misleading advertising; it can take place in the plush-lined palace of the modern entrepreneur, the pillar of respectibility in local society. As one investigator succinctly stated ,"it is an assembly line of ambiguity, little truths, big lies and contracts with hidden pockets of deceit."

Government Controls

The rule of "caveat emptor," although ostensibly negated by means of what has been considered brilliant legislation with far reaching social significance, is still with us, notwithstanding the

newly coined rule, "caveat venditor" (let the seller beware). The
buyer is still exploited and it doesn't appear he will ever actually
be fully protected as the delicate balance between complete non-
governmental interference and control and stifling restriction
must be maintained. Our society can exist only under this condition. But this doesn't mean that controls should be weakened or
employed only in certain areas. Today's marketing has become
too impersonal and complex for the buyer really to have actual
knowledge of his purchase, its amount, fitness and costs. In the
two general areas of thought, more versus less restrictions, legislators have been tusseling for years. There is a certain amount of
hysteria from both sides whenever the issue is raised. The socially
conscious side points the indignant finger of debased guilt in a
shotgun fashion at all retailers, insisting they are unmitigated
thieves and liars. The other side responds, or perhaps gets in the
first blow occasionally, in the same tone concerning the buyer
attempting to get something for nothing and to effectively
counter-balance the respective positions advocate the return to
the laissez faire doctrine.

One nationally syndicated feature writer in July, 1969 in discussing the Department of Health, Education and Welfare policy
and practice, commented on a speech by an Assistant Secretary
concerning the "Truth in Packaging Law" and said, "Well, hum-
bug." Underlying these moans, groans and trivial dithyrambs are
a couple of bogus assumptions. The first is that consumers
generally, and housewives particularly, are a bunch of ignorant
dolts; they cannot add, subtract, or divide; they are incapable
of learning by experience that one can of corn is soupier than
another; they are so gullible they cannot perceive that a box of
cereal is needlessly too large for the contents therein. And the
second assumption is that Mama Hitt (Asst Sctry), the Congress,
the home economists, and the Federal Trade Commission are
competent to make mankind shape up.

"Honest to goodness, there are times when an ordinary citizen wants to echo the exasperated demand for independence of
the girl in the TV commercials: 'Mother I'd rather do it myself'."
The editorial policy of the newspaper at the time of course could
have had some bearing on the import of the article.

It is the opinion of the authors that there is presently meaningful legislation. But, the need is not more law, it is the effective enforcement of what already exists. It requires the intelligent interest of both prosecutors and law enforcement agencies. But even this, with diligent and effective prosecution, is not going to place a shroud of invulnerability around the buyer. He will still have to take his chances in the market place. It will, however, reduce measurably the incidence of fraud and deceit. The only viable practical protection which is afforded the prospective buyer is still his ability to say "No," loud and clear to any questionable offer; his second line of defense is his ability to read, in its entirety and fully understand the provisions of any contract *before* signing.

The American public has been inured to being victimized. It seems to have become a part of the culture which is an outgrowth of the free enterprise system and appears to be sort of a protective veneer. The common jokes about used-car salesmen, the "Honest John" prefix jestingly used in reference, to not only politicians, but to vendors of many different wares has become a fixed part of the language. The unfortunate thing, however, and here the socially conscious legislators and interest groups are unquestioningly correct, is a large part of those victimized are those who can least afford it; the aged, many with little income and usually of a fixed nature or none at all, not permitting the absorption of a financial blow, and the under-priviledged groups who have the understandable human desire for material things which in themselves are accepted as mute testimony of the better life and which is constantly but ephemerally held out to them as achievable. Into this happy hunting ground moves the huckster with no apparent limitation upon the game he can bag.

The Dilemma

The greatest difficulty is the delineation between the legitimate and fraudulent vendor. All fields are replete with both types. It is impossible to ban all salesmen by law to catch the crooked or unethical ones. The legitimate businessman is mousetrapped right along with the victims as he is viewed with the same jaundiced eye as the illegitimate vendor by the collective victims of fraud. No one yet has come up with an answer to this problem. Apparently it is one of the calculated risks that must be assumed in business today. It was very clearly brought out in testimony in 1963 at a hearing before the United States Senate Special Committee on Aging that laws and education cannot, by themselves, protect people in the old age (and deprived and underprivileged) area. If they are to be fully protected responsible members of a community such as relatives, friends, neighbors, clergymen, lawyers, doctors and others who come in contact with the potential victims must be available for guidance. If our society really subscribes to the concept that we are our brother's keeper, should we not then assume the social responsibility for the aged and others who are unable to cope with these problems? At least it requires us to strengthen the forces of self-discipline within the business area coupled with a degree of public education.

Public education has been a continuous effort on the part of the Better Business Bureau, Consumer Research Counsel and various Federal, State and local agencies. But apparently Barnum's observation of many years ago that "one is born every minute" still has credence. The educational phase also has been accompanied by legislation at all levels resulting in a multitude of laws designed to protect the unwary buyer and establish equitable guidelines for the seller, but still the cheaters do prosper. It is self-evident that the need is not more laws but an emphasis placed on the proper enforcement of those which already exists.

The Nature of the Offense

Consumer frauds are essentially offenses involving the elements of theft by false pretenses (the intent of the victim to transfer title of funds to the seller) except for some statutory provisions which may be somewhat unique in their proscription and involve the elements of trick and device in that the victim does not intend to pass title to his funds, being misled as to amounts involved and payment commitments. Both, however, are predicated upon the import of the common law concept of theft. The California Legislature has enacted a number of statutes

relative to this type of crime and they are of some fa
significance if viewed properly.

Fake Advertising

One such law relates to false, untrue and misleading statements when advertising an item for sale. By amendment in 1955
it also covered the "bait and switch" scam (infra): "It is unlawful for any person, firm, corporation or association, or any employee thereof with the intent directly or indirectly to dispose of
real or personal property or to perform services, professional or
otherwise, or anything of any nature whatever or to induce the
public to enter into any obligation relating thereto, to make or
disseminated before the public in this State, in any newspaper or
other publication, or any advertising device, or by public outcry
or proclamation, or in any manner or means whatever, any statement, concerning such real or personal property or services, professional or otherwise, or concerning any circumstances or matter
of fact connected with the proposed performance or disposition
thereof, which is untrue or misleading, and which is known, or
which by exercise or reasonable care should be known, to be
untrue or misleading, or for any such person, firm or corporation
to so make or disseminate any such statement as part of a plan
or scheme *with the intent not to sell* such personal property or
services, professional or otherwise, so advertised at the price
state or as so advertised."

One Tactical Approach

A violation of the above quoted section and others in the
same chapter of the code are punishable as misdemeanors. From
the investigator's standpoint this and the plethora or similar provisions are a means to an end. If the elements of the offense can
be satisfactorily shown a prima facie case of theft can then be
established if there was the necessary reliance placed upon the
advertiser's statements by the victim and there were no intervening circumstances which would mitigate the situation such as
an admission to the buyer prior to consumating the sale that the
public statements were false. Thus, if theft per se can be alleged,
the false advertising would merely be a supportive item. From the

practical viewpoint it perhaps would be better, especially if
the seller has a long record of similar fraudulent practices with
minimal police interference, to allege, if the complete elements
are there, the false advertising violation initially, holding in abeyance the theft allegation until the lesser charge is adjudicated.
If it results in a conviction, plea of guilty (and this often is the
situation, the vendor viewing such a charge as a mere nuisance
and the payment of the nominal fine imposed as a "license" to
operate) or one of *nolo contendre,* then the charge of theft based
upon the same set of facts, but with the inclusion of a victim
suffering a loss through the sale (In re O'Connor (1927) 80 Cal
App 647): in other words a tactical approach of lulling the opposition into a false sense of security and invulnerableness. However, double jeopardy is a problem here. In those jurisdictions
having such laws proscribing false or misleading advertising, they
must be so written to clearly establish the offenses of theft and
false advertising are entirely separate and distinct and the latter
is not a necessary lesser included offense in the former. Even here
there is a problem as a number of opinions now hold a joinder is
demanded if the same act or *course of conduct* plays a significant
part in the commission of more than one offense. This holds
whether they are multiple felonies or a combination of felonies
and misdemeanors.

According to an opinion in an early case (*Peo vs Wahl* (1940)
39 Cal App 2nd Supp 771) a violation of the false advertising
statute can be achieved by the making of statements which are
"*merely misleading* and *without* the *specific* intent to deceive
as—the laws of this nature are passed to protect the general
public who read advertisements and are likely to know nothing
of the facts, and not for the benefit of dealers who publish them
or other experts on the item so advertised." A more recent case
interpreted the law much more stringently, holding that a person, in advertising matters, uses words having a *double* meaning
cannot escape the charge of misleading or deceiving by saying
the words were true as *he* meant them to be (*Garvai vs Chiro-
practice Examiners,* 216 Cal App 2nd 374.

There does exist a practical problem in this area for the investigator. If the protestations in the offending advertisement

are actually viewed as "puffing" and without any real misrepresentation as to the character, quality or quantity of the item being sold, it is questionable a complaint would issue. A case frequently cited (*People vs Morphy*, 100 Cal 84) held that a volume merchant who said he sold at lower prices than his competitors because of lower expenses and costs, even though his prices were higher, could not be charged, the court saying, "Customers are presumed to have sound knowledge of the value of what they purchase and if such representations were criminal, a crime is paraded in numerous show windows in every city."

A California Statute covers the "non-responsibility" of publishers: "This article does not apply to any visual or sound radio broadcasting stations or to any publisher of a newspaper, magazine, or other publication, who broadcasts or publishes an advertisement in *good faith without knowledge* of its false, deceptive, or misleading character." There seems to be a correlation here between the provisions of this statute and the theory of the late Dr. Edwin H. Sutherland, the sociologist, who alleged "practically all the newspapers and popular journals have participated in the dissemination of false advertisements" (*The Sutherland Papers*, Bloomington, Indiana University Press, 1956). He pointed out the variety of advertisements appearing in nationally known and distributed magazines and trade and professional journals which propounded in length and detail the virtues of certain cigarettes, using physicians for testimonials which were patently false and even ridiculous. His contention, and from the standpoint of ethics it cannot be challenged, was that the publisher is as culpable as the advertisers. Of course, sociological concepts are not necessarily legal precepts.

The situation presently has remained unchanged. United States Senator Frank Moss, Utah, of the Senate Consumer Committee stated that a number of publishers contacted regarding the use of restraint in cigarette advertising were vague, noncommittal or openly hostile to any suggestion that *they* bear any obligation to restrain the advertising of a legal product.

Another California law embodies the spirit of both the preceding sections (17500 and 17502) relating them to the sales of real estate: "It is unlawful for any person, firm, corporation or association or any employee or agent thereof, to make or disseminate any statement or assertion of fact in a newspaper, circular, or form letter or other publication published or circulated in any language in this State, concerning the extent, location, ownership, title or other characteristic, quality or attribute of a real estate located in this State *or elsewhere,* which is known to him to be untrue and which is made or disseminated with the intention of misleading.

"Nothing in this section shall be construed to hold the publisher of any newspaper, or any job printer, liable for any publication herein referred to unless the publisher or printer has an interest either as owner or agent, in the real estate so advertised." Sutherland's observations seem to gain some credence here, although it perhaps would pose an inordinate burden on a legitimate publisher or printer if he had to examine in detail the assertions in every advertisement brought to him for publication.

The Injunction

The discussion to this point has been limited to such provisions relating essentially to advertising. And, within the purview are two pieces of legislation which have proven their efficacy. The first is entitled, "Injunction Again Violation" and provides, "Any person, corporation, firm partnership, joint stock company, or any association or organization which violates or proposes to violate this chapter may be enjoined by any court or competent jurisdiction."

Further, "Actions for injunction under this section may be prosecuted by the Attorney General or any District Attorney in this State in the name of the people of the State of California upon their own complaint or upon the complaint of any board, officer, person, corporation or association or by any person acting for the interests of itself, its members or the general public."

The other remedial provision, "Civil Penalties" sets forth, "Any person who violates any provisions of this chapter, shall be liable for a civil penalty not to exceed $2,500 for *each* violation, which shall be assessed and recovered in a civil action brought in the name of the people of the State of California by the Attorney General or by any District Attorney in any court of competent jurisdiction. If brought by the Attorney General, one-half of the penalty collected shall be paid to the Treasurer of the County in which the judgment was entered, and one-half to the State Treasurer. If brought by a District Attorney, the entire amount of penalty collected shall be paid to the Treasurer of the County in which the judgment was entered."

The combining of these two statutory provisions into one action is probably the most effective way to erradicate and control the thieves and charlatans who prey upon the consumer. This can be directed not only against the company or firm, but also against its officers and employees and is a continuing situation, operating against them permanently. The Attorney General's opinion indicated that the acts of one group within the firm is corroborative evidence as to the practices of the entire firm.

The penalties ($2,500 for each offense) can prove costly to the offender. The California Attorney General has successfully obtained judgments in excess of $95,000 against single companies. This is the deterrent; take the profit out of fraud, "hit them where it hurts, in the cash register."

For the investigator this type of action can prove redeeming and saving both in time and expense. The People/State in this situation have the right of discovery, meaning depositions, subpoenas duces tecum and other avenues to develop information are opened. And, if the injuction procedure is upheld the operating records of the defendant for a stipulated period of time are available for examination to assure there has been no later violation of the court order. There is no requirement under this procedure to show an actual victim who suffered a loss. The crime is the misleading and false public advertisement. If this condition can be adequately established to the satisfaction of the court nothing else is required. Further, any transaction of a similar nature occurring anywhere within the State (and presumably outside the State) is admissable as corroborative evidence.

The fraudulent advertiser, by the myriad of laws enacted to control him, is a real consumer problem. But, he is not the only swindler with which the buyer must contend. Another area of deception is financing. It is probably greatest with the unscrupulous seller in the ethereal plane of contract financing. It appears in

the Civil Code, Sections 1801.1 through 1812.10. The act, too
lengthy to quote here, definitively sets forth the rights, obligations and liabilities of all parties to sales contracts; the format in
which it is to appear; the size of print which is to be used; purchase, interest and financing costs and expenses permitted; contract assignment procedures and third party rights and obligations; and prohibited contract provisions. A willful violation of
the act constitutes a misdemeanor.

A companion bill is the "Automobile Finance Act." It encompasses similar provisions of the other act, relating them solely
to the sales and purchase of motor vehicles.

Interest Rates Problems

The consumer revolt has enlarged with the Federal Government now enacting legislation to combat fraudulent practices
where feasible. This emphasis is presently in the area of interest
rates. Under the new "Truth in Lending Act" (Public Law 90–
327, The Consumer Protection Act. Title I) the vendors have to
notify the buyer of the true and accurate interest rates, finance or
"service" charges they have been or are going to pay when purchasing under installment sales contracts.

The average consumer was jolted out of his reverie when he
was informed that instead of paying what he thought was a "a
small service charge" of 1½% per month, he was actually paying
18% annual interest. The phrase "per month" was glossed over
by the vendor and the implication was lost on the buyer. Some
rates even proved out to be 36% annual interest as opposed to
the low sounding 3%. Banks, department stores, loan companies,
and motor vehicle dealers were all part of this interest scam. One
situation existing was the holder of a bank credit card who assumed his 3% rate on charged items was annually and that his
savings account interest of 4% was the same, thereby earning
him at least 1% net profit annually. He soon realized his card
was really 36% and his savings at 4% but with a loss differential
of 32%. He did not understand the savings interest was really
one-third of 1% per month or 1% every three months. California under its Usury Law has clearly outlined the interest rates
and computing methods permitted for several years. The "legal"

rate is set at 7% but by contract, clearly setting forth the provisions, the rate can be 12%. Pursuant to the Unruh Act (Conditional Sales), Section 1810.4 Civil Code, the allowable rates are the same as those contained within the new Federal Act; 1½% per month on such amount of the outstanding contract balance as does not exceed $1,000 and 1% per month on that amount which is in excess of $1,000. There is no change by the law in the allowable amounts charged, it merely clarifies semantically the situation. Full disclosure is one thing, reduction in usurious rates is another. But this in itself is a large step in the right direction.

The Boiler Room

The types of consumers' scams are as varied as there are people to dream them up. It is not possible to include in one chapter of a book all of the variegated swindles which are today victimizing the purchaser. They can only be, and will be, touched on briefly here to give the student some idea of the operations possible. A common one which reappears frequently despite unified efforts of law enforcement agencies at all levels, is the aluminum siding scheme. It usually commences with the "boiler-room" operation which is a rented premises equipped with multiple telephones and people hired to call at random or from prepared lists and make a phony sales pitch. A typical prepared "pitch sheet" is the following:

"Good afternoon Mr(s) . . . . this is Miss Zilch with the advertising department of XYZ Aluminum Co. I'm not on the telephone to sell you anything Mr(s) . . . . Do you own your home Mr(s) . . . .? You do live at . . . . isn't that correct? The reason I'm checking is that our field representative was in your neighborhood today and he recommended that your home is the type we can use to stimulate sales interest in a new type of stucco aluminum. Are you familiar with aluminum siding?

"If you will allow us to send our factory man out to your home to explain our program to you and your . . . . you will receive absolutely free 5,000 Red Seal stamps and in addition we are prepared to make other generous concessions for your cooperation.

"When would be the better time to see you and your .... together? Remember, Mr(s) .... you are under no obligation whatever. All we ask is that you merely hear our offer and give us a yes or no."

Of course within the context of the pitch the names of legitimate companies such as Alcoa, Kaiser, etc. are dropped. There is often alluding to "advertising discounts," "no down payments" and "easy terms" if the customer will "just allow" a demonstration to be made on his building: sometimes as an inducement there are even offers of cash monies.

Once the "lead" had been obtained (a verbal acquiescence however hesitatingly given will suffice) the salesman appears within a matter of an hour or so; sometimes even within a few minutes. He tries to time his arrival so that both the purchaser and spouse are there together. His sales pitch will last, if not interrupted, from one to four hours, depending upon the potential take and the sales resistance of the purchaser. He will represent himself as being from one of the acknowledged legitimate aluminum companies, even speaking deprecatingly of those phonies and fakes who have sullied the good name of the aluminum siding business; he will purport that his company has selected the buyer's house as the model to appear in a nationally circulated magazine advertisement as the "before and after" application of siding; and that his company will pay a certain amount of money for this. He may even make a blatant offer of a "kickback" to the buyer which he glossed over as a means "to pay up some old bills, etc."

The Lien Contract

If the offer is accepted in the usual halting confused way which is peculiar to, and normally results, in a high-pressure sales approach, the clincher is the statement the buyer will be given an inordinately large discount or a "cash commission" for each homeowner in "his area" who later purchases siding from the company. The whole purpose is to get the signature on the paper. It is usually represented that the sales contract can be financed over a long time period by the "company," then the path divides: either the salesman says the contract will not be secured by a trust deed on the buyer's home, or *conceals* the fact that the buyer is signing a trust deed as well as a contract by some no small degree of legerdemain. The buyer is handed a legitimate appearing contract form with copies to sign; under the top sheet which is entitled "Lien Contract" are two or more copies and followed by a blank trust deed form. After the buyer signs he is told the last copy wasn't in place and to please affix his signature to it also, the bottom edge only being exposed to his view. This, of course if later and at another place, completed and then recorded unknown to the buyer. What he does is encumber his home with a trust deed to secure his contract obligation into which he entered hastily and with no real reflection as to his needs or abilities to pay. The sales contract, now well secured by the trust deed, is assigned to a finance company at a discounted price (see *Buck vs Superior Crt* (1965) 232 Cal App 2nd 217).

The Assignment

The personal contract and assignment are usually followed by the sales firm's closing after a few months operation, because the area has run dry of good prospects. The buyer finds frequently that the work he receives is shoddy and incomplete, an exhorbitant contract price exceeding otherwise normal competitive prices for the same work has been charged, and no referral commissions are actually paid. Then the shocker comes when he is pressed for payments by a finance company he never knew existed, with whom he has had no previous contract, and which has no compassion for people and no compunction about dispossessing them, notifying him that it now holds his contract secured by a trust deed on his home.

Complaints the buyer may have as to improperly performed work cannot be addressed to anyone because the salesman and his crew have evaporated. By the time the assignment is completed, he has placed a third person between him and the buyer.

This situation can be overcome if the buyer acts promptly to assert some right or defense he may have under the contract. However, he is usually so confused and overcome by the anticipated costs and expenses, he fails to act within the time period.

Other Similar Scams

The scam described is not limited to the aluminum side field. The same set of circumstances can prevail in house painting, patios, and room additions; in fact in any situation in which the buyer desires or is led to believe he desires or needs, home improvements. This brings to mind the notorious "Williamson Gang" with their annual visitations selling "old Irish lace," roofing and driveway treatments. The lace is from Hong Kong and the emulsion put on the victim's roof or driveway is nothing but used crankcase oil which creates a need of a house paint job and a new driveway at the first rain storm of the season. The only difference, there are no assignments of contracts, everything being done for cash payment at the time of the job and probably a somewhat faster departure from an area.

The home freezer plan sometimes called the "package deal" or "wholesale meat" plan is another area of deceitful practices. The salesman, after a "boiler-room" pitch, circular letters (junk mail) or even just a door to door canvassing, assures the buyer that *all* arrangements have been made with a local wholesale packer and all the buyer has to do is sign the purchase contract, the freezer being installed immediately fully supplied. The actual purchase price for the plan is exhorbitant but cleverly concealed by masquerading the interest rates and other charges, notwithstanding the provisions of the Unruh Act and the Federal "Truth in Lending" law. The victim so overcome by the brilliant verbal footwork of the salesman and the sight of a beautifully constructed mechanical larder appealingly filled with beautiful meat supplies, ignores the operational expense and depreciation which are his to bear in addition to other costs. He soon learns to his amazement that the Grade "A" meats he thought he was receiving are actually Grade "C" or lower and can be purchased at much less cost from another source. His second shock is the assignment of the contract to the third party financing company.

Bait and Switch

The "Bait and Switch" scam is merely an extension of the old-time circus barker trick of "getting them inside the tent." In other works show some tantalizing item for sale to engender the interest but with the *intent not to sell it,* instead substitute another of probable less or comparable worth but of much higher price. The victim is induced to purchase the other article after a sales pitch deprecating the quality of the originally advertised item. In one variation of the scam, a case in point (*Electrolux Corp. vs Val-Worth Inc.,* 161 N.E. 2nd 197 & 190 NYS 2nd 977) held that where the defendants had advertised the sale of *rebuilt* vacuum cleaners at a very attractive price *in order to incite inquiry by the public* and after gaining admittance to homes under the guise of answering inquiries, the salesmen for the defendants would make the "switch" in the transactions by "knocking" or disparaging the rebuilt cleaners and introduce new cleaners which were in competition with the rebuilt cleaners manufactured by the plaintiff. The defendant's actions constituted "bait advertising" and an injunction was issued restraining such conduct.

Automobile sales were effected by the enforcement of the "bait ad" law. The indicator was the prominent showing of license plate numbers and often vehicle identification numbers on television commercials joined to the verbal admonishment "all cars subject to prior sale." This is apparently a technical compliance with the law.

The sewing machine distributors and stereo phonograph, radio and television vendors have also resorted to a gimmick which is being widely used. It is the letter informing the recipient that he had "won a prize" or the letter contains a card with a sticker to be removed which will disclose a number or combination of designs which will indicate the type of discount he is to receive on a purchase of an appliance at the sender's store. The context of the letter is very promising and interesting. These sales promotion scams are usually flooded into an area by mail three to four times a year. The "prize" of a $150.00 discount certificate or some similar purported form of credit such as a

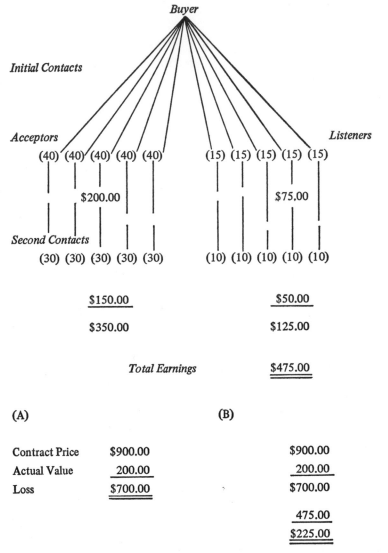

(A)   Loss experience if no referrals listened or accept
(B)   Loss experience if *all* referrals listen and accept

"free" machine and the recipient "only" has to purchase "the cabinet" or a "service policy" for an extended period of time. This, of course, is only a way to mask the actual value of the item being sold which normally would sell on the open retail market for an amount far less than the credit amount.

Referral Sales

The Frauds Division, Los Angeles Police Department in the early part of the 1960s while conducting inquiries into the burgeoning consumer swindling cases, found a unique artifice implemented by a number of the "suede-shoe salesmen" to induce buyers to become involved in referral sales scams as related to conditional sales contracts. The salesmen would tell the buyer that if he would furnish a list of friends who might possibly purchase the item or "even just listen to our offer" that an arrangement can be made whereby the buyer can receive stipulated amounts in return from the seller. He then would draw a diagram which graphically portrayed the "kick-back" amounts the buyer was to receive and how all this reduces the amount that actually must be paid, even to the point where the buyer could even receive his appliance, or whatever item is being sold, "free." The facsimile given above shows only the first few steps that the salesman's pitch says can result in great discounts as each succeeding contact which results in acceptance or "listening" also becomes a secondary remunerative contact for the buyer.

Of course the item purchased is overvalued and the sales contract is immediately assigned to the third person finance company with the salesman and his group departing the scene when the well runs dry. There have been a few occasions when some of the "profit sharing" checks (these soon dwindling away to no check at all) were actually sent to the buyer, but these were only a frosting on the cake, an enticement to others to join the act and a method of keeping the earlier buyers "off their back" until it was obvious the scam was running its course.

Some states have laws making the use of such a device a misdemeanor. It is called the "Endless Chain" (supra) scheme and states that anyone who induces a buyer to pay consideration (the purchase price or assumption of a contract obligation) for a chance to receive compensation for introducing additional persons to participate in the purchase scheme is a violation of the law.

The Auto Salesman

The automobile salesman, new and used, has been with us for over fifty years. Because we have become a highly mobile people his product ceased to be a luxury many years ago and is a necessity today. As a result everyone will periodically have contact with this type of merchant, and like any other enterprise of a mercantile nature, the ranks will have members who have the social instincts of a coyote. Probably the better way to classify them is equation with the reincarnated old-time horse trader, and with about the same conscience. This is nothing new, there were real sharp practices resorted to by people dealing in chariots in biblical times.

In California a discussion of con-artists in the automobile trade cannot be possible without a passing commentary on the operations of one group in the early 1950s. The entrepreneur utilized every means available to advertise his product accompanied by the use of altered contracts, reneging on contract obligations, the training and guidance of a sales force along lines to achieve the purposes unto the point of electronic control systems to assure the goals, and even alleged threats of physical violence to unhappy customers and frequently questionable products (*Peo vs Caruso,* 176 Cal App 2nd 272).

"He's the greatest" was an incantation heard a hundred times a day by listeners to radio and viewers of television in Southern California. This was accompanied by the usual "huckster" type music and prose format and eye appealing advertisements. By constant repetition apparently many people came to believe it, if sales volume is a criterion of success. However, the Los Angeles District Attorney began receiving numerous complaints from dissatisfied customers who protested the contracts which they had signed (some in blank while mesmerized by the salesmen) did not conform to the statements and assurances mouthed by the salesman at the time they signed. The investigations which resulted disclosed the accuracy of the complaints and later conviction and jailing of the dealer (upon a plea of guilty) and a number of his staff for grand theft and conspiracy.

A buyer, so the inquiries reflected, would trade in his old vehicle on a new or "re-conditioned" used car at one of the dealer's multiple car lots which abounded in the Los Angeles area. At the time of contract signing he would be offered a definite price on his old car, however, upon receiving a copy of the contract later through the mail (the customer was never given a copy at the signing time, vague and nebulous excuses being made usually about the mounting load of office work) he would find the amount of credit on his trade-in was much lower than he had been told. There were even disclosures of contracts which, because of more sophisticated customers, were not signed in blank, but were thereafter altered by members of the dealers staff. A constant complaint from buyers was his failure to put a vehicle in proper working order per contract. Sometimes there was a direct refusal to comply coupled with a threat of bodily harm if the customer did not leave the premises.

The main thing which evolved out of this dealer and his methods was a new legislation appearing in the Vehicle Code and the Civil Code (Rees-Levering Act) relating to the sales of motor vehicles and which at least gave the buyer some measure of protection against the more blatant practices of the dealers. The Vehicle Code provisions of greater importance are briefed as follows:

Section 11705: Disciplinary action to be taken against dealers for any violation of the Rees-Levering Act (2981–2982 Civil Code)

Section 11715: It shall be grounds for action against anyone who
(a) shall intentionally publish or circulate any advertising which is misleading or inaccurate in any material way or which misrepresents any of the products sold or furnished by a licensed dealer.
(b) To advertise or offer for sale or exchange in any manner, any vehicle not actually for sale ("bait and switch") at a premises of such dealer or available to said the dealer from the manufacturer or distributor of such vehicle *at the time of the advertisement of offer.*
(c) To fail within *48 hours in writing* to *withdraw* any advertisement of a vehicle that has been sold or withdrawn from sale.
(d) To advertise a vehicle as new when in fact it is not new.
(e) To include the cost of licensing and transfer to the sales costs when this has already been paid to the State.

The Fountain of Youth

With the advent of more leisure time for more people in keeping with the advances of our social order there has been an emphasis on individual physical conditioning and the embracing of those social amenities guaranteed to bring happiness and success. This opened the door to the patent-leather shoe shod Narcisstic operators who prey on the loneliness and feeling of inadequateness present in some people. The California Legislature in 1961 very succinctly declared its intent and purpose when enacting a law relating to Health and Dance Studios. It said that there was found to "exist in connection with a *substantial* number of contracts for health and dance studio services, sales practices and business and financial methods which have worked a fraud, deceit, imposition, and financial hardship upon people of this State; that existing legal remedies are inadequate to correct the abuses.........."; that the purpose of law was to safeguard the public against the fraud and related hardship and encourage fair dealing in these two areas.

As a result the contracts used in these two sectors are required to be in writing; separate contracts are precluded, everything included within one agreement; a contract shall not extend over two years; no contract will exceed $500.00; no right of action by the buyer (one subscribing to the service or treatment) can be cut off by assignment; the seller (one who provides service or treatment) will refund any prepaid amounts in case of the buyer's death or disability; and treble damages will be paid by the seller for failing to comply with the law. These provisions are self-indicative of the abuses which were, and can still be, present.

"Business Opportunities"

Business opportunities is a fertile field for the con-man in spite of the self-regulation resorted to by legitimate brokers and controlled by various State and local agencies. These operations prey upon people, often who are retired, disabled or otherwise so situated that any financial loss, whatever the extent, can be disastrous. The methods resorted to can include falsification of business account books to reflect larger assets, less liabilities and greater income than is factual; the sale of a business in which the source of raw materials is no longer available; the willful failure to disclose a highly competitive venture to be initiated soon; and "exclusive" franchise for an area where in fact there are, or will be, other holders.

For illustration, a graphic example is given of a variation of the old "Knitting Machine" fraud. There began to appear in newspaper classified sections under "Business Opportunities" column an advertisement which claimed a purchaser of a wire weaving machine manufactured by the seller, could, with an investment of about $2,000, start his own profitable business as an independent manufacturer of chain link fencing.

The contract entered into had an agreement in which the seller agreed to purchase from the buyer/investor all of his woven wire fencing. However, there were inserted very exacting specifications as to tolerances and types which would be acceptable; and, the seller was committed to buying *only* that production which met or conformed to specifications.

To induce the buyer/investor to take part the seller would purport "the company" had a back-log of orders for chain link fences and needs outside assistance to meet the contract committments; that there will be a free delivery of raw wire materials and pickup of the finished goods; that the investor will earn at least $8.00 per hour work; that if he is dissatisfied with the machine the seller will assist in its resale; that there will be close supervision and assistance from the seller to guide the machine's operations; that the machine can be set up in a small place such as a portion of a residential garage, shed or some similar building; and that normal household power input of 110 volts is adequate to operate the machines.

The machine is delivered. The buyer/investor is now engaged as a self-employed businessman, an independent contractor with thoughts of profits and being his own boss. He then finds the machine operates poorly on his standard 110 volts household current, necessitating changes at cost to him; that the machine keeps having adjustment problems with the result being that the specified tolerances he has to maintain per the buy-back agreement in the contract are not possible. Consequently, he ends up with a worthless monstrosity in his garage that takes up room and gathers dust; he has bales of rolled wiring which were delivered to him (at his own cost), not as agreed in the contract (the cartage man having nothing in his hauling contract about payment by the sender); and he has had little or no training, supervision or instruction on how to operate the machine. Thus, ends his dreams and more often than not, his savings, a blow from which he may not recover.

The Businessman Victim

The homeowner and daily shopper are not the only people who can be taken. A unique operation which has been controlled by a firm located at Long Island, New York, has for a number of years, been victimizing large companies, usually manufacturers, throughout the United States. One of the authors conducted an investigation in San Diego, Orange and Los Angeles Counties concerning this scam commonly called the "Hungarian Stationary Swindle" in 1964, culminating in testimony before the Federal Trade Commission at New York City in 1968. It was a sales swindle involving fake distress items. The unusual facet of this operation is that purchasing agents and other responsible officers of the victim companies, people who are trained and presumably knowledgeable in purchasing supplies and materials for their firms and who are normally the most difficult persons to convince, were the very ones who were susceptible to the blandishments and sob-stories of the phony Hungarians.

An officer of a victim company would be approached usually by two Hungarians, both speaking impeccable English but with strong accents, who purported to be refugees from the Russian occupation of their country. The younger and more personable of the two purported to have been a medical student in Vienna since leaving Hungary and had recently come to the United States when his father, who had come here directly after the 1956 debacle, had died. His father, the story went, had opened a wholesale stationery business in New York upon his arrival in this country, but now with his unexpected death there existed a problem of either foregoing his medical studies to continue the firm's operation or to liquidate completely and with the monies received continue his education. It would be at this point in the conversation a name of a highly placed company officer would be mentioned, one who was in the eastern part of the country. The younger Hungarian would say this absent officer was a close friend of his parents and who had advised him to sell out the business and return to school, urging him at the same time to contact, when on the west coast, his company's main office and gave him the local officer's name with assurances he would have a sympathetic ear for his (the Hungarian's) problem. The other member of the Hungarian duo would purport to have come to this country shortly after the Russian take-over and to have been employed by the other's father as sales-manager.

Both men carried briefcases in which they had sales order forms and lengthy inventory lists of stationery and other office supplies available at high discounts. These and their business cards had the company name and address (New York) printed thereon. With heartfelt sympathy for the young medical student's plight upper-most in their minds, the local company officers (especially when the absentee Chairman of the Board's name or a majority stockholder's name was used so intimately) would grant large purchase orders for office supplies of various kinds, whether needed or not. A number of weeks later the ordered supplies would arrive at the receiving docks, be checked off accordingly to amounts appearing on the manifests, purchase orders and sales invoices, processed through the normal accounting and paying channels, and sometimes later there comes the awakening. Everything was sub-standard, seconds and rejects, and most of it unusuable. The absentee officer would be contacted and it would be learned that he had never heard of the Hungarians, refugees or otherwise, accompanied with a few choice comments as to the ineptness and stupidity of the purchasing agent and local managers. Efforts would then be made by mail with the Hungarian's company in New York for an adjustment, but this, after lengthy and meaningless correspondence, never came to pass. The expense and costs incidental to any effort to rectify the situation was usually too much to merit further action; the whole thing then being marked off to an operating loss.

Upon their arrest in San Diego for attempted grand theft and conspiracy and while enroute to jail the younger Hungarian volunteered that he enjoyed a monthly income of about $2,000 after expenses; that he and his partners had obtained the name of the eastern Board Chairman by merely placing a telephone call to the local company office and inquiring from some unknown employee who complied in the best of public relations spirit the information, willingly furnishing all the facts even his New York residence and office addresses; that if this did not work, there were numerous trade journals containing lengthy and detailed stories about various personalities connected with most of the firms they hit; and that this was further enhanced by the "lead sheets" (3″ × 5″ cards) their Long Island manager or his Los Angeles area man would furnish them.

This young con-man further said, "I bet I buried my father a thousand times in the last three years. I'm a nice looking young man, and the story I tell about my being a medical student and my father being dead is a good story and people believe it. It's the sympathy people feel, although we do deliver some stuff. It's just a gimmick, everyone that is a salesman has some sort of gimmick; this is mine."

This young man had one previous arrest by a California Police Department for grand theft, but it was dismissed for lack of evidence, and he was merely charged with soliciting without a license. The Federal Trade Commission had attempted to stop his operations, but finally backed off being powerless to do anything.

He maintained, and unfortunately successfully for local pur-purposes, that his position was that of a "jobber" or "salesman," and that as he received only a purchase order from the victim and not cash monies, the victim's problem was with his Long Island manager and company. Further, he had no control over the quality or quantity forwarded to the buyer. He contended the victim paid nothing until receipt of the ordered items, and if he accepted them through some receiving clerk who was not overly intelligent and forwarded payment (even without the proper physical examination of the contents) that was the victim's error and misfortune.

The older "salesman" type Hungarian gave relatively the same story punctuated with the comment, "You should hear what I dream up when I go alone." He acknowledged that "perhaps morally the operation is not good, but then, everybody has a gimmick." An examination of their vehicle (per search warrant) disclosed countless order forms of varied company names, but all with the same address at Long Island. The purchase order copies indicated a nation-wide operation for at least nine years duration and correspondence showed the same pattern of misrepresentation and resulting losses experienced by the victims. Records also found reflected a Southern California District Headquarters for the group with interest parties named, but the indication was that everything was controlled from Long Island.

The inquiry was widened when reports in response to teletypes and letters began coming in from other agencies disclosing victims in several areas. There were developed within the next ten days complete documentation of sixteen similar acts and transactions in three counties; however, upon re-consideration of the matter there was forebearance of prosecution. There was, thankfully, no record of repeat performance locally for at least the following three years. The fourth year brought with it a couple of abortive attempts but circularizing by the Better Business Bureau had informed most of the business houses, thus preventing any sizeable losses. The total case, although no longer prosecutable locally, is still to be resolved by the Federal Trade Commission on the inter-state concept of fraud and deceitful practices. There were hearings held at Baltimore, Boston and New York City during the winter of 1968 but at this writing there is no indication that a cease and desist order is being issued or even considered.

The Investigation

From the investigator's standpoint there must be taken an overall view; determine what happened and the things needed to establish it, then *plan* the attack. When the word "plan" is used, it is not meant some unyielding, static, tunnel visioned approach, but a predetermined path that provides for alternatives and exceptions which can and will develop during any inquiry regardless of its nature.

During the interview of the complainant in a consumer fraud, the purpose is the same as in any other case involving false pretenses or misrepresentation——to determine exactly what was said or done in any manner which misrepresented any material fact related to the purpose, establish the manner in which the two parties (or more) came in contact such as the result of a widely disseminated advertisement campaign, referral, house to house canvassing, mail order type or some other method, show clearly, and to what degree, the reliance which was placed upon the representations of the seller by the buyer (was it reasonable?) and what was done in response to these two connecting elements, ascertain *in detail* and in *proper sequence* the documents and instruments subscribed to by both the buyer and seller (and anyone connected to the scam), the exact amounts involved, the dates and times there was contact between the parties (including any correspondence) and what was said and done on each succeeding occasion, who else was present, and where they took place, again in the proper sequence.

Three very important leads or evidence supplied by the complainant-buyer are the original documents and instruments, or the copies; the identification of other parties present during the negotiations who can be classified as witnesses; and persons who also became buyers. The documentation is the required corroborative means of proof. This is the "token" in the method of proving an allegation of theft by false pretenses or misrepresentation. The witnesses are another means towards the same requisite, and in effect, are cumulative in nature. The other buyers, of course, are the developed similar acts or transactions which go towards establishing a pre-determined pattern, scheme and design of the seller to cheat and defraud buyers.

Unfitness of Item

If the basis of the alleged misrepresentation is the unfitness of the item purchased, the investigator must be able to show that such a situation does in fact exist and that the seller was aware. To do this there is a two-pronged approach: (1) expert valuation of the item sold and (2) the seller's experience with, and knowledge of, the item. The first can be determined through the manufacturer and/or his representative, reputable dealers or independent laboratory testing either by a police agency or private firm. This grouping will furnish the actual performance rating and also the proper valuation in monetary terms. The second prong of the inquiry is sometimes the more difficult one to follow, but albeit an imperative one. The seller's source of supply must be identified and a history of his experience (wholesale purchases) with the particular item developed.

If the seller has purported in support of his representations to the buyer that certain tests have been made by others, either buyers, or Government laboratories, or independent testing agencies, and was found satisfactory, these "testers" must be identified and, if they do in fact exist, contacted for their actual valuations and the circumstances under which they had previously rendered reports attesting to the product. It is very important, if they are legitimate, to determine if what the victim had purchased was the same thing in every detail, quantitatively and qualitatively, upon which they had rendered the earlier tests and reports. It is not unusual for the seller to actually have a good report on an item he has for sale but what the buyer/victim received was something else again masquerading under the name and specifications of the legitimate product.

Know Your Man

The investigator must develop background information concerning the merchandising con-man to the same degree as inherent in other properly conducted fraud inquiries. *Know your man.* The County Clerk's files should be examined for certificates of "fictitious names" for a business operation, corporate and partnership information for obvious reasons or responsibility and culpability. The civil suit files, both plaintiff and defendant, must be perused, the pleadings are fruitful to show the preconceived scheme and design and other victims and also the defensive action the seller may frequently take, such as filing specious suits for defamation of character, money damages, money recovery, or even injunctive relief against official interference, and most frequently, attachments against the properties of his victims for nonpayment. The City Clerk's files and Business License Bureau data are important, the applications disclosing previous activities and often other parties of interest. Wholesale credit agencies and national business reporting agencies should be contacted for activity reports on the seller and disclosures of his finances and banking information of value on the con-man's in related fields often have information of value on the con-man's practices as he poses an unwanted threat to them by unfair competition. They can usually furnish names of several other persons who were victims. The

Better Business Bureaus are excellent sources, both in determining the finer points of the con-man's methods and the identity of other victims. The banks and finance companies who accept the con-man's contract assignments should be contacted to determine the actual scope of his activities. And, of course, the routine contacts with police and other public agencies must be made for whatever type of information as may be available. It is often the case that these sources have parallel cases going thus being of material assistance in establishing the pattern, scheme and design.

The Use of the Disenchanted Employee

One source, which if it can be developed, probably transcends the value of all others for current information and planned future activities; the dissatisfied and helpful (to you) present employee or one who was recently terminated either of his own or the seller's choice. This person is privy to conversations and activities, directives, instructions and orders, written and verbal, which too often are not part of the records or documentation available to the investigators, even those lawfully obtained by subpoena. He can disclose with pinpoint accuracy the methods, purposes, procedures and processes intricately concerned with the inner operations of the enterprise. He often has direct knowledge concerning the case in chief, perhaps even having taken part to some degree.

In situations in which the victim/buyer has, by some trick or device, been induced by the seller to hypothecate his property through the execution of a trust deed to secure a promissory note attendant to a conditional sales contract (supra), the seller can be charged with forgery in addition to grand theft. If a person who has no intention of selling or encumbering his property is induced to sign a paper having such effect, believing at the time of signing the paper or document to be something different, it is just as much a forgery as if the seller had himself signed the buyer's name (*Conklin vs Benson,* 159 Cal 785 and *Buck vs Superior Court,* 232 Adv Cal App 2nd 217).

"Shopping"

Another well tested technique is "shopping" the con-man merchandiser. If he had openly advertised his products, asking for customers from the general public, thus avoiding the perennial defense of entrapment, the investigator can properly send in pseudo customers to develop a case. The same situation prevails if the investigation concerns a referral type sales scams. The "You have won a contest" scheme is also amenable to such an investigative approach.

When employing such a procedure, there seems all too frequently to develop a laxity on the part of the "shoppers"; the lack of attention to detail. It is not enough to merely establish a prima facie case of false or misleading advertising, but it is essential to identify completely the persons involved, the parts they played and connect these factors up to the issue; misrepresentation.

The following is a suggested series of questions developed by the California Attorney General's Office to be put to victim's of consumer frauds. These questions, when answered in full, furnish the investigator with about as complete a picture as he can get of what he is dealing with, in terms of both victim and con-man vendor.

CONSUMER QUESTIONNAIRE

Name _____ Address _____
_____ Tel. No. _____

1. What is the name of the company you dealt with? _____
_____

2. What is the address of the company? _____
_____

3. What is the name of the first representative of the company you dealt with, and when did you first meet him, or talk to him? _____
_____

4. What is the name of the person with whom you dealt when you signed the contract, and when did you sign? _____
_____

5. Did the people with whom you dealt have a title, (manager, vice-president, consultant, etc.)? _____
_____

6. Were any other people present during any of your conversa-

tion with the representatives of this company? _____ Who were they, and what part of the conversation did they hear?

_____

_____

_____

7. How did you first become aware of the company?
   A. Was there an advertisement in the newspaper? _____
   What was the name of the newspaper, and when did you see the advertisement? _____ Do you still have a copy of the newspaper? _____ What did the advertisement say? _____

   _____

   B. Did you receive a pamphlet, throw-away, leaflet, booklet, or brochure? _____ When and how did you receive it? _____ Do you still have it? _____ If not, what did it say? _____

   _____

   _____

   C. Was the advertisement made over the radio? _____ On what station and at what date and time? _____

   D. Was the advertisement made over television? _____ On what channel, and at what date and time? _____

   _____

   What did the advertisement say? _____

   _____

   _____

   E. Were you first contacted by a person over the telephone? _____ Who did he say he was? _____
   When did he talk to you, and what did he say? _____

   _____

   _____

   F. Were you told about this company or product, or service through a friend? _____ What is his name? _____
   _____ When did he contact you and what did he say?

   _____

   _____

   G. Were you first contacted by a salesperson who came to

your door? _____ Did he come into your home? _____
Who did he say he was, and what did he say that caused
you to let him into your home? _____

_____

_____ What did he say after he was in your
home? _____

_____

8. If you bought the product in a store, did you buy the model
   or type that you thought was being advertised? If not, why
   not? _____

   Did you buy the model or type you had planned to buy? _____
   If not, why not? _____

   Did you pay what you had planned to pay (a) as a down
   payment? _____, (b) as a total price? _____, (c) for
   monthly installments? _____. If you paid more than you
   planned, what caused you to do so? _____

9. Did you receive what you purchased? _____ If not, why
   not? _____
   What did you receive? _____
10. When did you receive the product or service? _____

11. Did the salesman explain how the product you asked for
    worked or how long it would last? _____
12. Did the salesman say that the advertised item was of poor
    quality or would not do the job or was not what you wanted
    or lacked something? _____
13. Were you told that you must purchase something else in ad-
    dition to the product you wanted? _____

14. Did the salesman tell you anything about other items he had
    for sale? _____ Did he compare these items to the one you
    wanted to buy? _____ What did he say? _____

    _____

15. Were you offered something free or at no additional cost? _____ What was offered and when was the offer made?
_____

16. If you went to the store because of an advertisement, did the store have any of the products advertised? _____ If not, did the salesman explain why? _____
_____

17. When you were shown the product that was advertised, did it look like what you had expected it to be? _____ If not, why not? _____
_____

18. What did the salesman tell you about the guarantee? _____
_____
_____ Did you get a written guarantee? _____ Was the written guarantee different from what the salesman said it would be? _____.

19. After you began using the product, was it different from what the salesman told you it would be? _____ Did it perform the way the salesman said it would perform? _____

20. (Furniture) Did the salesman say anything about the upholstery or fabric that did not turn out to be true? _____
_____ Did the salesman say anything about the wood or other material that did not turn out to be true? _____

21. (Appliances) Did the salesman tell you how well the appliance would perform and what special features it had? _____
_____ Were these statements true? _____.

22. Did the salesman tell you anything about the regular price of the product or service? _____

23. Did the salesman tell you anything about the value of the product or service? _____
_____

24. Did the salesman tell you that you were getting a special deal? _____ What was the special deal? _____
_____

25. Did you first think that the product or service you bought

would be a certain price and then discover that the price you were paying was different than you had first thought? _____ What did you understand at first and what did the contract say that you were to pay? _____

26. How did you agree to pay for the product or service?
    A. (Payments) Did you agree to pay in weekly or monthly payments? _____ Were all the payments to be the same or was there to be one big payment at the end of the contract? _____
    Did the salesman tell you anything about what would happen if your payments were late? _____

    _____ Did you buy insurance at the same time you bought the product or service? _____. Did you have to buy the insurance? _____. What did the salesman tell you the insurance was for? _____
    _____ What do you believe the insurance protected you against? _____
    _____ Did you realize that you were buying insurance? _____ Were there any charges in the contract that you did not understand at the time you signed the contract? _____

    B. (Cash) If you paid cash did the salesman tell you you could buy the product or service cheaper than if you made payments? _____ Was the difference only the finance charge or interest or could you buy the product or service cheaper in addition to saving the finance charge or interest? _____

    C. (Loan) If you borrowed money from a finance company to pay for the product or service, did you borrow to only pay a down payment or to pay the whole thing? _____
    _____ How did you choose that particular finance company? _____

Did the salesman suggest that you go to that finance company? _____. Did he go with you to the finance company? _____ Did he help you arrange the loan? _____. Did he help you prepare any loan papers? _____. Did the finance company give you the check or did it send the check to the sales company? _____

Did you sign a contract for the product or service before you went to the finance company? _____. If so, what did the salesman say would happen if you couldn't borrow the money? _____

27. Had you ever bought a product or service from the sales company before? _____. If so, had there been any problems? _____ Was what happened to you this time different from what happened to you before? _____. If so, explain the difference.

_____

_____

28. Were you offered the chance to lower the price on what you were buying by referring or introducing other people? _____ If the product or service was sold to you in your home did the contract state that you had three days in which to cancel? _____ If so, did you attempt to cancel within the three days? _____

29. If the product or service was bought in a store, did you attempt to cancel? _____. If so, what reasons did you give to the store for wanting to cancel? _____ What did the store representative tell you? _____

_____

_____

30. Was the product new or used? _____. If it was used, what did the salesman say about its condition, its guarantee, its age, and its price compared to a new product? _____

_____

_____

31. Did the salesman tell you the product was a demonstrator or a floor sample or had been repossessed? _____. If so, what did he say about how much you would be saving by not buying a new factory fresh product? _____

32. By buying the product or service were you promised anything in the future such as the right to buy other items cheaper or at better rates of interest or at smaller monthly payments, etc.? _____

33. Did you get a copy of everything you signed? _____. If not, what did you get a copy of? _____. Is there anything you remember signing that you did not get a copy of? _____

34. If you signed a contract, did you know at the time you signed it that it was a contract? _____. If not, what did you think you signed and what did the salesman tell you you were signing? _____

35. Did the salesman tell you that the product or service you bought was better than another brand or kind? _____ If so, what did he say? _____

36. Did the salesman state that certain organizations or certain people or the government had approved or liked or preferred or recommended the product or service? _____ If so, what was said? _____

_____ If so, do you believe the salesman told the truth? _____

37. Did the salesman tell you anything about what you should do if you were not satisfied with the product? _____

38. In some businesses, a salesman talks to the customer and then turns the customer over to someone else for additional conversations about financing or price or the signing of a contract. Did this happen to you? _____. If so, did the second person tell you something different than the salesman had told you? _____

39. If you complained to the salesman or to the sales company about the product, were you sent to someone else such as the manufacturer or the distributor? _____

40. If you complained to the manufacturer or the distributor, were you sent to the store? _____.

41. Did you complain to:
    A. The owner or manager of the sales company? _____.
    B. The manufacturer? _____.
    C. Better Business Bureau? _____.
    D. An attorney? _____.
    E. Any governmental agency? _____.
    F. To your Assemblyman, State Senator, Congressman or Senator? _____.
    G. A local consumer group? _____.
    H. The finance company? _____. If you complained to any of the above, what were you told? _____

    _____

    _____

42. Some companies selling you products and services will sell the contract to a finance company or other company. This is different from you going to a finance company and borrowing money. In both cases you may be paying a finance company but your rights may be quite different. If you are making time payments, are you making them to a company that loaned you money or a company that your contract was sold to? _____

    _____

43. If your contract was sold to a finance company or other company, did you complain to that company? _____. If so, what were you told? _____

    _____

    _____

44. Has anyone filed a lawsuit against you as a result of a product or service you bought? _____. If so, when was the lawsuit brought? _____. In what court was it filed? (Superior Court or Municipal Court; what County?) _____ What is the case number and what is the name of the person or company suing you? _____

_____ Did the lawsuit result in a judgment against you? _____

45. Have you filed a lawsuit or did you file a claim in Small
Claims Court as a result of the purchase of the product or
service? _____. What was the result of the lawsuit or claim?

_____

46. Have you been contacted by a collection agency? _____ If
so, has this been by letter or by telephone or by both? _____
_____. If by telephone, what was said by the col-
lection agency? _____

_____

47. Do you know anyone else who had a similar problem with the
sales company or the finance company or the manufacturer?
_____. What is the name and address of the person who had
that problem? _____
_____ Do you know anyone who has had any problem with the sales company or the finance company or the
manufacturer? _____. If so, what was the problem and what
is the name and address of the person or persons? _____

_____

_____

_____

48. Before you bought the product or service had you compared
the price at other stores? _____.
49. Have you made any purchase from the sales company since
you had a problem? _____. If so, what occurred? _____

_____

_____

50. Is there anything that bothered you about the entire transaction that hasn't been covered by the other questions? _____

_____

_____

_____

_____

_____

_____

CHAPTER VI

MEDICAL FRAUDS

THE MOST heartrending fraud which confronts the investigator is the one involving the medical quack and victims. There are no swindlers who are as depraved and insouciant as those who prey upon the sick and lame, using, as a lever, the pain and fear of death that is inherent in the human animal, this often being coupled with religious overtones. The victims are usually pitiful creatures who are in advanced stages of debilitation caused by physical and mental diseases or injuries and frequently beyond remedial medical help; or those who can still receive and respond to some measure of medical assistance at least to the degree of arresting the condition; and those with psychomatic problems. The quack is totally aware of his victims and their real and/or imagined ills. He frequently is rendered the unconscious help of the victim's friends and family, who through compassion, fear and an overabundance of zealousness for what they consider righteous causes, lend impetus to the victim's approach to costly, ineffective and often fatal quasi-treatment.

The situation is frequently further compounded by the victims and their families and friends who prove reluctant to cooperate with investigators (infra). This can often be the result of a guilt-complex on the part of the family if the victim dies and on the part of the victim (if gratifyingly still in the world of the living) who has become mesmerized by the soothing, sympathetic attitude of the quack who manages to keep alive a faint spark of hope by his incantations and "therapy." There are even sometimes found victims who are actively assisting the quack to widen his practice, influencing other potential victims to embrace the theory of the charlatan. This, of course, is not done with a vicious turn of mind, but in the actual pious belief that help and cure can be given. The investigator should be conscious of this situation and appreciate the cause. When there is sufficient fear or apprehension, and admittedly this varies with individuals, it is only natural for the victim to turn to anyone who will succor his needs, real or imagined.

Another obstacle in the way of an effective investigation and prosecution is the reluctance of legislatures to propose and enact meaningful laws by which such cabalists can be controlled. A number of states do have statutory provisions which are designed to limit acts which are fraudulent and deleterious to health, but the larger part are classified at the misdemeanor level except those relating to cancer (which after the *third offense,* then can be viewed as a felony), and fictitious certificates, diplomas and degrees. Of course, if misrepresentation can be established, creating the sound basis for an allegation of theft, then the way is open for effective control. However, generally there seems to be a tendency to allege a lesser offense such as the practicing of medicine without a license as the quack usually is unlicensed besides being unprincipled and unethical. He does sometimes display a bona fide license as a chiropractor, chiropodist, physical therapist or some other such vocation as licensed by the state, his operation then being one beyond the scope of his recognized and lawful activity. More commonly though, he is in possession of a certificate or degree issued by some non-existent school or "diploma mill" which declares he is a "Doctor" of some weird occultism, the scientific basis of which is either untested, unknown, or rejected.

The California Business and Professions Code which relates to the practice of medicine without a license (a misdemeanor) sets forth those acts constituting a violation; "Any person, who practices or attempts to practice, or who advertises or holds himself out as practicing, any system or mode of treating the sick or afflicted in this State, or who diagnoses, treats, operates for, or prescribes for any ailment, blemish, deformity, disease, disfigurement, disorder, injury, or other mental or physical condition of any person, without having at the time of so doing a valid unrevoked certificate as provided in this chapter, is guilty of misdemeanor."

The unlicensed practice of medicine as a criminal act was unknown at common law. It was only after our social order became better educated and more knowledgeable that it was deemed necessary to exert the police powers of the sovereign state to protect the health, welfare and safety of the less sophisticated citizens by requiring certain occupations to adhere to predetermined levels of competence, ethics and necessary education to assure compliance. Medicine was one of these. This was not achieved without strenuous opposition. There always present a group of ignorant uninformed persons who object to any reform regardless of the area concerned. They are especially notable when problems involving the healing arts are being examined. These staunch believers in the mustard plaster—colonic irrigation—nature's way the best way—rabbit food—electric muscle palpitations theories always raise their unlearned and unlettered heads in vigorous protest. Unfortunately, their ideas, the genesis of which are lost in backwoods antiquity and in the aboriginal jungles, have some appeal. This is the result of that latent feeling of antipathy in many people towards the "educated" man; the intellectual. Physicians fall within this category. Consequently, if there is a failure to produce exciting success, or even the giving voice to a completely honest admission of inability to cope with an isolated situation, there is the immediate loudly vocal condemnation of all modern scientific medicine as a failure and fraud. This lunatic fringe displays a tendency to band together and they do create pressure groups when proposed legislation is under discussion and consideration.

A person's health is still viewed as a personal thing notwithstanding the tremendous advances of science and medicine. Self-treatment, resorting to questionable obscure remedies or submitting to the ministrations of someone outside the profession of medicine is extremely difficult to legislate against. Often there is closely interwoven with the treatment, the element of a religious belief. The last is the political kiss of death to any law-maker who would dare transcend that line, vague though it is, between the State and public welfare and the private inviolate religious beliefs of an individual. It is only when death in excruciating form usually results from the onset of the illness and medical science is

at last beginning to make some progress towards treatment and
cure, that legislation is enacted to exclude the phony, the fake,
and the quack from perpetrating his crime. The California Health
and Safety Code provisions relating to cancer is an example of
this, but even here it requires three offenses before the crime is
viewed as a felony. The constitutionality of such laws are continuously under attack.

The California Legislature in 1959 very succinctly stated it's
intent and logical reasoning with enactment of Chapter 7 H & S
Cde, (supra). It was stated in part, "Despite intense campaigns
of public education, there is a lack of adequate and accurate information among the public with respect to presently proven
methods for diagnosis, treatment and cure of cancer. Various
persons in this State have represented and continue to represent
themselves as possessing medicine, methods, techniques, skills, or
devices for the effective diagnosis, treatment or cure of cancer,
which representations are misleading to the public, with the result that large numbers of the public, relying on such representations, needlessly die of cancer, and substantial amounts of
the savings of individuals and families relying on such representations are needlessly wasted.

"It is therefore in the public interest that the public be afforded full and accurate knowledge—to that end there be provided means for testing and investigating—and protecting the
public from misrepresentations in such matters."

Under this chapter there is created an Advisory Council
within the State Department of Public Health which is to assure
the continued study of the cancer problem and empowered to
hold hearings and advise the Department on such matters. The
latter prescribes reasonable rules for the administration of the
chapter, investigates violations and cooperates with law enforcement agencies for prosecution. There is the requirement of a license for anyone who undertakes the treatment of cancer regardless of the method with the exception of those resorting to prayer
exclusively in accordance with some recognized religious sect.
There is also the power to require anyone engaged in or representing themselves as capable of treating and diagnosing cancer
to furnish all devices, compounds, formulas, drugs, medicines and

detailed data relating to a method, to the Department for examination and the failure to comply is presumptive evidence that it is valueless.

The chapter further states that anyone willfully and falsely representing a device, substance or treatment as effective to arrest or cure cancer is guilty of a misdemeanor. This would seem to negate the efficacy by false pretenses. However, it has been held since 1966 the fraudulent representations as to cures for cancer has not been preempted by the Health and Safety Code. The Court said it must be inferred that the Legislative intent was not to supplant the Penal Code provisions, but actually to supplement it, as the theft section requires proof a victim relied upon representations causing him to part with something of value, while the Health and Safety Code does not (*Peo vs Phillips*, 51 Cal Rptr 225).

There are some jurisdictions which have laws relating to "unlicensed practice." There are numerous ways in which its provisions can be violated. It includes the practice of hypnotism when intended to be used as a curative measure for a disease, or to cause the loss of weight, correction of bad habits. Usually this requires the "placing of hands" on the patient. It is not a defense that the accused person does not claim to be a doctor of medicine. If he has the requisite specific intent to violate the provisions of the law and commits an overt act in that direction the crime is complete.

Insofar as payment for treatment is considered, where it can be shown, even circumstantially, that a device claimed by the accused to possess curative powers is sold to a patient, regardless of the protestations that the money given was a mere "loan" or "donation" by the patient and the act of using the device was not a demonstration as asserted but a treatment, the elements of the crime are present (*Peo vs Marsh* (1962) 58 Cal 2nd 732). The charging for service by the accused is not essential to the offense if it can be shown he regularly treated patients in some manner. An allegation that the accused rendered a "diagnosis" can be supported by the acts and conduct as well as an representation made to the patient. Also the unlawful possession of narcotics by the accused, the type of which are normally related to medical treatment, can be used as circumstantial evidence supporting an assertion of practicing without a license.

The proof of other acts of a similar nature by the quack is admissable to establish pattern, scheme and design. It has even been held that a single treatment warrants the inference that quack was engaged, as a business, in the practice of medicine (*Peo vs Wah Hung* 79 Cal App 286). In relation to the time honored statement by a quack that the patient has been given up as incurable by the bona fide medical profession and his ministrations are merely an attempt to save a human life is without validity when it is obvious no actual emergency existed.

There are also some jurisdictions that have laws which preclude the unauthorized use of the word "doctor" as a title in any writing and in an combination of letters or abbreviations such as "M.D.," "Dr.," "Phys.," which directly or impliedly indicate he is a physician, surgeon or practitioner of the healing arts as licensed by the State, without having a properly issued certificate of such status. This also includes any other form of letters or abbreviations such as "N.D." (Doctor of Naturopathy) which will tend to confuse the public.

California, especially the southern part, notwithstanding Berkeley and the Haight-Ashbury district, has often been referred to facetiously as the land of fruits and nuts. This very generalized term includes the social lepers who prey upon the afflicted. There have been numerous cases of interest over the years in which the victims not only suffered great material losses due to the fraudulent practices foisted upon them, but also unwittingly denied themselves the proper medical attention which in a number of instances could have prolonged life or at least made it less painful. A classic operation along these lines was the mother-daughter combine of Dr. Ruth Drown and Dr. Cynthia Chatfield, both chiropractors with the former operating a "laboratory." The basis of their scam was the "diagnostic machine." The published material by Drown described her theory: "We diagnose by placing the patient (or his blood crystal) in a lateral hookup to the instrument. When we treat we hook up the patient (or blood crystal) in series with the instrument, using an electrode on the solar plexus of the patient (or with the blood crystal hooked up to the electrode) which causes the patient to take the place of a drycell battery. We turn the dials to the disease rates and areas of the body affected, and the instrument is grounded. The patient is treated by his own energy." They claimed to diagnose a person's ailment through his blood specimen and to photograph the cell structure of the part involved, whether the patient is in the same room or at a distance.

The California Department of Public Health in 1963 initiated an investigation of the Drown scam, having one of their agents submit blood samples from a turkey, a sheep and a pig to Chatfield, labeling them as from three children. The price was $50.00 for each sample diagnosed. The report rendered stated the children were suffering from chicken-pox and mumps. The agent was then supplied with a "Drown Machine" for an additional cost of $600.00 with the instructions regarding its operation and how to set the dials to treat the children for the diagnosed conditions.

The same agent later was examined by Drown at the "laboratory." This consisted of the placing on the feet and abdomen of metal plates wired to the diagnostic machine. Drown said the agent had aluminum poisoning of the stomach and gall bladder, a malfunction of the left kidney and right reproduction organ. An employee explained the treatment costs as $50.00 per month for direct treatment by the laboratory instruments, $35.00 per month for "indirect" therapy accomplished by "broadcasting" the treatment through the blood specimen. The agent had supplied the blood specimen five years earlier on a previous contact. The treatment machine consisted of a black box with nine dials, an ammeter and two metal electrodes. An examination of the device at the UCLA Medical Center reflected it had the same therapeutic value of a flashlight battery.

Drown *et al* were "treating" epilepsy, cancer and just about any serious illness or affliction which could be conceived. She had successfully, if it can be thus described, operated for over thirty years with not too much interference, or apparently even interest, by law enforcement agencies, and boasted openly she had treated at least 35,000 persons. The action was so profitable she opened offices in San Luis Obispo, Hollywood and Twenty-Nine Palms in the desert area. Her devices began to wend their way out of the state at the usual exhorbitant cost thereby creating an interest in her and her activities by the Federal Food and Drug Administration. She was prosecuted and convicted in Federal Court in 1951, being fined $1,000.00 for shipping a misbranded device in interstate commerce. This punative measure of course had little or no effect on her as she continued to operate another twelve years.

The wide scope of the Drown operation defies the imagination. In 1963 when she was finally arrested again along with her daughter and a few employees and co-conspirators for multiple counts of grand theft this time (instead of the usual misdemeanor count of unlicensed practice of medicine), she had a monthly patient load in excess of 300 in the Los Angeles area and another 80 patients at the San Luis Obispo center. This gave her a gross monthly income of about $19,000. This calloused, unfeeling unrepentent, unmitigated parasite stated at the time of her arrest that the attendant publicity in the news media would increase her business immeasurably. Unfortunately the wheels of justice turn very slowly, Drown died in 1965 before she could be brought to trial. However, in 1966 the remaining jackals of this performing troup were tried and convicted in the Superior Court, the Judge commenting at the time that the Drown instruments and theories had about the same validity as witchcraft.

Further comment should be made concerning Drown's res gestae remarks at the time of arrest relative to publicity being beneficial to her purposes. She was not wrong in her assumption. It seems to be a part of the phenomenon in quackery scams. The victims, the ones who should resent and revile such a person, are often the first ones forward in defense of the charlatans. Their reasons being many and varied, but usually evolve into diefied belief in the omniscience of the quack because of his appealing approach to them in their time of need.

Nick Smith (fictitious name for an actual person) with his "Aeroclave Device" was a somewhat different personality from Ruth Drown. Smith was almost as pitiful as his patients. He reflected none of the obvious feelings of avarice and greed so common to the quack, however, the irreparable harm he did to his ignorant victims was as great. His attitude, personality and responses during interviews, tended to develop a feeling of compassion on the part of the listener, that is, until one of his victims was seen. He seemed to be on an ethereal plane, not completely in contact with or aware of things around him. But despite this seeming detachment from reality he was quite vocal in defense of his theories and devices.

The "Aeroclave" (see photo) was a combination of an electric ¼ hp motor, two mercury tubes, numerous flat pieces of thin copper cut in varied splayed patterns, these held in position by two

Aeroclave
Photos
San Diego Sheriff's Department

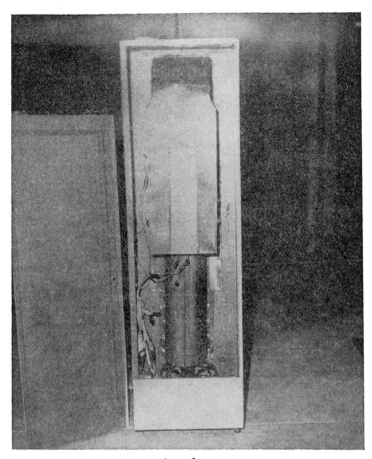

Aeroclave
Photos
San Diego Sheriff's Department

hollow copper tubes in a vertical position all of which was contained within a sheet-metal cabinet about 6½ feet tall. At the top
there protruded a copper attachment which in effect was an air
duct with the funnel extending downward. At the bottom of the
machine there was a grating through which air was sucked, much
the same as a vacuum cleaner. This air went upward as it was
warmed from the surface heat of the motor and additionally
warmed by the mercury tubes, going through the maze of copper

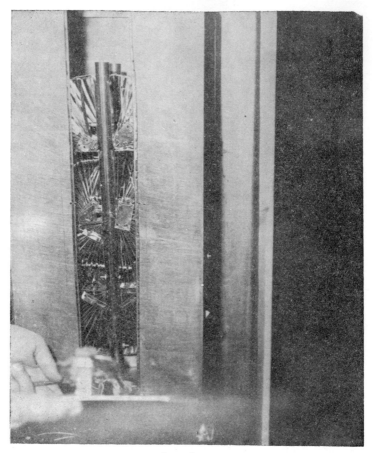

Aeroclave
Photos
San Diego Sheriff's Department

sheeting above, thence escaping outward via the funnel attachment and downward onto a patient who would lie upon a table placed adjacent to the front of the device with his head directly below the funnel aperture. The Smith theory as implemented was somewhat vague at best. He purported that "when the exterior air was drawn into the device the nitrogen was removed leaving charged oxygen, which was warmed prior to inhalation by the patient; and this warmed air was charged with electrons." Naturally, laboratory examination, as is required in the course of such inquiries, disclosed no production of ozone or oxides of nitrogen, just normal warmed air was produced following its circulation through the device.

Smith was exemplificative of the average medical con-artist. His formal education was terminated at the grade school level. He stated he had developed his scientific knowledge from the reading (unsupervised and also undirected) of various texts, one of which was "Anatomy and Physiology" by Mary R. Mulliner, M.D. published in 1938. He supplemented this with the pocket edition of Einstein's "Theory of Relativity." He professed an interest in and a study of astronomy, astro-physics and microbiology. He also indicated he was greatly influenced by the "scientific fact, bacteria may be destroyed by physical means." He talked at length in a disjointed manner about expending in excess of $75,-000.00 in his "research," losing his wife in the process. He said he *never* charged anyone for treatments as he was trying to help mankind, and he wanted to put his machine and theory in the hands of the medical profession, forebearing any financial rewards himself.

When Smith first came to the attention of the California agencies in 1960 he was interviewed concerning his "aeroclave" operation. He indicated he had been "testing" and "researching" his device for a period of 14 years in Arizona and California and it had proved beneficial in the treatment of breast cancer, lung cancer, heart disease, infection of the uterus, hemorrhoids, asthma, emphyzema and other respiratory illnesses. There appeared to be nothing he was in the least bit apprehensive to treat. He also dropped the names of a number of people who he purported to have successfully treated for a variety of ailments, including himself, saying he was self-cured of cancer of the mouth. His discourses were usually long and rambling with the frequent misuse of medical and scientific terminology. After listening to him for a period of time the interviewer came to the conclusion that Smith's intellectual development was at about the level of a 14 year old child. He made one think of a child playing at being a doctor with homemade tools, but even a child can cause death.

Smith apparently was not too active for about three years as he did not come to the attention of the California Department of Public Health again until 1964 when he was operating in a suburban area of San Diego. He was found then to be set up in an old frame house situated on the edge of a third rate trailer court occupied by elderly and unemployed persons, most of whom were receiving public assistance. The conditions in and around the premises were singularly lacking in cleanliness. Inquiries prior to arrest by warrant and statements of Smith and one female helper (a Mexican woman in the terminal stages of breast cancer) at the time disclosed the larger part of his clientele was from Mexico being referred to him by various doctors in Tiajuana. His fees were actually very small when compared to other quacks such as Drown.

The investigative process employed in this case was the same as normally used in similar situations; undercover agents. Two female agents, ostensibly unknown to each other insofar as Smith was concerned, approached him for treatment after conversation with other "patients" who publicly praised his efforts and "passed the word" as to his location and availability to those who sought help. They both underwent treatments separately, each paying a nominal "donation." They were told by Smith that they were breathing "hot electrons" and the blue shaded light which reflected itself on the interior surfaces of the air-duct was an "ultraviolet ray" (the mercury tubes) and this had a curative effect. On the date of the arrest both agents again were on the premises to keep their pre-arranged appointments, however, this time wired for sound. After a half-hour's conversation between Smith and the two agent-patients while both were undergoing simultaneous treatment for their purported sinus and lung pluerisy conditions (diagnosed by Smith) all of which recorded in an investigator's receiving set and tape recorder located in a vehicle parked nearby, the arrest was made. In the search incidental to the arrest (infra), two "aeroclave" devices which were in use on the agents were confiscated as were the records in which Smith was making entries relative to the agents. These consisted of two large loose-leaf binders completely filled to capacity with typewritten and handwritten pages disclosing his "treatments" for two years of cancer and other disease afflicted patients. The prose therein was in the same style and continuity as his spoken word, but it clearly indicated in excess of one hundred people had undergone his ministrations. The diagnoses described, with related treatment apparently rendered, sounded like a script from a comedy of errors with Mrs. Malaprop as the protagonist except for the tragic overtones of the situation when one considered the patients were human beings suffering immensely from their illnesses.

Smith was charged with two counts of 2141 Business and Professions Code (unlicensed practice) and two counts of 488 Penal Code (petty theft). He entered a plea of *nolo contendre* in the San Diego Municipal Court, sentencing held in abeyance until a sanity hearing conducted by the Superior Court. He was later placed on three year probation and was given permission to move to another state to reside with some relatives. There has been no indication of a resurgence of the Smith theory in that area.

The American Arthritis Foundation over the years has kept abreast of the quacks working in that particular field making an effort to educate the public. This affliction is probably the nation's one greatest crippler, effecting at least 13 million people. It has become a lucrative area for the medical fakir and his witchcraft. There is a report concerning some arthritics paying three dollars an hour for the priviledge of sitting in wheelchairs in a worked out uranium mine near Boulder, Montana inhaling radon gas which they have been told has curative benefits. Radon is a radioactive gaseous element produced in the disintergration process of radium.

There are machines, devices and medications sold to victims at exhorbitant cost with the healing capabilities of a sack full of dried rattlesnake skins. The gadgeteering goes into the field of radiology, electricity, ice water and varied heat treatments. The medication consists of mysterious elixers of horse radish, honey, vinegar, mud and vitamin shots. The field is replete with every conceivable kind of concoction and equipment that the human mind at its twisted best (or worst) can dream up to swindle a mark.

The field is not unknown to medical rogues who have been

banished from the profession. Canada is the work base of a former physician from the United States who dispenses "Liefcort," a highly toxic item of no value which he sends to patients all over the northern hemisphere. Even the Indian medicine-man has gotten into the act selling odorous compounds to the ailing whiteman. Maybe this is retribution. The arthritic is no different from the cancer victim; he is in pain, fears death and is an easy mark for anyone or anything promising him a modicum of relief.

Comparable to the "Liefcort" treatment for arthritis are the better known and discredited compounds, "Krebiozen", a mixture of horse blood, horsemeat and horse plasma; and "Laetrile", ground up apricot kernels which is highly toxic; both of these used for the purported treatment of cancer. Krebiozen is the brainchild of one Steven Durovic, a Jugoslavian who induced a respected American physician to assist him in its promulgation. They both were indicted on multiple counts of fraud but acquitted. The Laetrile compound was the result of efforts by Ernest T. Krebs and his son in San Francisco. They both have been subjected to various legal actions, but still manufacture their drug. It is sold in Europe and central-south America.

William F. Koch, presently residing in Brazil, uses the "therapy" approach while Harry M. Hoxsey of Dallas, Texas uses a combination of internal medications and external compounds. Both men are viewed with disapprobation by legitimate medical people and have been in and out of courts so often that they have more trial experience than their attorneys.

Iridology is another gimmick utilized by quacks. Most patients know that authentic physicians (with unquestioned training, knowledge and proper equipment) examine the eyes. However, this is not the same theory employed by the quack. According to the "iridoligist" he can tell if a leg bone is fractured by looking into the iris of his patient's eye; that the spots which appear are an indicator of any disablement or disease which may affect the body (also a full pocketbook). This approach is a favorite of the charlatans who operate health ranches, spas and rural clinics. It is usually combined with the "naturopath's" treatment of clear air, sunshine and "organically grown vegetables, etc." The patients in these places normally end up not only paying for a useless diagnosis and medication, but also for the priviledge to work in the "Master's" truck gardens, which is no slight savings for him as an operating expense.

When the element of religion appears in the quack's performance, the investigator and legislator both are confronted with an almost insurmountable obstacle. The quack knows this and uses it to his advantage. The law in its creation and in its enforcement is thwarted. The American public has not yet gone beyond the bible-thumping, downsouth-camp-meeting perspective towards religious beliefs. Any time efforts are made at effectively curbing the fakirs who use religion as a veil of immunity the cry is raised, and very effectively, of religious persecution. These Psalm singers and their nostrums receive the vigilent protection of their hoodwinked victims.

The late (1967) Adolph Hohensee was a past-master of this dubious art. He combined his considerable knowledge of Bible quotations with his "Ambrosia of the Gods." He literally took unto his bosom hundreds of God-fearing elderly people in Southern California. On his first appearance in San Diego in excess of 1,000 people attended his lecture at a downtown hotel which had been widely advertised. He traveled with an entourage of from three to seven persons complete with an advance-man. He would give a series of "free" lectures (and he was a real four karat spellbinder) then follow it up with a pitch for his "health course" which was sold to the unsuspecting at twenty-five dollars a copy. His compound, the "Ambrosia" which upon analysis turned out to be pure (?) honey, was added free of charge by the charity-minded Apostle of good health and contendedness. He lectured at length on causes and his cure of cancer, besides berating the American Medical Association, the Pure Food and Drug agents in general and the medical profession in particular. He contended "science has become a part of life only so drug firms can get your money." This had a certain amount of appeal to his audience, most of whom were in the medicare age bracket; and the propitious news articles at the time regarding the profiteering by the pharmaceutical firms were of no little help also.

Hohensee, who had more than thirty years experience in the

quackery field and was convicted previously for fraud, was again convicted along with some of his group for conspiracy to defraud and obtaining money under false pretenses. His trial was something to behold. The courtroom was constantly filled each day whether for trial, law of motion calender, or any time he might be in attendance, by his clack of indignant elderly people who frequently had to be admonished for their individual and collective outbursts interrupting the decorum. He died in Pennsylvania sometime after his release from prison in California, "ambrosia" apparently not prolonging his eventful life.

Another California case permeated with the religious facet was that of "Bishop" Stanton L. Jamison and his "New Age" movement. Grant Leake of the California Department of Public Health's Fraud Section and members of local law enforcement agencies in a north central valley County were able to develop sufficient evidence to effect a conviction of the ecclesiastical phony and his apostles for violations of the Health and Safety Code and the Medical Practices Act. Jamison, who created his own position of "Bishop", organized his "Church" along with four helpers. This theological front was used as a wholesale outlet for a variety of devices which he claimed could be used for the cure of cancer, heart disease and other ailments. His unique approach was the granting, at a price, of sales franchises for the devices to anyone who joined his "church." Appealing to the sacred consciousness which he calculated to be present in most people, there was bestowed upon the joiners the status and title of "Minister." Three State agents, a Deputy District Attorney, two Police Sergeants and an Assistant Attorney General joined and were immediately made "Ministers," the State officers later being promoted to the exalted position of "Bishop." Apparently Jamison was somewhat discrimnatory against local people, as they remained merely as "Minister" without the exhaltating recognition and status symbol.

During the inquiries it was disclosed Jamison and one of his disciples were treating a victim for throat cancer. The diagnosis in this particular instance was arrived at by the unusual use of a pendulum. There was supposed to be a transmitted effect involved, flowing from the apparatus to the patient. This was achieved by the patient writing his signature on a piece of paper which was placed under a small cardboard cone or pyramid, and from this the curing treatment flowed to the patient, evidently without regard to where he might be at the time.

Jamison and his crew also employed what he termed a "Multiple Wave Oscillator" which was a version of an old model "T" spark coil. This device cured the patient of any illness whatever by supposedly passing 70,000 volts of electric energy through his body.

Jamison's contraptions which he sold through his "church", were manufactured in a purported "laboratory" at Tumtum, Washington. This is not to be confused with the town of Tumwater in the same state, the source of a better brand of elixer. There was also an ancillary operation of the "church" and its organizers, the sale of naturopathic diplomas or degrees emanating from a correspondence mill in England known as the "Drugless Practitioners Society of Great Britain."

The foregoing cases were briefly touched on primarily to present to the student investigator the classic types of scams he would usually meet with and the personalities (on both sides of the street) involved. It must be appreciated that they were not all inclusive, as there can be, and are, multiple variations and also other methods employed, however, with the same common denominator always present; the desire to separate the victim/patient from his funds by worthless and ineffective treatment and the calloused indifference of the quack.

Experience has shown the most effective method to be employed during the inquiry stage of medical frauds is the proper use of undercover operators or agents. If actual police personnel are to be used in this capacity there is created a need to establish a complete new identity. There should be kept in mind that if the quack has a large lucrative practice coupled with perhaps some local public support, he is in a position with his connections to conduct counter inquiries of his own, especially of new patients. He will encounter no problems in making discreet inquiry to determine the background, financial, employment/occupational and social position of a new patient who approaches him for treatment. The use of police personnel who have had some length of service is, of course, fatal to this type of an investigation. Public exposure limits their usefulness; civil service records of employment, also credit agency records, are too readily available to anyone who will pay the necessary fees or has a friend who has access to the files. The normal practice is to implement the newer officer, regardless of sex, who preferably is unmarried permitting a freer movement, unencumbered with domestic obligations. There should be established a new residence under his fictitious name with at least one cooperative neighbor who can attest to a lengthy period of association; a vehicle registered in this same name; fictitious employment with a public-spirited cooperative employer who can develop a comparable work record and payroll number; the depositing of funds in a checking account under the fictitious name with the help of a cooperative bank officer who can and will set up a false opening date and also a fictitious savings account with false four figure balances to make it more attractive. It is advisable to establish a credit rating at a retail outlet in this name, also done with fictitious opening dates and balances. The larger stores with their internal security sections can enlist the aid of the company auditor and store manager for this purpose. If a person outside of the agency is to be used, and there is no obvious connection between her (or he) and the regular personnel, there exists no real need for a new identity.

The next step, and a very important one, is the series of complete detailed clinical examinations of the undercover agent, the first one prior to any approach or contact with the quack for treatment. This, however, must be done within a matter of hours before the initial contact. The physician must submit a detailed report to be maintained on file. This seldom poses a problem as most medical societies make strong efforts at eradicating the quacks from their midst. The second examination must be made during the course of any treatment being given by the quack to determine any possible change in the agent's condition while undergoing these administrations. The third examination should be made without any delay immediately following the last period of treatment; all of course being reported by the physician in detail for the case file. The reasons are obvious; these will refute by legitimate authoritative medical knowledge, any claims of debilities in the patient by the quack. There is often a fourth examination which can be made and prove very useful. This is just prior to the trial to show, even after a period of time, no disorders developed which the quack avers are present.

The agent must be an actor. He plays a role of duplicity that can really lay a heavy hand on both his emotional and physical being. He must possess an inordinate supply of self-control and be able to feign an illness or injury with such finesse that he will not inadvertently lapse into physical appearance or movement, or by way of conversation, which reveals his position. His introduction to the quack must have an authentic appearance. It should not deviate from the manner in which actual victims have come there. Any change in the normal process is immediately noticeable. The quack as a matter of course will lay traps in which to catch a phony patient. He is as suspicious of new (and often even old) patients as investigators are of him. He will protect his position like a lioness with her cubs. He knows the agent-patient is a constant threat to his business and will use everything he can to thwart them.

The agent's primary duty is to obtain a diagnosis and treatment of a disorder, actual or false. To carry out this mission he must in some manner record simultaneously (infra) or otherwise all conversation he has with the quack and his known assistants. He must, in detail record in proper sequence for a later time all treatment received, all tests performed, all specimens given, any device, mechanism, medication employed and the prognosis related to him by whom, when, where and how. He must also be able to report to whom he made any payments in what manner, for what purpose, the date, time and place concerned, and under what conditions. He must gather, either surreptitiously or in such an open manner so as not to excite suspicion, any brochure, photographs, diagrams, devices, medications and other items which are relevant to the mission he is performing. All of these must in some way be passed to the officer who is directing the inquiry, and of course be properly marked to maintain the chain of identification of evidence which may be used later in trial.

Medications, compounds and similar items which are given

to the patient-agent must be secretly taken in such quantities
that chemical analysis can be made and with a sufficient amount
left over for exhibit. This is often a difficult problem for the
agent because frequently the quack is present or at least in near
proximity during this period. This, then, is a matter of individual
ingenuity of an agent, each act being based upon the exigency
and expediency of the moment. There is no set rule which can
be applied other than *theft cannot* be an element. Such an act
would vitiate the whole operation by violating constitutional
guarantees against unlawful search and seizure. Only those items
as are made available to the agent can be taken.

Photography and listening-transmitting-recording devices can
and are used effectively by agents. However, here a clumsily
performed act can destroy any other effective efforts. The danger
of surveillance by the quack can limit any achievement along
these lines. Also, searches of a patient's personal effects are not
unknown, especially at "health farm" operations where he is
shuttled from quack to quack during the day, ostensibly receiving the attention of "specialists" in the course of his stay. Much
thought and consideration must be given by the investigator
regarding the use of such devices. Conditions, not only physically
on the premises, but also electronic/radio/magnetic files must be
proper. Often the physical set-up is ideal for their use, but recep-
tion outside is ruined by faulty radio waves; many times the
electronic equipment used by the quack will jam very effectively
any transmissions making them unintelligible even if they are
reduced to a recording tape and this "cleaned" of excess and
interfering noise. Here again, a decision must be made on the
merits of the individual situation alone and not upon wishful
thinking.

Written reports and verbal reports by the agent to the investigator are the life-blood of the inquiry. Again, it must "be
played by ear." Any contact between the parties during the
course of the investigation is tenuous at best. There is always
the possibility of disclosure. This can come about by some ill-
advised meeting which can be observed by the quack or someone of his group or even indirectly revealed because a third party
who may have seen the conclave will in all innocense comment
on it within the hearing of the quack. But the fact remains re-

ports must be made, thus a calculated risk is taken. The undercover agent must be able to reduce to writing things heard, seen and done within a relative short time after their occurance to assure accuracy and continuity in recording. Another element to consider, and positive efforts should be made to manuever in that direction, is having a third party witness to the action related to the quack or his representatives.

If two agents are working in conjunction with each other this poses no problem. If not, then the use of another uninformed patient can be effected. Sometimes this is even more acceptable to a jury who must judge the authenticity and integrity of an agent's statements. But the problems which can evolve here are numberless if the actual patient is the least bit reluctant. The investigator must avoid at all cost be placed in a position that it can be alleged he in any manner "pressured" the witness (*Smith vs U.S.* (1965) 344 Fed 2nd 545).

The suspect, the quack, the focal point of the whole investigative effort must be completely identified. Before any real work is extended to other phases of the inquiry, know your man. A police agency often receives its initial information concerning a medical fraud from a reputable physician whose patient has undergone some of the quack's ministrations or from a local medical society, friends or relatives of a victim and from disinterested persons who have observed a certain amount of activity on or near the quack's premises. Regardless of the manner in which the data comes to the investigator, start with the quack. This requires a detailed examination of his background and personal history.

The first step is a physical description complete with any oddities he may have. Included with this should be developed comparable information concerning his wife and children if any. Inquiries should be directed to the Department of Motor Vehicles, Division of Driver's Licenses requesting copies of the operator's permits, with photograph if available and driving records. This last shows all citations and arrests concerned with automobiles giving insight into the other areas frequented by them. Also there should be requested vehicle registration information in the quack's name, his wife's and children's names. If his business is functioning under a registered (or even unregistered) fictitious or business name all vehicles registered thereto should be developed. Such data will disclose the legal owner if different from the quack who will have a record of the purchase contract, its inception, amount, payments and balances. Also the contract will disclose the insurance contract underwriter who has a detailed background dossier on the insured.

Simultaneously, descriptive information should be forwarded to State, FBI, and local agencies for any criminal record of applications made for vocational, professional, Armed Forces and defense industry employment.

Upon receipt of any response from the above agencies inquiries are then made in the directions indicated. If criminal records reflect an arrest, don't stop with the "rap sheet." Contact the arresting agency for the arrest and case report, the booking sheets with any photographs and other information of record. If the case actually came to trial review the pleadings, court docket and any transcript as may be available. Some authorities demand certified copies of all records; actually at the investigative phase this is really not necessary. If a complaint or indictment is assured there is then sufficient time before any hearings to obtain the certified documents and instruments. Doing so beforehand is an assumed expense which may not only prove prohibitive but also unnecessary. The contract information on the vehicles and insurance is not only useful for observation purposes but also discloses an application of the quack's funds and location of his bank accounts and other useful data. The driving history as indicated not only shows accidents and citations etc. but these in themselves are very useful in determining the quack's travel habits, areas of operations and other residences.

Credit agencies are an invaluable source. It must be remembered however, the information furnished normally cannot in itself be used in support of any allegation. The investigator uses this only as "leads." It is incumbent upon him to conduct follow-up inquiries personally following or paralleling, if he desires, the footsteps of the credit man, but he still must do this himself. Usually the credit reports are so clear, especially when disclosing purchases contracts, location of bank accounts, loans, law suits, both as plaintiff and defendant, places and periods of employment and education, that the investigator will have no trouble in authenticating the information (*see* Chapter, "Investigative Sources" for limitations imposed by Federal and State laws).

If the quack purports to have a specialized education such as a lawyer, physician, dentist, osteopath, chiropractor, teacher or minister of some denomination, or in practically any vocational or professional field for that matter, there exists excellent sources at the public library and with the Department of Professional and Vocational Standards. Every profession or vocation in which there is a required licensing process involved in order to practice in California is recorded by Department at Sacramento. Every licensee has to furnish accurate personal history information and this is available to the investigator, as is data on those who were unsuccessful in their application and those who have been suspended or revoked. From this other similar acts can be determined and other areas of operations to which inquires can be directed. The public library is replete with directories and registers which have fairly comprehensive personal information such as "Martindale and Hubbard" for attorneys. There are others for members of the Armed Forces (Commissioned and Warrant, Regular and Reserve), medical and dental and related professions or occupations, accountants, engineers, ministers and priests of various religious sects. Also available are catalogues and year books of most universities, colleges and junior colleges. The registrar's offices at these institutions have a wealth of information available on former students. Most of the vocations and professions also publish membership directories of fraternal and occupational association related to the various fields which are available. The quack usually purports to have a professional background disclosing diplomas and degrees to this effect, fictitious ones from actual schools and institutions or actual ones from diploma mills and similar phony schools. The validity can soon be determined by checking these reliable sources. Here again these sources are merely investigative leads. They must be followed through to the actual sources indicated and documented thoroughly.

The Registrar of Voters files, in the form of affidavits, has information as to place of birth, residences, party affiliation and employment. These are public record and are kept up to date and in file for a number of years. Changes are noted when new affidavits are filed permitting the investigator to determine past occupations claimed and former addresses.

The Plaintiff and Defendant files of the County Clerk's Office and the Clerk of the Municipal Court are invaluable. The pleadings and often transcripts of civil trials are filed with information in detail concerning the quack. This is a good place to start when attempting to develop similar acts and transactions to support collateral information regarding pattern, scheme and design (infra). The marriage license files located in the County Clerk's Office are useful for personal history, as are the divorce files also located there. These last frequently disclose real and personal property interests which otherwise would remain hidden. All partnership, corporate and sole proprietorship businesses are recorded by the County Clerk and the business/ fictitious names which may be used, disclosing all parties of interest.

The Office of the Clerk of the United States Court, the Office of the Referee in Bankruptcy and the Office of United States Marshal can be contacted for the same purposes concerning anything at the Federal level. The County Recorder's files have all the information concerning the ownership and interests in real estate. A trust deed, which is security for a promissory note (loan) will disclose the amount involved, the third party beneficiary, the trustee's identity and the file number, the detailed description of the parcel of land, the date of the transaction, the escrow number and location (company), and the mode of payment. The grant deed (conveyance) will show essentially the same information and the total valuation of the property involved (the I.R.S. stamps appearing on the face of the document indicate the tax paid; .55 for every $500.00). All this data is important when attempting to develop the quack's net worth, source and application of funds. Many other documents and instruments are also recorded in the public files such as chattel mortgages on personal property, tax liens, Federal and State, all mechanics liens and such other encumbrances as may be alleged against property, real or personal. In conjunction with the

Recorder's data, the files of the Assessor and County Tax Collector should be examined for parallel information. The Civil Division Records of the Sheriff's Department and the Municipal Court Marshall's Office should be queried. This will cover any processes emanating out litigation at either level of the court system, showing the amounts and properties involved and parties of interest.

If the quack has children, the census files in the various school districts' offices are useful in determining former addresses and occupations, other members of the family or guardians, current location, ostensible destination and actual place of new location, if different, as transcripts are normally forwarded.

All Federal, State, County, City and Township licensing bureaus should be contacted to determine the quack's exact operational status. These agencies have on file all fees paid, dates, parties of interest, location, lessor if any, type and nature of business and frequently the background or professional qualifications.

Everything heretofore said regarding the quack is not to be construed as limited to him. If a thorough investigation is being made the same processes and techniques are to be directed at his colleagues or any other person important to the case. The sources as related are not to be deemed all-encompassing or complete. They are set out primarily as guideposts for the investigator. Often the data he can develop from these will lead him to other agencies or individuals who can present even more detailed and accurate knowledge concerning the quack. This is something which is incumbent upon the investigator; develop his own routines, processes and sources and above all, if they are of the confidential type, protect them.

Similar acts and transactions are an important part of any case. This is the better means to support are allegation of specific intent to commit the offense. If they can be developed every effort should be made to document them in detail with the same care as is given the case in chief. Notice of related incidents come to the investigator in a variety of ways; other victims, concurrent operations of undercover agents, medical groups, individual doctors, Coronor's Office, Bureau of Vital Statistics, friends, relatives, etc. Publicity and advertising on the part of the less obscure quacks is often a lucrative source of data. The Hohensee species of medical con-men blatantly advertise to the world at large their operations and defy police interference. This, on occasion, can and does work against them. But the veneer of self-confidence is a tremendous weapon in their arsenal.

Current and former employees of the quack, especially those who might have become disenchanted, usually can provide the better insight into his scam. Before any approach is made, however, just as thorough background examination should be conducted on them as on the quack himself. Too often they prove to be as unstable as some of the victims and even more difficult to handle. It must be considered here, the investigator to a degree even under the most favorable conditions (to him at least) is, in essance, asking the employee to violate a trust and this is viewed with disapprobation even by quasi-con-men. They often do just this, but they don't like to be asked directly. The situation is further complicated by their justifiable fear of being too closely related to the scams unto the point of being declared co-principals or co-conspirators; even the other facets or embarrassment or shame become a part of the problem. Each one, then, must be evaluated on his relative merits and probable contribution to the total investigation.

In developing the similar acts it will be frequently found that inquiries will have to be initiated in widely separated areas. Medical quacks are usually peripatetic by nature and will seldom remain for extended periods in a single place unless the action is so good, official interference or surveillance so minimal and their capital outlay too great to disregard (health farms, resorts, etc.) to force their movement. Most of them are actually reincarnations of the old-time snakeoil peddlers who sold their products to the local yokles and then moved on to other lucrative spots. The widely flung places of activity, which must be covered by the investigator if he intends to establish a complete case, can cause real expense problems. Again, he must evaluate each possible source as to its merits to the total case. If the information and evidence is material then he should cover it; as a last resort an agency in the jurisdiction concerned can be requested to conduct some inquiries, but this is not as satisfactory as a personal on-the-spot investigation, regardless of the high degree of competency the corresponding agency may possess.

During the course of the background investigation the indentities of other quacks and related associates should be examined and the degree and nature of relationship ascertained. "Health Food Stores" and "Health Faddists" with their wheat-germ, vitamins, organic and otherwise grown concoctions are frequently panderers for the quack. It is not unusual for the "storeman" or the "faddist" to refer potential victims to the medical con-man, either innocently in misbegotten good belief or maliciously for profit similar to the condemned "fee-splitting" scheme. The oversale of vitamins which the human body cannot assimilate or need is not uncommon with this gentry. Those things which they as a group promote perhaps cannot in themselves be medically questioned, but their funneling of hapless victims into the web of the quack, urging in the circumvention of available ligitimate medical attention can and should be. If such a situation can be proven there should be no hesitancy in alleging a conspiracy. The manner, of course, in which this is established is by the agent/customer purchases over a period of time and surveillance (visually, photographically, electronically) to show personal contact between the suspects.

If the quack dispenses some sort of "medication" his source of supply must be identified. If the item is a legal and harmless compound which he would more likely purchase in bulk form, the chemist or pharmacist is usually an innocent party and normally cooperative. *After* the investigator has had his own laboratory analyze the item for its quantitive parts, interviews are proper. A complete documented sales record must be obtained. If, however, it is a narcotic, drug, poison or some other prohibited element, narcotics detectives should be consulted and their advice adhered to for possible additional felony counts of possession and sales. They have the knowledge of the sources of illicit drugs and the technical competence, through training and experience, to handle this facet of the investigation and should nominally direct proceedings. This should not be construed to mean the fraud investigator will take no part; he should, but in this phase be guided by the specialist.

Devices and equipment that are employed by the quack

must be examined if possible. If not, at least their source ascertained and those involved in their manufacturing and installation identified. Plans, diagrams, blue-prints and photographs are to be developed in detail with an analysis of each component, including serial and model numbers clearly set forth, their limitations and ostensible purpose. Again purchase orders and other forms which will document a sales record must be secured. Normally the investigator will contact machinists, carpenters, plumbers, electricians and electronic people, all of whom are usually called upon for basic installation by the quack. He may take care of the final adjustments, changes, alterations and repairs, but often legitimate technicians are used for the initial work involved. Take into consideration, there are only three normal sources of power and energy in a structure; electricity, gas and water, all must be handled and inspected by the utility company employees. The uses to which these items are put normally must be channeled by the appliance people whose work is also inspected. To this point the information is available to the investigator who has enough initiative to review the city and county building permit files, utility company records and contact various appliance firms. Each of these will have information which can be put together affording a fairly comprehensive picture of what the quack is using on the premises.

The premises occupied by the quack is of material interest to the case; the ownership should be determined, including all parties of interest. If it is a leased structure, the lessor must be contacted if feasible (without jeopardy to the inquiry) and all points of the lease discussed and copies obtained. If the quack is the owner of record and necessary information can be obtained by examining the Recorder's files which in turn will lead to the escrow and title company records (supra). All utilities companies should be contacted as their records will denote inception dates, operational expenses, installation costs and types and energy loads. Surveillance should be maintained as continuously as possible, not only during the working hours, but *after* hours also. Frequently previously undisclosed associates and other parties can be identified. The trash receptacles are of prime importance. Vital records, surgical instruments, bandages, discarded equipment, fixtures and other interesting items of probative value and investigative interest often end up there. The investigator should either examine the contents surreptitiously or make arrangements for a detailed search at the dumpsite. If the latter method is used and the debris can be logically traced from the premises to the disposal point without intervening interruption or contamination there is, at least at this time in legal history, no probable constitutional problems concerning search and seizure to be raised.

The medical con-man like any other proprietor of a business, either sales or service, must purchase on a fairly continuous basis, operating supplies. A surveillance usually will pinpoint most legitimate vendors. These should be contacted, again with the same admonishment to the investigator regarding possible jeopardy to the case. If the move is deemed proper and expeditious, the purchased items or supplies by amount, nature, grade, condition, cost and frequency pattern must be determined. The nature can be anything which is endemic to a medical business, whether concerned solely with ambulatory patients or those who take up temporary residence, such as a clinic, resort or health farm. For example, one profitably operating "health farm" placed great emphasis on the curative value of "organically grown food which is planted and cultivated in our own truck gardens located on the ranch." However, a surveillance disclosed almost daily deliveries from a produce market located in a nearby suburban community. Inquiry with the cooperative market manager, documentarily supported and later confirmed by agents/patients at the farm, disclosed at least 85% of the vegetables consumed by the patients and quacks alike came from the very prosaic public market and not from the highly touted "organic gardens." Of course the patients were unaware of the substitution in their daily diet and were paying outrageous prices for so-called emendatory foodstuff. This situation was admissable to show cumulative acts of misrepresentation.

The quack, as can be seen, is not adverse to public proclamation. Advertising is a recognized operational expense, often his greatest next to legal and accounting advice. The investigator must contact the advertising agencies, job-printers, photographers (artists also) collecting all the exemplars available. The contracts and agreements entered into between the quack and the suppliers are material to the case. It is of prime importance to obtain the *original* and *corrected* matrixes of any printed matter, including written forms submitted by the quack. If multilithic or mimeographic reproductions are used, the situation is not changed; *get those things which he submitted.* They tend to show the intent and frame of mind existent at the time of making or preparing a public representation. If they can be shown as false or misleading the investigator has taken a long stride towards establishing his case. Also, if the quack has submitted to any interviews for the news media regardless whether television, radio, newspapers magazines or any form of public statement, contact the reporter and obtain his original notes, recorded tapes or such form of transcription which he may have.

An actual victim of the medical con-man is the best evidence which can be developed. As previously pointed out they are not always inclined to be helpful but they can on occasion be approached through the medium of friends, relatives or even physicians. Even these frequently will create problems, the physician because he lacks the time or is disinclined to become involved, the others for a wide variety of rationalizations. However, if the impediments are overcome and contact is made, a complete medical history of the victim is outlined. This shows the deleterious effect or the lack of effect of the quack's ministrations on the victim, physically and emotionally. There must be a detailed interview in which is developed the method of inducement employed to cause the victim to undergo the treatment, the representations made by the quack and his agents acting at his behest and under his direction, the diagnosis, prognosis, treatments, and amounts expended as to form and purpose (bank records are invaluable here), any written agreements and the dates, times, places in their proper sequence in which any action related to the scam occurred and any other persons present who may be witnesses.

The victim must, if lucid, furnish information concerning all persons who were directly, and even indirectly, involved in the quack's operation. Not only the "doctor", "nurses" and "technicians," but disclosures unto even the laboring help on the premises, delivery people, vendors and other patients and their respective debilities.

The reason for developing an actual victim to supplement the undercover agent is the salient effect it has at trial. This is not a sub-rosa, unethical tactic as the defense will aver, protesting entrapment, but an honest disclosure of the actual situation. The quack, then, is not viewed merely as a thief who was caught in his false representations to, and proven by, a police agent, but in fact a dangerous and deadly growth in the community which must be eradicated.

This last appelation is not unfair or even challengeable. The Los Angeles Superior Court just recently (and finally), after an original conviction in 1962 had been overturned by the Appelate Court and the Supreme Court, was the scene of the conviction of a chiropractor for second degree murder. He had treated an 8-year old girl for cancer by a method of iodine water and vitamins. The Appelate Court, in its great wisdom upon reversing the lower court at the first trial, said "the crime itself was not inherently dangerous to human life. The chiropractor/ quack had induced the parents of the child to remove her from a hospital one day before she was to undergo critical eye surgery. He assured them he could cure her of cancer. The child died about two months later. He, however, still had the sheer gall to hand the parents a bill of $739.00 for his "services." He was indicted and tried on the technical charge of murder which results when a death occurs during the commission of a felony, in this case, grand theft. The Supreme Court overruled this as a misapplication of the felony murder rule. However, upon retrial in July, 1969 he was again convicted of the same offense.

Many pitfalls are in the investigator's pathway when he nears the end-purpose of his work, the arrest and trial. It cannot be urged too strongly, never arrest without a warrant based upon information and complaint or an indictment. There is no hurry. If the quack is successful enough to merit attention, he is not going to run away. The nature of his business precludes obscurity. He basks in the glow of quasi-public adulation and approval, and he will not leave a good thing easily or quickly. The methodical, steady, inexorable, relentless investigative approach without deviation at the last moment because of baseless anxiety is the better way. File the affidavit for the warrant of search covering everything on the premises which is relevant to the case (if the investigative reports have been clear, concise, accurate and detailed, there should be no problem here). Be prepared for photography and diagraming in detail and have sufficient vehicles to transport and impound devices, machinery, equipment, medications and records. The peril at this point is the inadvertant taking of something which is considered material to the case based upon the theory of search incidental to arrest and not covered by the warrant. A recent U.S. Supreme Court case (*Chimel vs Calif.*) apparently has curtailed this police technique for some time to come. Any evidence developed later through such an error (as now construed) would be inadmissable and possibly vitiate the whole case by invocation of the "poisoned tree doctrine," thus destroying perhaps months of long tedious work. There is no excuse for such a development.

Occasionally the purveyors of questionable compounds sold openly to the public can be restrained. The District Attorney of Santa Clara, California in 1968 filed a *civil* complaint against a quack firm advertising and selling a panacean program including a variety of concoctions purporting to give relief to, and curing persons afflicted with arthritis, diabetis, heart and vascular diseases. The complaint was based upon the findings of the California Department of Public Health laboratories which declared the compounds as useless and having no effect. The injunctive measure is useful to law enforcement to prevent further harm to the public. If the investigator finds himself at an impasse and evidently can go no further, the statute of limitations perhaps being a factor coupled with the inability to develop sufficient evidence to support an allegation of theft by false pretenses, the injunctive process can be an answer. But, it is no substitute for an intensive properly conducted criminal investigation to put the quack where he belongs; out of circulation, not just temporarily out of business.

CHAPTER VII

"INVESTIGATIVE SOURCES"

IN 1969 there was appointed to the White House special staff a veteran investigative reporter, Clark R. Mollenhoff. For twenty-five years he had created and maintained an enviable reputation for being able to develop information on a variety of important issues among which were labor racketeering and other facets of organized crime. It was always mystifying to less endowed and diligent colleagues how he seemed to be able to find some investigative leads which for unknown reasons eluded them in spite of their numerous "reliable" and "personal" contacts within and without the government. An analysis of his approach to a situation under inquiry disclosed that a larger part of his success was due to his indefatigable examination of public records. Many of his best leads came from checking records other reporters and/or investigators just did not know how to find, and even if they did happen to be confronted with the information in its recorded form, would not recognize it as such. He once told a friend that he liked the County Courthouse best of all government buildings because the records there were easily available in contrast to most state and federal buildings and offices, besides many of the records found at the latter were frequently duplicated at the county level because the impetus of the transaction in question was usually there. Mollenhoff taught many young neophyte reporters and investigators how to use the records to their best advantage the way he did.

What is related here about Mollenhoff is applicable to fraud investigators. The wealth of determinative information and investigative leads which is available in public records to anyone who will just take the time and make the effort is astounding. When one considers that just about every human activity in our society is touched on, directly or indirectly, by some regulatory or registering agency, both public and private, the value of such records is self-evident. To paraphrase what a veteran detective, who was widely experienced in both fraud and warrant-fugitive investigations, used to say, when instructing young new officers assigned to his division, "Remember, a man to live, must have something to eat, clothes to wear, a place to sleep, transportation, a source of funds and some social contact. These are the economic-legal-social fundamentals in our concept of society. All of these, because of the manner in which they are obtained, are the genesis of some sort of record. What you have to be able to do, is locate the record. Analyze each one of the necessities in the light of personal experience and think of things and persons which can be effected in some way when you obtain one of them. Logic, then, will indicate to you the path to take when ascertaining the same thing concerning someone else, whether it be a victim, suspect or a witness."

In other chapters of this book when discussing the investigative techniques which can be employed, a number of federal, state, county, municipal and private offices and agencies have been referred to as highly remunerative sources. This chapter will cover the operations of a number of these, other than the regularily constituted police type, so that the student is furnished a graphic example of their worth to him as an investigator. It is not inferred the list is all conclusive, but merely some of the avenues to be explored. Nor is it implied that the information available should be viewed as an end in itself. These are *leads* (other than those denominated official recordings—and even those) in the full meaning of the term; or an indication to the investigator what direction he possibly should take to authenticate such information he may already possess. Regardless of California legal connotations of the text the sources and their functions are uniform and applicable throughout the country.

County Assessor

It is the responsibility of a County Assessor to assess all property in his county (except public utilities) in uniform proportion to the market value. He must prepare an annual assessment roll and index wherein is shown the individual legal description and assessed value of all taxable land, the assessed value of improvements, and the assessed value of personal property. He is charged with the processing of all claims for property tax exemption for veterans, churches, welfare and other organizations of a charitable or eleemosynary nature. In addition, he is required to maintain many books and related records showing ownership, location, description and valuation of all taxable property within his county. The evaluation (appraisal) process is a continuing one and requires periodic review if level of uniformity in assessments as required by law is to be achieved.

Most assessors have a personal property appraisal division which evaluates all locally assessable personal property within the county in compliance with conditional and structural requirements. This includes, but is not limited to, commercial and industrial firms, livestock, farm equipment, machinery, poultry, boats, aircraft and related marine and aviation personality.

The Revenue and Taxation laws of most states require that every person owning a taxable personal property having an aggregate cost of thirty-thousand dollars or more shall file a written property statement. The code further provides that every person owning personal property which does not require the filing of a written property statement or owning real property, shall sign a real property statement upon the *request of the assessor*. The statement shall be made under penalty of perjury to the assessor of the county in which the property is situated.

All such property statements are subject to review and audit by the assessor. Certain of the audits are mandatory pursuant to law, others are discretionary upon the assessor. The review and processing of exemption claims is another responsibility of this division.

Information relating to hundreds of thousands of parcels of property is prepared and assembled by the assessor. The Records Division, as it is usually denominated, maintains the "Master Property Records" whereon are shown the latest recorded ownership, assessed valuation, location, legal description, tax code area and parcel number.

The assessor maintains cadastral maps of the county accurately detailing the complete inventory of all assessable land units or parcels. These maps are for the public convenience and for use in the field by the assessor's appraisers. Related to this, the assessor prepares "cuts" (land divisions caused by a sale or a portion, combination, new subdivision, etc.) for mapping and processing. There is also a continuing sales ratio program which is a statistical comparison of actual parcels to appraised values resulting in a sales ratio useful to the assessor (and others) in measuring the quality of the appraisals in a given area or any other grouping of appraisal results.

The assessor also makes investigations for tax roll corrections and Appeals Board action. He prepares tax roll corrections requests and maintains control and files of such corrections.

County Clerk

The County Clerk is required by law to provide a depository for the care and custody of a variety of official public records. He issues marriage licenses and, as an agent of the Federal Government, processes applications for passports. By determination of the County Board of Supervisors, he enforces collection of revenue due and owing the County for various services rendered by the County to individuals within the community. He accounts for all monies received or deposited with his office.

In many states he is frequently the ex officio clerk of the Superior Court and as such performs a number of functions related to the Court and its proceedings:

(1) He attends, via the person of a courtroom clerk who is a Deputy County Clerk, the sessions of the Court

(2) He keeps Registers of Actions and Indexes of Proceedings

(3) He issues Process and Notices, e.g. Summons, Writs, Subpoenas etc.

(4) He enters Judgments and Orders

(5) He keeps Records and Papers

(6) He is the custodian of Court exhibits

(7) He charges and collects statutory fees

The office which the County Clerk uses normally to handle

the daily transactions with the public is usually called the "Business Office." This Division of the Clerk's office:

(1) Receives the initial filing of any legal proceeding with the Superior Court in domestic, civil and criminal actions and in adoption and probate petitions, assigns case numbers and makes appropriate settings

(2) Receives for filing or deposit other documents and records such as fictitious names, articles of incorporation, medical and dental license registrations, etc. which are required by law to be filed locally

(3) Issues marriage licenses and processes passport applications

(4) Collects the statutory fee prescribed for each of the above processes

(5) Examines all applications and orders for the publication of summons in Civil cases and all orders submitted to the Court in connection with the Divorce Law (now called Family Relations) and Motion Calender

The Master Calender Division sets all Civil cases for pre-trial, schedules settlement conferences and mails notices of such settings to the attorneys involved, and assists the Presiding Judge in setting Civil cases for trial. The Division also is responsible for calling individually the number of jurors required for civil and criminal jury trials and for maintaining records of their service.

Many counties have created a separate Juvenile Court Division within the Clerk's office. This entity provides to the Juvenile Department of the Superior Court the same support and services as are provided by several other Divisions to the remaining Departments of the Court. It prepares the Juvenile Court calender; prepares notices of hearings on petitions, judgments, order and decrees; maintains a Register of Actions, drafts written orders on each matter heard by the Court; provides a courtroom clerk for each of the Juvenile Departments. In addition, they provide information to the Revenue and Collections Division on all detentions of juveniles in order timely efforts can be made to recoup detention charges from the parent(s) or the juvenile, or from some other responsible person.

The Probate Division examines and processes all documents

filed in connection with the guardianship of minors or incompetent persons, conservatorships, the estates of deceased or missing persons, proceedings for the determination in inheritance tax and adoption proceedings. It also provides advice and assistance on these matters to the Judge of the Probate Court. It maintains the Register of Actions for Probate and Adoption matters, prepares the Probate Calendar, and prepares and mails or posts all required notices.

The Records Division is responsible for the following:
(1) Processing all incoming documents in connection with Civil, Criminal, Domestic and Mental Health matters through the appropriate Register of Actions
(2) Prepares Criminal, Mental Health and Law and Motion Calendars and enters defaults
(3) Maintains and safeguards Superior Court records and archives
(4) Processes all appeals to the Superior Court from judgments and other orders of the Superior Court to the Court of Appeals
(5) Provides microfilm and photocopy services

The Superior Court Division staffs each department of the Court with a clerk who serves as a Constitutional Officer of that Court and attends each session, administers oaths to witnesses and interpreters, maintains case records, safeguards and accounts for exhibits and prepares minutes, orders and judgments of the Court.

The Revenue and Collections Division enforces the collection of revenue due and owing to the County primarily for various services performed by the County for individuals. The bulk of the accounts have been established for care rendered at the County Hospital but also accounts for care in various State and County Juvenile Detention facilities and to collect child support for both recipients and non-recipients of welfare aid. There are a number of Units or Bureaus within the Division to expedite the operations:
(1) Collections: Hard-core collection activity, using legal action, court order etc., while trying to avoid undue hardship on families.

(2) Skiptrace: Locating debtors who have moved, locating assets, verifying employment and general investigations concerning those who owe monies to the County

(3) Lien Service: Maintain property liens granted by the recipients of County aid, examine real estate transactions mortgages, trust deeds and quit-claims, thereby protecting the County's interests

(4) Support: Maintain vigilant surveillance to assure that those required by law to make support payments do so, initiate appropriate legal action when they do not, appear in court when required and maintain liaison with Family Service Division of the District Attorney's Office and the Welfare Department.

(5) Intake: Establish accounts, maintain files, assist collectors and skip-tracers.

The Accounting Division consists of a number of Units or Bureaus, two of which are of interest to investigators:

(1) Hospital and Insurance Billing: Bills of County patients receiving care at the County Hospital and the Community Mental Health Center. Searches medical records and liens. Prepares the necessary claims under Medi-Care and Medi-Cal for eligible patients as well as claims against other commercial insurance companies.

(2) Departmental Accounting: Maintains all departmental accounting records; records, controls and deposits receipts; administers all departmental trust fund activity; and controls budgetary transactions for the County Clerk;

County Recorder

The function of this office is best understood by considering the necessity of having a central place of record to which the public may have access for determining what has transpired that may have affect on some interest they may possess. A unique situation was created in the southwestern areas of this country many years ago. Under the Spanish and Mexican governments, there were no registry or recording laws and the first California

Legislature adopted a recording system in 1850. The primary purpose was to make property safely transferrable so it was necessary to create a device by which title to, or an interest in land, could be located in a convenient and safe place in order that persons intending to purchase or otherwise deal with land could determine ownership and the condition of the title. Recording of executed conveyances of real property imparts constructive notice to subsequent purchasers and encumbrancers. The Recorder is also the administrator of the Documentary Transfer Tax and collects the tax due on sales of real property within the county. The cities are entitled to half the tax collected on sales within their boundaries and the Recorder prepares a tax collection report by area to be used in apportionment of the tax revenue.

To enable the public to locate expeditiously the records they wish, the Recorder maintains alphabetic indices of the daily recordings by grantor and grantee (see exemplars). A numerical index is also available if one wishes to scan the recordings of a particular day without referring to the filmed record. To facilitate rapid searching, the daily grantor and grantee indices are consolidated monthly during the current period and semi-annually as the year progresses. The preparation of the index is accomplished by punch cards and verified by index clerks who are familiar with the finely defined details of all types of real estate transactions. A tabulating section then processes the cards to produce the indices promptly and accurately. The San Diego Recorder processes, with cross indexes, over two-hundred thousand multiple name recordings each year. Other Recorders handle comparable amounts in ratio to their size and population.

Some examples of records to be found in Recorder's office are:

Maps: Subdivision, Record of Survey and Parcel Deeds, mortgages, trust deeds, partnership certificates and agreements, assignments, notices of sale, transfer, pendency of action (Lis Pendens) and completion, mechanics liens, abstracts of judgments, Financing Statements filed under the Uniform Commercial Code, lien contracts, bills of sale, releases, satisfaction of judgments and reconveyances of trust deeds
Marriage records
Death records

The indices and records are open to the public and the Recorder's staff is available to assist anyone in becoming familiar with the manner of locating a record. The exemplars on the following pages illustrate typical recordings and the indices which are prepared as a means of locating the record. The contents of each exemplar discloses the informative data which the fraud

TEMPORARY WORK SHEET

INDEX OF GRANTEES

UNLESS OTHERWISE INDICATED DOCUMENTS ARE COPIED IN OFFICIAL RECORDS

SEE PAGE ONE FOR LIST OF STANDARD ABBREVIATIONS   DATE   JUN 4 1968   1968

GRANTEES AND PLAINTIFFS — ALSO MORTGAGEES, LESSEES, VENDEES, ASSIGNEES APPOINTEES, PARTIES WHOSE MORTGAGES ARE RELEASED ETC	GRANTORS AND DEFENDANTS — ALSO MORTGAGORS, LESSORS, VENDORS, DOING ASSIGNORS, APPOINTORS, PARTIES RELEASING, JUDGMENT DEBTORS, WILLS, BONDS, PARTIES AGAINST WHOM LIENS ARE CLAIMED OR ATTACH, MENTS ISSUED, MINING LOCATOR, NAME OF MINE, PROOF OF LABOR ETC	TITLE OF INSTRUMENT	NO	DAY	YR	FILE NO / PAGE
A B I INC	LOUISVILLE TITLE CO	TRUSTEES DD	6	04	68	987665
	ANDERSON JOHN	TRUSTEES DD	6	04	68	987665
	ANDERSON MARY	TRUSTEES DD	6	04	68	987665
DOE JANE	DOE JOHN	DEED	6	04	68	987660
DOE JOHN	SMITH MARY	DEED	6	04	68	987654
DOE JOHN	SMITH JOHN & MARY	TR DEED ASGT RENT	6	04	68	987654
DOE JOHN	A B C ELEC CO	RELEAS	6	04	68	987661
DOE JOHN	BLACK MARY	BILL SALE	6	04	68	987668
DUNBAR JAMES	SECUR TITLE INS CO	CANCELLATN	6	04	68	987669
	BROWN DONALD	CANCELLATN	6	04	68	987669
JONES JULES	BURR JAMES & VIOLA	MECH LIEN	6	04	68	987662
LIGHT HAROLD	BEAN CELIA	POWER ATTY	6	04	68	987663
MATTHEWS MARILYN	MATTHEWS JIM	REV P ATTY	6	04	68	987670
SMITH JOHN & MARY	DOE JOHN	DEED	6	04	68	987659
SMITH JOHN & MARY	DURBIN JAMES	ASGT TR DEED	6	04	68	987658
	DURBIN NANCY	ASGT TR DEED	6	04	68	987658

This represents the recordings indexed alphabetically by grantees.

NOTICE TO THE PUBLIC: THIS IS A TEMPORARY SHEET COMPILED FOR THE CONVENIENCE OF THE RECORDER IN THE PERFORMANCE OF THE DUTIES OF THAT OFFICE AND ALLOWED TO BE USED BY THE PUBLIC ONLY WHILE THE PERMANENT INDEX IS IN COURSE OF PREPARATION SEE PAGE 1 FOR STANDARD ABBREVIATIONS

TEMPORARY WORK SHEET
INDEX OF GRANTORS
UNLESS OTHERWISE INDICATED DOCUMENTS ARE COPIED IN OFFICIAL RECORDS
SEE PAGE ONE FOR LIST OF STANDARD ABBREVIATIONS

DATE   JUN 4 1968   BOOK   1968

GRANTORS AND DEFENDANTS — ALSO MORTGAGORS APPOINTORS PARTIES RELEASING JUDGMENT DEBTORS BILLS BONDS PARTIES AGAINST WHOM LIENS ARE CLAIMED OR ATTACHMENTS ISSUED ALL MINING NOTICES NAME OF DEBTOR	GRANTEES AND PLAINTIFFS — ALSO MORTGAGEES LESSEES VENDEES ASSIGNEES APPOINTEES PARTIES WHOSE MORTGAGES ARE RELEASED ETC ADDRESS OF DEBTOR		TITLE OF INSTRUMENT	WHEN RECORDED MO	DAY	YR	FILE NO / PAGE
A B C ELEC CO	DOE JOHN		RELEAS	6	04	68	987661
ANDERSON JOHN	A B I INC		TRUSTEES DD	6	04	68	987665
ANDERSON MARY	A B I INC		TRUSTEES DD	6	04	68	987663
BEAN CELIA	LIGHT HAROLD		POWER ATTY	6	04	68	987672
BLACK ANDREW J	DOC 456789 FEB 12 66	UCC	TERMINATION	6	04	68	987668
BLACK MARY	DOE JOHN		BILL SALE	6	04	68	987664
BROWN DONALD	DOC 87438 MAY 9 63		DEFAULT	6	04	68	987669
BROWN DONALD	DUNBAR JAMES		CANCELLATN	6	04	68	987655
BURR JAMES & VIOLA	JONES JULES		MECH LIEN	6	04	68	987642
DOE JOHN	SMITH JOHN & MARY		DEED	6	04	68	987655
DOE JOHN	DOC 22055 AUG 9 67		REG NTC	6	04	68	987697
DOE JOHN	DOE JANE		DEED	6	04	68	987660
DURBIN JAMES	SMITH JOHN & MARY		ASGT TR DEED	6	04	68	987658
DURBIN NANCY	SMITH JOHN & MARY		ASGT TR DEED	6	04	68	987658
GREEN JOHN A	5353 ROSE DR S D	UCC	FINCG STMT	6	04	68	987671
LOUISVILLE TITLE CO	A B I INC		TRUSTEES DD	6	04	68	987665
MARSH JANET			HOMESTEAD	6	04	68	987659
MARSH WILLIAM			HOMESTEAD	6	04	68	987659
MARSHALL JOHN & MARY			CESSN LABOR	6	04	68	987667
MATTHEWS JIM	MATTHEWS MARILYN		REV P ATTY	6	04	68	987670
SECUR TITLE INS CO	DUNBAR JAMES		CANCELLATN	6	04	68	987656
SMITH JOHN & MARY	DOE JOHN		TR DEED ASGT RENT	6	04	68	987657
SMITH JOHN & MARY	DOC 22055 AUG 9 67		REQ NTC	6	04	68	987657
SMITH MARY	DOE JOHN		DEED	6	04	68	987654
STONE DONALD	DOC 87438 MAY 9 63		DEFAULT	6	04	68	987664
STREET GORDON & JUNE			NTC COMPL	6	04	68	987666
WHITE THOMAS MOSES	5204 SUBMARINE WAY S D	UCC	CONTR STMT	6	04	68	987673

This represents the recordings indexed alphabetically by grantors.

investigator can use as documentary proof of some issue and as authoritative leads establishing affinity between persons and their joint or individual activity and interest.

The following listed agencies, public and private, with some of the activities falling within their jurisdiction and areas of op-

INSTRUMENTS FILED IN THE OFFICE OF THE COUNTY RECORDER OF SAN DIEGO COUNTY

GRANTOR	GRANTEE		DATE	TITLE OF INSTRUMENT	FEES	FILE NO./ PAGE
SMITH MARY	DOE JOHN			DEED	2 00	987660
DOE JOHN	SMITH JOHN & MARY			DEED	2 00	987660
SMITH JOHN & MARY	DOE JOHN			TR DEED ASGT RENT	2 00	987660
DOE JOHN		DOC 22055 AUG 9 67		REG NTC	2 00	987667
SMITH JOHN & MARY				REG NTC		
DURBIN JAMES	SMITH JOHN & MARY			ASGT TR DEED		987660
DURBIN NANCY				ASGT TR DEED		
MARSH WILLIAM				HOMESTEAD	2 00	987660
MARSH JANET				HOMESTEAD		
DOE JOHN	DOE JANE			DEED	2 00	987660
A B C ELEC CO	DOE JOHN			RELEAS	2 00	987661
BURR JAMES & VIOLA	JONES JULES			MECH LIEN	2 00	987660
BEAM CELIA	LIGHT HAROLD			POWER ATTY	2 00	987660
BROWN DONALD		DOC 87438 MAY 9 63		DEFAULT	2 00	987660
STONE DONALD				DEFAULT		
LOUISVILLE TITLE CO	A B I INC			TRUSTEES DD	2 00	987665
ANDERSON JOHN				TRUSTEES DD		
ANDERSON MARY				TRUSTEES DD		
STREET GORDON & JUNE				NTC COMPL	2 00	987666
MARSHALL JOHN & MARY				CESSN LABOR	2 00	987667
BLACK MARY	DOE JOHN			BILL SALE	2 00	987660
SECUR TITLE INS CO	DUNBAR JAMES			CANCELLATN	2 00	987660
BROWN DONALD				CANCELLATN		
MATTHEWS JIM	MATTHEWS MARILYN			REV P ATTY		987670
GREEN JOHN A	5353 ROSE DR S D		UCC	FINCG STMT	2 00	987671
BLACK ANDREW J		DOC 456789 FEB 12 66	UCC	TERMINATION	2 00	987672
WHITE THOMAS MOSES	5204 SUBMARINE WAY S D		UCC	CONTN STMT	1 00	987672

This represents the recordings indexed numerically and the amount of recording fee paid.

TOTAL FEES → 40 00 40 00

erations are basic sources for the investigator. The intelligent use of teletype inquiry, letter or personal contact with them will provide the investigator with a wealth of useful information from which he can establish his guidelines and areas of activity:

Department of Motor Vehicles

(1) Automobile and small craft registration data
(2) Division of Driver's licenses; certified copies of drivers' licenses with vehicle offenses history, photographs and fingerprints of licensee, former and current addresses

State Departments of Corporations and Federal Securities Exchange Commission

(1) Individuals, personal histories and complaints
(2) Companies, histories and complaints
(3) Fraud schemes, past and current
(4) Technical assistance of Departmental Investigators

Department of Justice (Some States)

(1) Bureau of Criminal Identification (Records)
(2) Bureau of Investigation (Special Agents) furnishes technical and field assistance to local agencies
(3) Statistics
(4) Crime Laboratory furnishes technical and scientific support to local agencies
(5) "M.O. Technicians" (method of operation) maintain up-to-date information concerning a wide variety of con-men and their current and past operations
(6) Registrar of Charitable Trusts has complete data, including Federal tax filings (contributions and all parties of interest) for all organizations which are viewed as "non-profit," tax-free groups
(7) Business Crimes and Trust Fund Unit is a specialized section within the agency (lawyers, accountants and investigators) which concerns itself with major frauds and will furnish technical and field assistance to local agencies

State Divisions of Real Estate and Federal Office of Interstate Land Sale Registration

(1) Real estate agents and brokers; personal histories and past and current complaints

(2) Real estate fraud schemes
(3) Technical assistance to local agencies

Legislative

(1) State Senate Committee reports on a variety of topics and subject-matter which is the basis of legislative concern and action; the reports cover witness testimony under oath and documentary evidence
(2) State Assembly Committee reports; same
(3) United States Senate Committee reports; same and on occasions technical assistance from investigators
(4) United States House of Representatives reports; same and assistance from investigative staffs

Registrar of Voters

(1) Birthplace of voter
(2) Residences, past and present
(3) Party affiliation

Merchants Credit Associations *

(1) Residences, ownership and other interests
(2) Personal histories
(3) Education and training
(4) Employment
(5) Bank and savings and loan associations, credit and loans
(6) Law suits, criminal and civil and domestic situations
(7) Purchasing patterns and habits

Business Analyses Firms *

(1) Personal histories of participants, past complaints
(2) Net worth of operations
(3) Background of operations and potential

---

* See note one; page 288

Better Business Bureau *

(1) Personal histories of participants, past complaints
(2) History of operations
(3) Past and current complaints

City Clerk's Office

(1) Comparable to the County Clerk in structure and purpose
(2) Municipal Court Records
(3) Legislative records of the City Council

American Insurance Association

(1) Individual histories
(2) Fraud schemes relating to insurance, fire, accident, etc.
(3) Policy-holder identification
(4) Previous claims
(5) Technical assistance from Special Agents to local agencies

National Auto Theft Bureau

(1) Complete history of a vehicle from factory to present owner
(2) Fraud and arson schemes
(3) Policy-holder information
(4) Previous claims
(5) Technical assistance from Special Agents to local agencies

Referee in Bankruptcy

(1) Background of petitioners
(2) Location of Assets
(3) Identity of persons with whom the petitioner has been dealing

(4) Detailed information concerning new worth (assets as opposed to liabilities)

Department of Public Health

(1) Personal histories of medical con-artists
(2) Medical fraud practices, past and current
(3) Technical assistance to local agencies

Federal Aviation Agency

(1) Licensed pilots, engineers and related personnel
(2) Aircraft registration

Alcohol Beverage Control Board

(1) Applications of all licensees with some personal history
(2) Current and past locations
(3) All parties of interest
(4) All offense and complaints, past and present
(5) Business activity level and potential
(6) Creditors

City Engineering Department

(1) City contracts with all parties of interest identified
(2) Private property permits
(3) Mapping section
(4) Sub-division processing

City Treasurer

(1) Business licenses
(2) All parties of interest in licensed business
(3) Claims and collections

Public Utility Companies

(1) Identity of subscribers
(2) Former addresses
(3) Employment of subscribers

Department of Consumers Affairs

(1) Accountants; personal history, past and present complaints
(2) Architects; same
(3) Athletes (boxing and wrestling), trainers, managers and promoters; same
(4) Cemetary operators, same
(5) Chiropractors; same
(6) Contractors; same
(7) Cosmetologists, beauticians and barbers; same
(8) Dentists; same
(9) Electronic repairmen and dealers; same
(10) Morticians; same
(11) Physicians, Surgeons and Osteopaths; same
(12) Optometrists; same
(13) Private Investigators; same
(14) Short-hand Reporters; same
(15) Veterinarians; same
(16) Registered Nurses; same
(17) Licensed Vocational Nurses; same
(18) Pharmacists; same

Department of Corrections

(1) Location and activities of parolees
(2) Associates of parolees
(3) Personal histories of parolees

National Crime Information Center

(1) Stolen, missing or recovered firearms
(2) Stolen articles

(3) Wanted persons
(4) Stolen or wanted vehicles
(5) Stolen license plates
(6) Stolen, embezzled or missing securities

This last named item is of prime importance to the fraud investigator. The files contain serially numbered identifiable securities which have been the object of theft, embezzlement or otherwise missing from their proper holder. Securities, for this purpose, include currency (real and counterfeit) and those documents or instruments which are of the type traded in securities exchanges. Included are warehouse receipts, traveler's checks and money orders. It does not presently (1969) carry personal notes, checks, cashier's checks or certified checks.

Securities are basically described in terms of type, serial number, denomination, issuer and owner (and social security number if the owner is a person). Other descriptive expressions which are helpful to identify a security are readily available from observation of the item and are termed "sinking fund," "Series A," "collateral trust," "cumulative," "convertible," etc. The date of the theft, the identity of the agency holding the theft report and case number are included in the file.

The files are useful because of the mobility of the security thieves and the speed at which NCIC can advise an agency whether a questionable security has been entered as a stolen or embezzled item. To make a proper inquiry it is essential to furnish type, serial number and the denomination although it is possible to obtain information concerning a security taken from one person by giving type, owner and/or social security number of the owner.

One of the best resources an investigator can avail himself to is the annually published Government Organization Manual. This book, obtained from the Government printing office at a very nominal price, lists every office or function within the federal structure and in fair detail outlines the activities and the recorded information available to the public. It is astounding, when on occasion an examination is made, the prolixity of agencies which have parallel interest. All of these can make a worthwhile contribution to the investigator's case information. Most states publish a comparable book furnishing data concerning agencies at that and the local level which are readily available to the investigator. Don't ignore these resources as being too mundane. No one can know or anticipate all areas of vested interests in any matter. They all can and will contribute.

---

* Note 1

The enactment by Congress in 1970 of the "Fair Credit Reporting Act" has placed a number of limitations on the sources of non-criminal information and the methods which can be employed to obtain such data. Sections 604 and 608 are of particular interest as they relate to the "permissible purposes of reports" and limited type available to governmental agencies. The act also creates civil and criminal sanctions for violations of its provisions. There are a number of states which have enacted similar statutes. The investigator is cautioned to familiarize himself with these various laws before making any inquiries which could be viewed as an encroachment. The only feasible avenue open is to conduct, as far as possible, a parallel investigation covering the same ground as the credit agency. This means in a large part, extensive use of *public records,* surveillance and personal contact, when deemed advisble, with the suspect's associates. In other words an interpolative process, which in fact is the essence of the investigative process anyway.

CHAPTER VIII

REAL ESTATE FRAUDS

R EAL PROPERTY, one of man's most coveted, yet probably most troublesome and costly of his possessions, notwithstanding domestic and vehicle problems, is an area replete with sharp practices and charlatans of all hues. A fraud inquiry in this sector creates unusual demands on both the investigator and prosecutor. They both must be conversant with real property law, terminology endemic to sales, title, escrow and the procedures, processes and practices employed. To achieve this they must have a working knowledge of applicable provisions of the Civil Code, Real Estate Code, Penal Code and publications of the Division of Real Estate such as the "Reference Book": to name a few.

The subject-matter of this chapter is real property, ground if you wish; that expanse upon which is constructed buildings for various purposes or used for growing crops or even a buffer zone between the holder and others. As students and investigators we are primarily interested in the methods and means of transferring and hypothecating title, legally and otherwise, and the machinations resorted to by both buyers and sellers to achieve their goals. First, in developing this expertise, determine the nature of real property. It includes all of the "freehold" interests together with such things closely associated with the land; fixtures, structures, growing crops, minerals and water, and the rights thereto. "Freehold" means the interest one has in the land and is basically of two qualities: (1) immobility, in other words immovable, a fixed thing and (2) of undetermined duration. Next, all land is governed by the laws of the state or territory wherein it is located (lex loci). And third, any conveyance (transfer of title) of real properties must be done by instruments in writing. This last is the key to many intricate puzzles which will attract inquiries.

The term instrument means, as we have seen in other chapters of this text, an agreement expressed in writing, signed and delivered by one person to another, transferring or effecting in some manner the title to a debt of duty. All other writings then are technically documents. Those instruments which normally relate to real property are grant deeds, quit-claim deeds, trust deeds, mortgages and promissory notes.

The grant deed passes title, rights and interest with the implied warranty the land or property is free from defects and encumbrances except those disclosed by the grantor (seller) and that the grantor is in fact the owner with power of sale. The quit-claim deed merely conveys the grantor's interests without any warranty; it gives up any and all interest or rights the grantor may have or may be forthcoming although unknown to him; it is used to quiet title.

The requisites for a conveyance of real property are as follows: (a) The grantor/seller must have actual title or a marketable interest in the land, (b) There must be a grantee/buyer, (c) The land must be sufficiently described in the legal manner, (d) There must be operative words of conveyance (e) There must be an acknowledgment by the grantor/seller if there is to be a recordation, (f) Both the grantor/seller and the grantee/buyer must be competent to enter into a contract.

The trust deed is an instrument, in some jurisdictions, which conveys property to a third person or corporation, partnership called a trustee for the purpose of securing a debt (usually in the form of a promissory note), with the power of sale in the trustee, upon default, to apply the proceeds in payment thereof. The trustee acts only upon default and until such time has none of the legal powers incident to ownership. It is a three-party instrument, the debtor/trustor conveys to the trustee to be reconveyed upon his satisfactory performance, but in case of his failure to perform, to be sold for the satisfaction of his obligation to the beneficiary who loaned him the funds.

The word "title" in this connection is somewhat misleading as it gives the trustee only such interest as is necessary to carry out the terms of the trust. In effect, it is little more than a mortgage with power to convey, the trustee getting title for security purposes only, leaving a legal estate and normal rights or occupancy and ownership with the trustor.

The mortgage is an instrument which is used to pledge property to another as security for the performance of an act such as the payment of a debt but title to, and possession of the property covered does not change hands from the mortgagor to the mortgagee. Upon the mortgagor's failure to perform his obligation (payment of the debt) the mortgagee then takes title *after* he goes through foreclosure proceedings, a court action. It is a two-party instrument.

In some jurisdictions, trust deeds are normally used in hypothecating or securing property transfers, although, infrequently the mortgage can, and is, used. The main differences are the number of parties involved, the situation of the title, the statute of limitations, the remedies available and redemption. The parties have been given above. The title is a factor in that when mortgaged, it is not conveyed but merely a lien thereon is created; if a trust deed is important, as an action to foreclose on

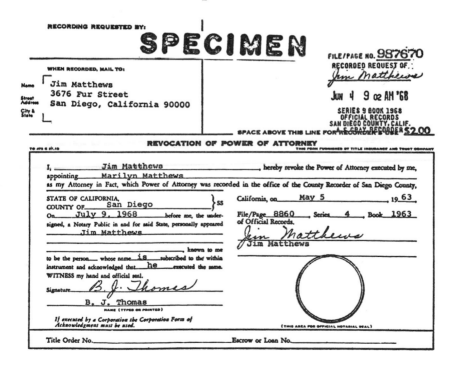

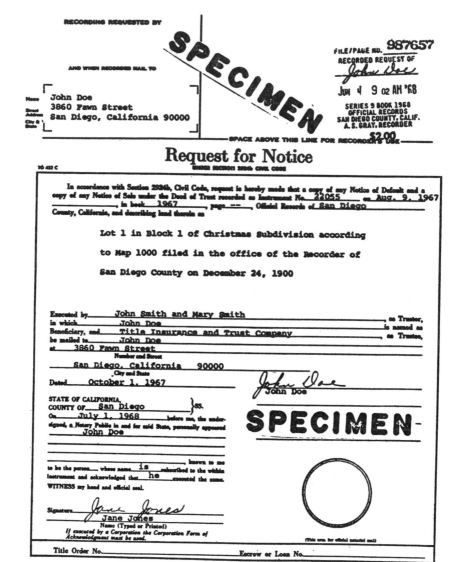

STATE OF CALIFORNIA
UNIFORM COMMERCIAL CODE—TRANSITION CONTINUATION STATEMENT—FORM UCC-T

82432   IMPORTANT—Read instructions on back before completing form

SPECIMEN

This **CONTINUATION STATEMENT** is presented for filing pursuant to the California Uniform Commercial Code

1. DEBTOR (LAST NAME FIRST)		1A. SOCIAL SECURITY OR FEDERAL TAX NO.
White, Thomas Moses		3920-49-4957

1B. MAILING ADDRESS	1C. CITY, STATE	1D. ZIP CODE
5204 Submarine Way	San Diego, California	90000

2. ADDITIONAL DEBTOR (IF ANY) (LAST NAME FIRST)		2A. SOCIAL SECURITY OR FEDERAL TAX NO.

2B. MAILING ADDRESS	2C. CITY, STATE	2D. ZIP CODE

3. SECURED PARTY

NAME	Open Door Finance Company	3A. SOCIAL SECURITY NO., FEDERAL TAX NO. OR BANK TRANSIT AND A.B.A. NO.
MAILING ADDRESS	5725 Smiley Avenue	
CITY San Diego STATE California ZIP CODE 90000		9357-27-3738

4. ASSIGNEE OF SECURED PARTY

NAME		4A. SOCIAL SECURITY NO., FEDERAL TAX NO. OR BANK TRANSIT AND A.B.A. NO.
MAILING ADDRESS		
CITY STATE ZIP CODE		

5. The original Security Agreement described below between the foregoing Debtor(s) and Secured Party(ies) is still effective. (Describe original Security Agreement.)

Chattel Mortgage

6. The original Security Agreement was filed or refiled, recorded or rerecorded with (check one)   [ ] Secretary of State

[X] Recorder of _____San Diego_____ County

It was filed or refiled, recorded or rerecorded on _____September 3_____ 19_63_

File number or recordation data is as follows_____12345_____

6A [ ] Check if no filing or recording was required to perfect a security interest prior to January 1, 1965.

SPECIMEN

7.

(Date)_____June 4_____ 19_68_

8. This Space for Use of Filing Officer (Date, Time, File Number, Filing Office)

Open Door Finance Company

By: *Robert Strong*   _Manager_
(SIGNATURE OF SECURED PARTY)   (TITLE)

FILED UCC 987373

9.   Return Copy to

NAME	Open Door Finance Company
ADDRESS	5725 Smiley Avenue
CITY, STATE AND ZIP	San Diego, California 90000

(1) FILING OFFICER COPY
STANDARD FORM—FILING FEE $2.00   UNIFORM COMMERCIAL CODE—FORM UCC-T
Approved by the Secretary of State

RECORDER'S USE ONLY

FILE/PAGE NO. 987665
RECORDED REQUEST OF
LOUISVILLE TITLE COMPANY

JUN 4 9 02 AM '68

SERIES 9 BOOK 1968
OFFICIAL RECORDS
SAN DIEGO COUNTY, CALIF.
A. S. GRAY, RECORDER
$2.00

SPECIMEN

UNINCORPORATED AREA

DOCUMENTARY TRANSFER TAX $22.00
TRANSFER TAX PAID
A. S. GRAY, COUNTY RECORDER

TRUSTEE'S DEED

Executed by _____ **Louisville Title Company** _____, a corporation, and herein called Trustee, to _____ **A.B.I., Inc.** _____

The Deed of Trust hereinafter referred to was recorded on **April 3, 1965**, in Book **1965**, Series **6**, Page **143614** of Official Records of **San Diego**, County, State of California. In this deed, this county and state will be referred to as "said County and State". The Deed of Trust was made to secure obligations stated therein and the payment of the Note or Notes for the total sum recited on the face of the Deed of Trust, with interest, and to secure any other money or obligations, the repayment of which was secured by that Deed of Trust.

Default occurred as set forth in a notice of default and election to sell under said deed of trust, which notice of default was recorded in Book **1968**, Page/Series **45765** of Official Records of said County and State.

Trustee has complied with all requirements of law regarding the giving of notices. After three months elapsed from the recording of said notice of default, trustee posted a written notice of the time and place of sale in a public place where said property was to be sold, caused publication of said notice in the **Daily Transcript** published at **San Diego**, California, a newspaper of general circulation printed and published in the city or judicial district in which said property or part thereof is situated; and by posting a copy of said notice of sale on the real property described in said deed of trust, as required by law. The posted notices and the published notice contained the description of the property to be sold.

Said publication and posting continued for a period not less than 20 days prior to the date of sale contained in said notice and thereafter Trustor offered the property described in said deed of trust for sale at public auction on **July 9, 1968** at **11** o'clock at the **south door of County Courthouse** in said county and state.

Trustee sold said property, which is hereinafter described, according to law, to the Grantee above named for **$20,000.00**, subject, however, to all prior liens and encumbrances. Said Grantee was the highest bidder for said property. No person offered to take any part of said property for the amount of principal, interest, advances, and cost.

In consideration of the foregoing recitals and $ **20,000.00** paid to Trustee by Grantee, trustee by power vested in it by said deed of trust, does hereby grant, bargain, sell and convey, but without warranty of title, to grantee, all that certain real property situate in said County and State, Described as follows:

Lot 246, Pleasure Manor according to the map thereof
No. 2546 filed in the office of the County Recorder
March 6, 1938

Trustors: John Anderson and Mary Anderson

without covenant or warranty, express or implied, regarding the title to said property or any encumbrance thereon.

DATED _____ **July 15, 1968** _____

SPECIMEN

LOUISVILLE TITLE COMPANY   AS TRUSTEE

By *R. B. Gregg*
R. B. Gregg   Vice President

By *Malva Stone*
Malva Stone   Asst. Secretary

STATE OF CALIFORNIA } ss.
COUNTY OF SAN DIEGO

On _____ **July 15** _____, 19 **68**, before me, the undersigned, a Notary Public in and for said County and State, personally appeared _____ **R. B. Gregg** _____ known to me to be Vice President and _____ **Malva Stone, assistant secretary** _____, the corporation that executed the within instrument as trustee, and known to me to be the persons who executed the within instrument on behalf of the corporation therein named, and acknowledged to me that such corporation executed the same as trustee, and acknowledged to me that such corporation executed the within instrument pursuant to its by-laws.

In witness whereof, I have hereto affixed by signature, and my official seal of office, in said County, on the date of this certificate.

Joan Cord
Joan Cord, Notary Public in and for said County and State.

FP 832

Form 855—4-52   THIS FORM FURNISHED BY UNION TITLE INSURANCE AND TRUST COMPANY   Order No._____

NOTICE OF CESSATION FROM LABOR

NOTICE is hereby given that:

1. Cessation from labor on work of improvement on the hereinafter described property actually occurred on the____9th____

day of_____July_____, 19_68_.

SPECIMEN

2. That such cessation from labor continued until the giving of this notice.

3. The name of the CONTRACTOR, if any, for such work of improvement as a whole was_____

_____Roy Ricks Construction Company_____
(If no contractor for work of improvement as a whole, insert "none.")

4. The property on which said work of improvement was being done is in the City of____San Diego____,

County of San Diego, State of California, and is described as follows:

Lot 3, Block 2 in Middletown Addition according
to map No. 756 filed May 6, 1925

5. The NAMES, ADDRESSES AND NATURE OF TITLE OF ESTATE OR INTEREST of every person (including the undersigned) owning any interest in said property is as follows:

NAME IN FULL	COMPLETE ADDRESS	NATURE OF TITLE OF ESTATE OR INTEREST
John Marshall	7200 Maya Drive San Diego, Calif. 90000	husband and wife as joint tenants
Mary Marshall	7200 Maya Drive San Diego, Calif. 90000	husband and wife as joint tenants

6. Dated____July 10____, 19_68_.

John Marshall
John Marshall

State of California } ss.
County of San Diego }

____John Marshall____

being first duly sworn, deposes and says that_____ owner of the property described in the foregoing notice, that __he__ has read the same, and knows the contents thereof, and that the facts therein stated are true.

(SIGNATURE) *John Marshall*
John Marshall

Subscribed and sworn to before me this__10th__ day of____July____, 19_68_.

Jane Smith
Jane Smith
Notary Public in and for said County and State

(If this notice is executed by a corporation, use corporate form of verification below and affix corporate seal)

State of California } ss.
County of San Diego }

being first duly sworn, deposes and says: That he is an officer, to wit,_____of_____

a corporation, which is the owner of the property described in the within Notice of Cessation executed by said corporation; that he has read the same and knows the contents thereof and that the facts therein stated are true of his own knowledge; that he makes this verification for and on behalf of said corporation.

(SIGNATURE)_____

Subscribed and sworn to before me this_____ day of_____, 19___.

_____
Notary Public in and for said County and State.

When recorded, this instrument is to be mailed to:

____John Marshall____

____500 Oak Street____

____San Diego, California   90000____

SPACE BELOW FOR RECORDER'S USE ONLY

SPECIMEN

FILE/PAGE NO. 987667
RECORDED REQUEST OF
John Marshall

JUN 4 9 02 AM '68

SERIES 9 BOOK 1968
OFFICIAL RECORDS
SAN DIEGO COUNTY, CALIF.
A. S. GRAY, RECORDER
$2.00

RECORDING REQUESTED BY

FILE/PAGE NO. **987663**

RECORDED REQUEST OF

Harold Light

WHEN RECORDED MAIL TO

JUN 4 9 02 AM '68

SERIES 8 BOOK 1968
OFFICIAL RECORDS
SAN DIEGO COUNTY, CALIF.
A. E. GRAY, RECORDER
$2.00

Name
Street
Address
City &
State

Harold Light
4656 Dark Street
San Diego, California
92101

(SPACE ABOVE THIS LINE FOR RECORDER'S USE)

POWER OF ATTORNEY

GENERAL

Know All Men by These Presents: That I, _____ Celia Beam _____

the undersigned (jointly and severally, if more than one) hereby make, constitute and appoint _____ Harold Light _____

my true and lawful Attorney for me and in my name, place and stead and for my use and benefit:

(a) To ask, demand, sue for, recover, collect and receive each and every sum of money, debt, account, legacy, bequest, interest, dividend, annuity and demand (which now is or hereafter shall become due, owing or payable) belonging to or claimed by me, and to use and take any lawful means for the recovery thereof by legal process or otherwise, and to execute and deliver a satisfaction or release therefor, together with the right and power to compromise or compound any claim or demand;

(b) To exercise any or all of the following powers as to real property, any interest therein and/or any building thereon: To contract for, purchase, receive and take possession thereof and of evidence of title thereto; to lease the same for any term or purpose, including leases for business, residence, and oil and/or mineral development; to sell, exchange, grant or convey the same with or without warranty; and to mortgage, transfer in trust, or otherwise encumber or hypothecate the same to secure payment of a negotiable or non-negotiable note or performance of any obligation or agreement;

(c) To exercise any or all of the following powers as to all kinds of personal property and goods, wares and merchandise, choses in action and other property in possession or in action: To contract for, buy, sell, exchange, transfer and in any legal manner deal in and with the same; and to mortgage, transfer in trust, or otherwise encumber or hypothecate the same to secure payment of a negotiable or non-negotiable note or performance of any obligation or agreement;

(d) To borrow money and to execute and deliver negotiable or non-negotiable notes therefor with or without security; and to loan money and receive negotiable or non-negotiable notes therefor with such security as he shall deem proper;

(e) To create, amend, supplement and terminate any trust and to instruct and advise the trustee of any trust wherein I am or may be trustor or beneficiary; to represent and vote stock, exercise stock rights, accept and deal with any dividend, distribution or bonus, join in any corporate financing, reorganization, merger, liquidation, consolidation or other action and the extension, compromise, conversion, adjustment, enforcement or foreclosure, singly or in conjunction with others of any corporate stock, bond, note, debenture or other security; to compound, compromise, adjust, settle and satisfy any obligation, secured or unsecured, owing by or to me and to give or accept any property and/or money whether or not equal to or less than the amount owing in payment, settlement or satisfaction thereof;

(f) To transact business of any kind or class and as my act and deed to sign, execute, acknowledge and deliver any deed, lease, assignment of lease, covenant, indenture, indemnity, agreement, mortgage, deed of trust, assignment of mortgage or of the beneficial interest under deed of trust, extension or renewal of any obligation, subordination or waiver of priority, hypothecation, bottomry, charter-party, bill of lading, bill of sale, bill, bond, note, whether negotiable or non-negotiable, receipt, evidence of debt, full or partial release or satisfaction of mortgage, judgment and other debt, request for partial or full reconveyance of deed of trust and such other instruments in writing of any kind or class as may be necessary or proper in the premises.

Giving and Granting unto my said Attorney full power and authority to do and perform all and every act and thing whatsoever requisite, necessary or appropriate to be done in and about the premises as fully to all intents and purposes as I might or could do if personally present, hereby ratifying all that my said Attorney shall lawfully do or cause to be done by virtue of these presents. The powers and authority hereby conferred upon my said Attorney shall be applicable to all real and personal property or interests therein now owned or hereafter acquired by me and wherever situate.

My said Attorney is empowered hereby to determine in his sole discretion the time when, purpose for and manner in which any power herein conferred upon him shall be exercised, and the conditions, provisions and covenants of any instrument or document which may be executed by him pursuant hereto; and in the acquisition or disposition of real or personal property, my said Attorney shall have exclusive power to fix the terms thereof for cash, credit and/or property, and if on credit with or without security.

The undersigned, if a married woman, hereby further authorizes and empowers my said Attorney, as my duly authorized agent, to join in my behalf, in the execution of any instrument by which any community real property or any interest therein, now owned or hereafter acquired by my spouse and myself, or either of us, is sold, leased, encumbered, or conveyed.

When the context so requires, the masculine gender includes the feminine and/or neuter, and the singular number includes the plural.

WITNESS my hand this ___ 17th ___ day of ___ July ___ 19 68

Celia Beam
Celia Beam

State of California,

County of: San Diego } ss. **SPECIMEN**

On ___ July 17, 1968 ___, before me, the undersigned, a Notary Public in and for said State, personally appeared ___ Celia Beam ___

known to me to be the person ___ whose name ___ is ___ subscribed to the within instrument and acknowledged that ___ she ___ executed the same.

(Seal) *Sarah Bright*
Sarah Bright

Witness my hand and official seal

NAME (TYPED OR PRINTED)
Notary Public in and for said State.

SPECIMEN

AND WHEN RECORDED MAIL TO

> Jane Doe
> 5555 Quint Street
> San Diego, California 90000

Name
Street Address
City & State

MAIL TAX STATEMENTS TO

> Moon Mortgage Company
> 5000 El Moro Boulevard
> San Diego, California 90000

Name
Street Address
City & State

SPACE ABOVE THIS LINE FOR RECORDER'S USE

DOCUMENTARY TRANSFER TAX $ —0—

TO 402 CA (9-66)

Quitclaim Deed

AFFIX $_____ I. R. STAMPS ABOVE

THIS FORM FURNISHED BY TITLE INSURANCE AND TRUST COMPANY

FOR A VALUABLE CONSIDERATION, receipt of which is hereby acknowledged,

John Doe

hereby REMISE(S), RELEASE(S) AND FOREVER QUITCLAIM(S) to

Jane Doe

the following described real property in the   city and   county of San Diego,
state of California:

> Lot 6, Block 3 of Black Bounty Subdivision,
> according to Map No. 9000 filed in the
> office of the Recorder of San Diego County
> on January 3, 1920.

Dated _____ June 1, 1968 _____

John Doe
JOHN DOE

SPECIMEN

STATE OF CALIFORNIA
COUNTY OF__San Diego__ } SS.
On _____July 1, 1968_____ before me, the under-
signed, a Notary Public in and for said State, personally appeared
__John Doe__

_____, known to me
to be the person___whose name__is__subscribed to the within
instrument and acknowledged that__he__executed the same.
WITNESS my hand and official seal.

Signature __*Jane Jones*__
Jane Jones
Name (Typed or Printed)
If executed by a Corporation the Corporation Form
of Acknowledgment must be used.

(This area for official notarial seal)

Title Order No._____   Escrow or Loan No._____

MAIL TAX STATEMENTS AS DIRECTED ABOVE

AND WHEN RECORDED MAIL TO

Name **Mr. and Mrs. John Smith**
Street Address **100 Christmas Way**
City & State **San Diego, California 90000**

FILE/PAGE NO. **987655**
RECORDED REQUEST OF
Mary Smith

JUN 4   9 02 AM '68

SERIES 9 BOOK 1968
OFFICIAL RECORDS
SAN DIEGO COUNTY, CALIF.
A. S. GRAY, RECORDER
$2.00

MAIL TAX STATEMENTS TO

Name **Same as above**
Street Address
City & State

DOCUMENTARY TRANSFER TAX $ *16.50*

TRANSFER TAX PAID
A. S. GRAY, COUNTY RECORDER

SPACE ABOVE THIS LINE FOR RECORDER'S USE

AFFIX $
I. R. STAMPS IN SPACE ABOVE

TO 404 CA (11-66)

SPECIMEN

Joint Tenancy Grant Deed

THIS FORM FURNISHED BY TITLE INSURANCE AND TRUST COMPANY

FOR A VALUABLE CONSIDERATION, receipt of which is hereby acknowledged,

John Doe

hereby GRANT(S) to

John Smith and Mary Smith, husband and wife,
, AS JOINT TENANTS,

the real property in the   City and
County of **San Diego,**   State of California, described as:

Lot 1, Block 1 in Christmas Subdivision according

to Map 1000 filed in the office of the Recorder of

San Diego County on December 25, 1900.

SPECIMEN

Dated: **July 9, 1968**

John Doe
John Doe

STATE OF CALIFORNIA
COUNTY OF **San Diego** } SS.
On **August 9, 1968** before me, the under-
signed, a Notary Public in and for said State, personally appeared
John Doe

, known to me
to be the person whose name **is** subscribed to the within
instrument and acknowledged that **he** executed the same.
WITNESS my hand and official seal.

Signature *Jane Jones*

Jane Jones
Name (Typed or Printed)

(This area for official notarial seal)

Title Order No. Escrow or Loan No.

MAIL TAX STATEMENTS / DIRECTED ABOVE

RECORDED REQUESTED BY

WHEN RECORDED MAIL TO

Name: Jules Jones
Street: 6420 Overbright Street
City & State: San Diego, California
92101

FILE/PAGE NO. 987662
RECORDED REQUEST OF
Jules Jones

JUN 4   9 02 AM '68

SERIES 9 BOOK 1968
OFFICIAL RECORD
SAN DIEGO COUNTY, CALIF.
A. S. GRAY, RECORDER $2.00

SPACE ABOVE THIS LINE FOR RECORDER'S USE

MECHANIC'S LIEN

NOTICE IS HEREBY GIVEN that: Pursuant to the provisions of the California Code of Civil Procedure,

Jules Jones

hereafter referred to as "Claimant" (whether singular or plural) claims a lien upon the real property and buildings, improvements or structures thereon, described in Paragraph Five (5) below, and states the following:

(1) That the demand of Claimant after deducting all just credits and offsets, is **$60.25**

(2) That the name of the owner(s) or reputed owner(s) of said property, is (are) **James Burr** and **Viola Burr, husband and wife**

Name, or state "unknown"

(3) That Claimant did from **July 8**, 19 68, until **July 8**, 19 68,
perform labor and/or supply materials as follows: **50 ft. of electric wire, two switches, three hours labor**

General statement of kind of work done or materials furnished, or both.

for the construction, alteration or repair of said buildings, improvements or structures, which labor, or materials, or both of them, were in fact used in the construction, alteration or repair of said buildings, improvements or structures, the location of which is set forth in Paragraph Five (5) below.

(4) Claimant was employed by **James Burr**
and furnished materials, if any, to **James Burr**

(5) That the property upon which said lien is sought to be charged is situated in the City of **San Diego**
County of **San Diego**, State of California, commonly known as **6568 Easy Street**,
San Diego

Street Address

and more particularly described as **Lot 236, Horton's Purchase, according to the map thereof No. 256, filed in the office of the County Recorder June 15, 1921**

as per Map recorded in Book _____ at Page _____ of _____ Records of _____
County, California.

DATED: This **10th** day of **July** 19 68

Jules Jones
JULES JONES

(Verification for Individual Claim)	(Verification for other than Individual Claim)
STATE OF CALIFORNIA, } ss.	STATE OF CALIFORNIA, } ss.
County of **San Diego**	County of _____
Jules Jones	_____ July sworn, deposes and says: That _____
being first duly sworn, deposes and says: That ____ he is the _____ Claimant named in the foregoing claim of lien, that ____ he has read the same and knows the contents thereof, and that the statements therein contained are true; and that it contains, among other things, a correct statement of h **is** demand, after deducting all just credits and offsets.	_____ that _____ and for that reas____ affidavit on behalf of said _____ that he has read the sa____ contains there-of, and that the statemen____ood are true; and that it contains, among t____rrect statement of the demand of Claim____ting all just credits and offsets.
Jules Jones (Signature of affiant) Jules Jones Subscribed and sworn to before me	(Signature of affiant) Subscribed and sworn to before me
July 10, 19 68 _Mava Smith_ Mava Smith	_____, 19 ____
NAME (TYPED OR PRINTED) Notary Public in and for said State.	NAME (TYPED OR PRINTED) Notary Public in and for said State.

MECHANIC'S LIEN—1024—Rev. 6-64

8 pt. type or lar...

SPECIMEN

AND WHEN RECORDED MAIL TO

Name
Street Address
City & State

John Doe
3860 Fawn Street
San Diego, California 90000

SPACE ABOVE THIS LINE FOR RECORDER'S USE

MAIL TAX STATEMENTS TO

Name
Street Address
City & State

Same as above

DOCUMENTARY TRANSFER TAX $ 11.00

TRANSFER TAX PAID
A. S. GRAY, COUNTY RECORDER

Grant Deed

AFFIX I.R.S. $_____ Above

THIS FORM FURNISHED BY TITLE INSURANCE AND TRUST COMPANY

TO 408 C (4-67)

FOR A VALUABLE CONSIDERATION, receipt of which is hereby acknowledged,

Mary Smith

hereby GRANT(S) to

John Doe, a single man,

the following described real property in the   City of San Diego,
County of   San Diego   , State of California:

Lot 4 of Block 8 in Nick's Subdivision according to

Map 3400 Filed in the office of the County Recorder

July 10, 1908

SPECIMEN

Dated June 5, 1968

Mary Smith
Mary Smith

STATE OF CALIFORNIA
COUNTY OF San Diego   } SS.
On   June 5, 1968   before me, the under-
signed, a Notary Public in and for said State, personally appeared
Mary Smith

_____ known to me
to be the person___ whose name is subscribed to the within
instrument and acknowledged that she executed the same.
WITNESS my hand and official seal.

Signature *B. J. Thomas*
B. J. Thomas
Name (Typed or Printed)

(This area for official notarial seal)

Title Order No._____   Escrow or Loan No._____

MAIL TAX STATEMENTS AS DIRECTED ABOVE

SPECIMEN

DECLARATION OF HOMESTEAD
(Joint Declaration of Husband and Wife)

KNOW ALL MEN BY THESE PRESENTS: That the undersigned, to wit: **William Marsh**

and **Janet Marsh**

(Name of husband)   (Name of wife)

do severally certify and declare as follows:

(1) They are husband and wife.

(2) _____**William Marsh**_____ is the head of a family, consisting of himself and wife

(Name of husband)

and **a son – Lawrence and a daughter – Jean**

(3) They are now residing on the land and premises located in the City of _____

County of **San Diego** State of California, and more particularly described as follows:

Lot 30, Nortonia Resubdivision No. 1 according to Map No. 5120

(4) They claim the land and premises hereinabove described together with the dwelling house thereon, and its appurtenances, as a Homestead.

(5) They estimate the actual cash value of the land and premises hereinabove described to be **twenty-five thousand dollars** ($**25,000.00**) Dollars.

(6) No former declaration of homestead has been made by them, or by either of them, except as follows: [1]

(7) The character of said property so sought to be homesteaded, and the improvement or improvements which have been affixed thereto, are as follows: [2]

3 bedroom stucco house and attached garage

IN WITNESS WHEREOF, they have hereunto set their hands this **29th** day of **July** 19**68**

William Marsh

William Marsh   (Husband)

Janet Marsh

Janet Marsh   (Wife)

Footnotes 1 and 2: See Reverse Side.

STATE OF CALIFORNIA } ss.	STATE OF CALIFORNIA } ss.
COUNTY OF **San Diego**	COUNTY OF **San Diego**
On **July 29** 19**68**	**William Marsh**
before me, the undersigned, a Notary Public in and for said State, personally appeared **William Marsh**	and **Janet Marsh** husband and wife, each, being first duly sworn, deposes and says: That he/she is one of the declarants in the foregoing declaration of homestead; that he/she has read the foregoing declaration and knows the contents thereof; and that the matters therein stated are true of his/her own knowledge.
and **Janet Marsh**	*William Marsh* (Husband)
	Janet Marsh (Wife)
known to me to be the persons whose names are subscribed to the within instrument, and severally acknowledged to me that they executed the same. Witness my hand and official seal.	Subscribed and Sworn to before me on **July 29** 19**68**
(Seal) *Margaret Jones*	(Seal) *Margaret Jones*
Notary Public in and for said State.	Notary Public in and for said State.

SPECIMEN

■■■   CANCELLATION **SPECIMEN**
of
Notice of Default and Election to Sell Under Deed of Trust

WHEREAS, _____James Dunbar_____
by deed of trust dated __May 8__, 19_60_, recorded __May 9__, 19_60_ in Book __1960__ page __87638,Official__ Records of
__San Diego__ County, California, did grant and convey to __Security Title Insurance Company__
a corporation, as trustee, all that certain real property situate in the ___City and___
County of _____San Diego_____, State of California, described as follows:

      Lot 8, Block 13 of East Ridge Subdivision filed in

      the office of the Recorder of San Diego County on

      February 8, 1917

WHEREAS, A written Declaration of Default and Demand for Sale was executed and delivered to said trustee, and thereafter
a Notice of Default and Election to Sell under the terms of said deed of trust was recorded __Aug. 8__, 19_63_, in Book __1963__
page __129630__ of __Official__ Records, in the office of the County Recorder of said County, to the record of which Notice of
Default reference is hereby made; and

WHEREAS, The undersigned owner and holder of the obligations secured by said deed of trust desires to cancel said Declaration
of Default and Demand for Sale, and also said Notice of Default and Election to Sell;

NOW, THEREFORE, Notice is hereby given to said ___Security Title Insurance Company___
_____, trustee as aforesaid, and all other persons, that said Declaration of Default and Demand for Sale,
together with said Notice of Default and Election to Sell, is hereby cancelled, rescinded and annulled, and is of no further force or effect
whatsoever.

IN WITNESS WHEREOF, The owner and holder of said note and obligation has executed and delivered this notice to said trustee,
and has caused the certificate hereto attached to be executed by said trustee this __20th__ day of __July__, 19_68_.

                                        Donald Brown
                                        Donald Brown

_____Security Title Insurance Company_____, trustee named in the
deed of trust hereinabove referred to, hereby certifies that written notice of the cancellation of said Declaration of Default and
Demand for Sale of the property described in the deed of trust hereinabove mentioned was delivered to said trustee on the
__20th__ day of __July__, 19_68_, and further certifies that prior thereto, no sale was made
of the title and interest conveyed to said trustee by said deed of trust

                                   SECURITY TITLE INSURANCE CO. Trustee

STATE OF CALIFORNIA
COUNTY OF   } ss.
San Diego   By *Sally Miller*
On____July 20, 1968____before me,   Sally Miller, Secretary-Treasurer
the undersigned, a Notary Public in and for said County and   SPACE BELOW FOR RECORDERS USE ONLY
State, personally appeared
      Sally Miller, Secretary
      Treasurer   FILE/PAGE NO. **987669**
                                       RECORDED REQUEST OF
known to me to be the person____ whose name __is__
subscribed to the within instrument, and acknowledged to   SECURITY TITLE INSURANCE COMPANY
me that__she__executed the same.
WITNESS my hand and Official Seal   JUN 4 9 02 AM '68

      Jack Crate   SERIES 9 BOOK 1968
      Jack Crate   OFFICIAL RECORDS
Notary Public in and for Said County and State.   SAN DIEGO COUNTY, CALIF.
AFTER RECORDING MAIL TO   A. S. GRAY, RECORDER
                                       $2.00
__Security Title Insurance Company__
__Third and "A" Streets__
__San Diego, California   90000__

RECORDING REQUESTED BY

SPECIMEN

FILE/PAGE NO. 987656
RECORDED REQUEST OF
John Doe

JUN 4   9 .02 AM '68

SERIES 9 BOOK 1968
OFFICIAL RECORDS
SAN DIEGO COUNTY, CALIF.
A. S. GRAY, RECORDER
$2.00

AND WHEN RECORDED MAIL TO

Name John Doe
Street Address 3860 Fawn Street
City & State San Diego, California 90000

———— SPACE ABOVE THIS LINE FOR RECORDER'S USE ————

TO 498 C (OPEN END)   SHORT FORM DEED OF TRUST AND ASSIGNMENT OF RENTS

This Deed of Trust, made this   8th   day of   July, 1968   , between

John Smith and Mary Smith

, herein called TRUSTOR,

whose address is   100 Christmas Way,   San Diego,   California   90000   ,
(number and street)   (city)   (zone)   (state)

TITLE INSURANCE AND TRUST COMPANY, a California corporation, herein called TRUSTEE, and

John Doe

, herein called BENEFICIARY,

Witnesseth: That Trustor IRREVOCABLY GRANTS, TRANSFERS AND ASSIGNS to TRUSTEE IN TRUST, WITH POWER OF SALE,
that property in   San Diego   County, California, described as:

Lot 1, Block 1 of Christmas Subdivision according

to Map 1000 filed in the office of the Recorder

of San Diego County on December 24, 1900.

TOGETHER WITH the rents, issues and profits thereof, SUBJECT, HOWEVER, to the right, power and authority given to and conferred upon Beneficiary by paragraph (10) of the provisions incorporated herein by reference to collect and apply such rents, issues and profits.
For the Purpose of Securing: 1. Performance of each agreement of Trustor incorporated by reference or contained herein. 2. Payment of the indebtedness evidenced by one promissory note of even date herewith, and any extension or renewal thereof, in the principal sum of $ 10,000.00 executed by Trustor in favor of Beneficiary or order. 3. Payment of such further sums as the then record owner of said property hereafter may borrow from Beneficiary, when evidenced by another note (or notes) reciting it is so secured.
To Protect the Security of This Deed of Trust, Trustor Agrees: By the execution and delivery of this Deed of Trust and the note secured hereby, that provisions (1) to (14), inclusive, of the fictitious deed of trust recorded in Santa Barbara County and Sonoma County October 18, 1961, and in all other counties October 23, 1961, in the book and at the page of Official Records in the office of the county recorder of the county where said property is located, noted below opposite the name of such county, viz.:

COUNTY	BOOK	PAGE	COUNTY	BOOK	PAGE	COUNTY	BOOK	PAGE	COUNTY	BOOK	PAGE
Alameda	435	684	Kings	792	833	Placer	895	301	Sierra	29	335
Alpine	1	250	Lake	362	39	Plumas	151	5	Siskiyou	468	181
Amador	104	348	Lassen	171	471	Riverside	3005	523	Solano	1105	182
Butte	1145	1	Los Angeles	T2955	899	Sacramento	4331	62	Sonoma	1851	689
Calaveras	145	152	Madera	810	170	San Benito	271	383	Stanislaus	1715	456
Colusa	296	617	Marin	1858	339	San Bernardino	5567	61	Sutter	572	297
Contra Costa	3978	47	Mariposa	77	292	San Francisco	A332	905	Tehama	401	289
Del Norte	78	414	Mendocino	579	530	San Joaquin	2470	311	Trinity	93	366
El Dorado	568	456	Merced	1547	538	San Luis Obispo	1151	12	Tulare	2294	275
Fresno	4636	572	Modoc	184	851	San Mateo	4078	420	Tuolumne	135	47
Glenn	422	184	Mono	52	429	Santa Barbara	1878	860	Ventura	2062	386
Humboldt	657	527	Monterey	2194	538	Santa Clara	5336	341	Yolo	653	245
Imperial	1091	501	Napa	639	86	Santa Cruz	1431	494	Yuba	334	486
Inyo	147	598	Nevada	305	320	Shasta	684	528			
Kern	3427	60	Orange	5889	611	San Diego	Series 2 Book 1961, Page 183887				

(which provisions, identical in all counties, are printed on the reverse hereof) hereby are adopted and incorporated herein and made a part hereof as fully as though set forth herein at length; that he will observe and perform said provisions; and that the references to property, obligations, and parties in said provisions shall be construed to refer to the property, obligations, and parties set forth in this Deed of Trust.
The undersigned Trustor requests that a copy of any Notice of Default and of any Notice of Sale hereunder be mailed to him at his address hereinbefore set forth.

Signature of Trustor

John Smith
John Smith
Mary Smith
Mary Smith

STATE OF CALIFORNIA
COUNTY OF San Diego } SS.

On July 9, 1968 before me, the undersigned, a Notary Public in and for said State, personally appeared
John Smith and Mary Smith

, known to me
to be the person**s** whose name**s** **are** subscribed to the within instrument and acknowledged that **they** executed the same.
WITNESS my hand and official seal.

Signature _Jane Jones_
Jane Jones
Name (Typed or Printed)

Title Order No.

Escrow or Loan No.

(This area for official notarial seal)

SPECIMEN

SPECIMEN
BILL OF SALE

For value received, the undersigned Vendor hereby sells, assigns and transfers to _____

_____ John Doe _____

as Vendee all right, title and interest of the Vendor in and to the following property situated

_____ A. B. C. Cafe, 1130 Union Street, San Diego, California _____

_____

to-wit:

      1 - Chest Type Freezer

      1 - Walk-in Box

FILE/PAGE NO. 987668
RECORDED REQUEST OF
John Doe
JUN 4 9 02 AM '68
SERIES 9 BOOK 1968
OFFICIAL RECORDS
SAN DIEGO COUNTY, CALIF.
A. S. GRAY, RECORDER
$2.00

SPECIMEN

and said Vendor does hereby represent to and covenant to and with said Vendee that at the time of execution hereof, Vendor is lawfully possessed in his own right of a good title to the above described property and that he has good right and lawful authority to sell and deliver the same, and that the same is free of all encumbrances of whatsoever kind or nature. The singular as used herein includes the plural.

WITNESS the hand and seal of the Vendor this _____ 15th _____ day of

_____ July _____, 19 68.

RETURN TO:

A.B.C. Cafe
1130 Union Street
San Diego, California

Mary Black
_____ Mary Black _____
Vendor

RECORDING REQUESTED BY

SPECIMEN

AND WHEN RECORDED MAIL TO

FILE/PAGE NO. **987658**

RECORDED REQUEST OF

John Smith

JUN 4 9 02 AM '68

SERIES 9 BOOK 1968
OFFICIAL RECORDS
SAN DIEGO COUNTY, CALIF.
A. S. GRAY, RECORDER
$2.00

```
Name      Mr. and Mrs. John Smith
Street    3000 Oak Street
Address   San Diego, California 90000
City &
State
```

————— SPACE ABOVE THIS LINE FOR RECORDER'S USE —————

Assignment of Deed of Trust

TO 414 C   THIS FORM FURNISHED BY TITLE INSURANCE AND TRUST COMPANY

For Value Received, the undersigned hereby grants, assigns and transfers to __John Smith__
_____and Mary Smith_____
all beneficial interest under that certain Deed of Trust dated____January 5, 1955_____,
executed by_____John Doe_____
_____, Trustor ,
to_____Security Title Insurance Company_____ Trustee,
and recorded as Instrument No.__1043_____ on __January 6, 1955___ in book __7830__
page __340__, of Official Records in the County Recorder's office of_____San Diego_____County,
California, describing land therein as:

      Lot 3, Block 9 in Read's Subdivision filed in the

      office of the Recorder of San Diego County on

      May 5, 1928

Together with the note or notes therein described or referred to, the money due and to become due thereon with
interest, and all rights accrued or to accrue under said Deed of Trust.
Dated____July 5, 1968_____

STATE OF CALIFORNIA,
COUNTY OF____San Diego_____}ss.
On____July 5, 1968___ before me, the under-
signed, a Notary Public in and for said County and State, personally
appeared____James Durbin and____
      Nancy Durbin

James Durbin
James Durbin
Nancy Durbin
Nancy Durbin

SPECIMEN

_____, known to me
to be the person _S_ whose name _S_ **are** subscribed to the within
instrument and acknowledged that __they__ executed the same.
WITNESS my hand and official seal.

(Seal)
Signature *Jack Henry*
     Jack Henry
     Name (Typed or Printed)
Notary Public in and for said County and State

If executed by a *Corporation the Corporation Form of*
Acknowledgment must be used.

Title Order No._____

Escrow or Loan No._____

STATE OF CALIFORNIA

UNIFORM COMMERCIAL CODE — FINANCING STATEMENT — FORM UCC-1

IMPORTANT — Read instructions on back before filling out form

SPECIMEN

This FINANCING STATEMENT is presented for filing pursuant to the California Uniform Commercial Code

1. DEBTOR (LAST NAME FIRST)		1A. SOCIAL SECURITY OR FEDERAL TAX NO.
Green, John A.		0505-55-1234
1B. MAILING ADDRESS	1C. CITY, STATE	1D. ZIP CODE
P. O. Box "A"	San Diego, California	92000
1E. RESIDENCE ADDRESS (IF AN INDIVIDUAL AND DIFFERENT THAN 1B)	1F. CITY, STATE	1G. ZIP CODE
5353 Rose Drive	San Diego, California	92000

2. ADDITIONAL DEBTOR (IF ANY) (LAST NAME FIRST)		2A. SOCIAL SECURITY OR FEDERAL TAX NO.

5. SECURED PARTY
NAME   XYZ Finance Company
MAILING ADDRESS 3003 Money Avenue
CITY San Diego STATE California ZIP CODE 90000
5A. SOCIAL SECURITY NO., FED. TAX NO. OR BANK TRANSIT AND A.B.A. NO.
2232-02-3345

7. This FINANCING STATEMENT covers the following types or items of property (if crops or timber, include description of real property on which growing or to be grown):

Household goods located at 5353 Rose Drive, San Diego, Calif.

SPECIMEN

By: *John A. Green* (Date) June 4 1968
XYZ Finance Company
By: *Robert Strong* manager

11. Return Copy to
XYZ Finance Company
3003 Money Avenue
San Diego, California 90000

(1) FILING OFFICER COPY
STANDARD FORM—FILING FEE $2.00
Approved by the Secretary of State

FILED - UCC 987671

STATE OF CALIFORNIA
UNIFORM COMMERCIAL CODE—FINANCING STATEMENT CHANGE—FORM UCC-2
IMPORTANT—Read instructions on back before completing form

SPECIMEN 987672

This STATEMENT is presented for filing pursuant to the California Uniform Commercial Code

1. FILE NO. OF ORIG. FINANCING STATEMENT	1A. DATE OF FILING OF ORIG. FINANCING STATEMENT	1B. DATE OF ORIG. FINANCING STATEMENT	1C. PLACE OF FILING ORIG. FINANCING STATEMENT
456789	2-12-66	2-10-66	COUNTY RECORDER

2. DEBTOR (LAST NAME FIRST)		2A. SOCIAL SECURITY OR FEDERAL TAX NO.
Black, Andrew J.		0076-54-3210

2B. MAILING ADDRESS	2C. CITY, STATE	2D. ZIP CODE
2121 Diamond Place	San Diego, California	90000

3. ADDITIONAL DEBTOR (IF ANY) (LAST NAME FIRST) — 3A. SOCIAL SECURITY OR FEDERAL TAX NO.

3B. MAILING ADDRESS	3C. CITY, STATE	3D. ZIP CODE

4. SECURED PARTY

NAME	Joe Friendly Loan Company	4A. SOCIAL SECURITY NO., FEDERAL TAX NO. OR BANK TRANSIT AND A.B.A. NO.
MAILING ADDRESS	4857 Sunny Lane	
CITY	San Diego STATE California ZIP CODE 90000	9384-46-3847

5. ASSIGNEE OF SECURED PARTY (IF ANY)   5A. SOCIAL SECURITY NO., FEDERAL TAX NO. OR BANK TRANSIT AND A.B.A. NO.

NAME	
MAILING ADDRESS	
CITY STATE ZIP CODE	

6.
A ☐ CONTINUATION—The original Financing Statement between the foregoing Debtor and Secured Party bearing the file number and date shown above is continued. If collateral is crops or timber, check here ☐ and insert description of real property on which growing or to be grown in Item 7 below.

B ☐ RELEASE—From the collateral described in the Financing Statement bearing the file number shown above, the Secured Party releases the collateral described in Item 7 below.

C ☐ ASSIGNMENT—The Secured Party certifies that the Secured Party has assigned to the Assignee above named, all the Secured Party's rights under the Financing Statement bearing the file number shown above in the collateral described in Item 7 below.

D ☒ TERMINATION—The Secured Party certifies that the Secured Party no longer claims a security interest under the Financing Statement bearing the file number shown above.

E ☐ AMENDMENT—The Financing Statement bearing the file number shown above is amended as set forth in Item 7 below. (Signature of Debtor required on all amendments.)

F ☐ OTHER

7.

SPECIMEN

8.

(Date) June 4 1968	CODE	9. This Space for Use of Filing Officer (Date, Time, Filing Office)
	1	
By: *Andrew J. Black*	2	
SIGNATURE(S) OF DEBTOR(S) (TITLE)	3	
Joe Friendly Loan Company	4	
By: *William Kelly* *manager*	5	FILED - UCC
SIGNATURE(S) OF SECURED PARTY(IES) (TITLE)	6	FILE/PAGE NO. RECORDED REQUEST OF SECURED PARTY Jun 4 9 02 AM '68 SERIES 9 BOOK 1968 OFFICIAL RECORDS SAN DIEGO COUNTY, CALIF. A. S. GRAY, RECORDER $2.00

10.
Return Copy to	7	
NAME Joe Friendly Loan Company	8	
ADDRESS 4857 Sunny Lane		
CITY AND STATE San Diego, California 90000	9	

(1) FILING OFFICER COPY

STANDARD FORM—FILING FEE $2.00   UNIFORM COMMERCIAL CODE—FORM UCC-2
Approved by the Secretary of State

WHEN RECORDED PLEASE MAIL TO:

Donald Brown

4555 El Dorado Street

La Mesa, California

SPECIMEN

RECORDERS USE ONLY:

FILE/PAGE NO. **987664**

RECORDED REQUEST OF

Donald Brown

JAN 4 9 02 AM '68

SERIES 9 BOOK 1968
OFFICIAL RECORDS
SAN DIEGO COUNTY, CALIF.
A. S. GRAY, RECORDER **$2.00**

Notice of Default and Election to Sell Under Deed of Trust

NOTICE IS HEREBY GIVEN:

THAT PACIFIC COAST TITLE INSURANCE CO., a corporation, is Trustee under that certain deed of trust dated ___May 8, 1963___, executed by ___Donald Stone___, and recorded on ___May 9, 1963___, as Instrument No. ___87438___ in the Official Records of the County of San Diego; covering the real property in the City of ___San Diego___, County of San Diego, State of California, described as:

    Lot 8, Block 10 of West Ridge Subdivision, filed in the office of the Recorder of San Diego County on February 8, 1917

THAT said deed of trust was given to secure payment of_____ promissory note for $___25,000.00___, payable with interest thereon as therein provided, which note was dated ___May 6___, 19_63_, and payable to Donald Brown

THAT a breach of the obligation for which said Deed of Trust was given as security has occured in this, that default has been made under the terms of said Note and Deed of Trust in that the installment of principal and interest due upon said Note on ___April, 1968___, was not then paid; that the same has not since been paid;

THAT an amount of $___22,325.65___, representing the unpaid balance of the principal sum of said note and interest thereon from ___April, 1968___, is owing and unpaid.

THAT by reason of said default the undersigned, present beneficiary under such deed of trust, has executed and delivered to said Trustee a written Declaration of Default and Demand for Sale, and ha surrendered to said Trustee said deed of trust and all documents evidencing obligations secured thereby, and ha declared and do hereby declare all sums secured thereby immediately due and payable, and ha elected and do hereby elect to cause the above described trust property to be sold, after three months shall have elapsed following the recordation hereof, to satisfy the obligations secured thereby.

Dated ___June 5, 1968___

STATE OF CALIFORNIA
COUNTY OF San Diego } ss.

On ___June 6___, 19_68_, before me, the undersigned, a Notary Public in and for said County and State, personally appeared

    Donald Brown

known to me to be the person___whose name _is_ subscribed to the within instrument and acknowledged that _he_ executed the same. WITNESS my hand and official seal.

Laura Gains

(Seal)   Laura Gains
Notary Public in and for said County and State
My Commission expires ___February 4, 1970___

Donald Brown
Donald Brown

SPECIMEN

Order No.

FP 186

Recording Requested By

SPECIMEN

FILE/PAGE NO. **987666**
RECORDED REQUEST OF
owner

JUN 4 9 02 AM '68

SERIES 9 BOOK 1968
OFFICIAL RECORDS
SAN DIEGO COUNTY, CALIF.
A. S. GRAY, RECORDER
$2.00

When Recorded Mail To
Mr. Gordan Street
6872 More Street
San Diego, California 92101

Order No.
Escrow No.

SPACE ABOVE THIS LINE FOR RECORDER'S USE

NOTICE OF COMPLETION

NOTICE IS HEREBY GIVEN THAT:

1. The undersigned is owner of the interest or estate stated below in the property hereinafter described.
2. The FULL NAME of the undersigned is .... June Street
3. The FULL ADDRESS of the undersigned is .. 2632 Britt Street, San Diego
4. The NATURE OF THE TITLE of the undersigned is: In fee.
   (If other than fee, strike "In fee" and insert, for example, "Purchaser under Contract of Purchase," or "Lessee.")
5. The FULL NAMES and FULL ADDRESSES OF ALL PERSONS, if any, who hold title with the undersigned as joint tenants or as tenants in common are:

   NAMES   ADDRESSES

   Gordon Street
   June Street

6. The names of the PREDECESSORS in interest of the undersigned, if the property was transferred subsequent to the commencement of the work of improvement herein referred to are: (If no transfer made, insert "none.")

   NAMES   ADDRESSES

7. A work of improvement on the property hereinafter described was COMPLETED on .. July 16, 1968
8. The name of the CONTRACTOR, if any, for such work of improvement was: (If no contractor for work of improvement as a whole, insert "none.")
   A. B. C. Plumbing Company
9. The property on which said work of improvement was completed is in the City of .. San Diego
   County of .. San Diego .. , State of California, and is described as follows:

   Portion Lot A, Block 12, Ales Tract, according to the
   map filed in the office of the County Recorder
   August 10, 1948

10. The street address of said property is: (If no street address has been assigned, insert "none.")
    6872 More Street
    San Diego, Calif. 92101

Dated .. July 22, 1968
June Street
(SIGNATURE of owner named in paragraph 2. Also sign verification at right at X) June Street

SUBSCRIBED AND SWORN TO BEFORE ME

on .. July 22, 1968
(Seal) .. *Shirley Pitt*
Shirley Pitt
NAME (Typed or Printed)   NOTARY PUBLIC IN AND FOR
                              SAID COUNTY AND STATE

STATE OF CALIFORNIA
COUNTY OF .. San Diego   (VERIFICATION)
The undersigned, being duly sworn, says: That ....he is the owner of the aforesaid interest or estate in the property described in the foregoing Notice; that ....he has read the same, and knows the contents thereof, and that the facts stated herein are true.

x *June Street*
(Signature of Owner Named in Paragraph 2 above)
June Street

STATE OF CALIFORNIA   (If this notice is executed by a corporation, use form below and
COUNTY OF ....   corporate seal)
The undersigned, being first duly sworn, says .... er, to wit, ...of

SPECIMEN

(Owner ... oration)
a corporation, which .... said interest or estate in the
property described .... executed by said corporation; that
he has read .... e contents thereof, and that the facts
therein .... n knowledge; that he makes this verification
for .... rporation.

(SIGNA ...)

FP 872

RECORDING REQUESTED BY

SPECIMEN

AND WHEN RECORDED MAIL TO

FILE/PAGE NO. **987661**
RECORDED REQUEST OF
Joe Mitchell
JUN 4 9 02 AM '68
SERIES 9 BOOK 1968
OFFICIAL RECORDS
SAN DIEGO COUNTY, CALIF.
A. S. GRAY, RECORDER
$2.00

Name   John Doe
Street Address   5644 Oak Lawn Street
City & State   San Diego, California
              92101

SPACE ABOVE THIS LINE FOR RECORDER'S USE

Release of Mechanic's Lien

TO 420 C   THIS FORM FURNISHED BY TITLE INSURANCE AND TRUST COMPANY

Know All Men by These Presents:

THAT the Mechanic's Lien claimed by___A. B. C. Electric Company_____

against *___John Doe_____

upon the following described real property in the___City and_____
County of___San Diego_____, State of California:

     Lot 4 of Block 8 in Nick's Subdivision according

     to Map 3400 filed in the office of the County

     Recorder July 10, 1908.

is hereby released, the claim thereunder having been fully paid and satisfied, and that certain Notice of Mechanic's Lien recorded as Instrument No.___120002___ on ___August 10, 1955___, in book ___6500___ page__30__, Official Records of___San Diego___County, California, is hereby satisfied and discharged.

Dated___July 20, 1968_____

STATE OF CALIFORNIA
COUNTY OF___San Diego___ } SS.
On___July 20, 1968___before me, the undersigned, a Notary Public in and for said State, personally appeared ___Joe Mitchell___
___President of A.B.C. Electric Co.___
to be the person whose name__is__subscribed to the within instrument and acknowledged that__he__executed the same.
WITNESS my hand and official seal.

Signature ___Jane Jones___
        Jane Jones
        Name (Typed or Printed)

A. B. C. Electric Company

By ___Joe Mitchell___
    Joe Mitchell, President

SPECIMEN

Title Order No.___

Escrow or Loan No.___

(This area for official notarial seal)

*Owner or purported Owner and Contractor as named in Notice of Mechanic's Lien.

the mortgage is barred if the statute has run on the debt being secured; with the trust deed, title is with the trustee who can sell it to pay off the debt to the beneficiary. The remedy is important as the foreclosure is the only one available in a mortgage situation but with the trust deed the trustee sale or a form of foreclosure proceedings both are available. The redemption is a right the mortgagor has for one year after foreclosure but with a trust deed situation there is no redemption and the trustee's sale is absolute.

To this point we have defined in a limited way various instruments related to sale and transfer of real property, however in a singular manner. Frequently financing demands finding beyond that capable by the initial loan secured by the trust deed or mortgage. Consequently, a second loan is obtained usually with a higher interest rate and also secured by a trust deed or mortgage called a "Second". In case of default on this second loan the holder of the second takes title (at trustee's sale) subject to the pre-existing first trust deed. To protect himself he files with the County Recorder simultaneously with the second trust deed and secured note, a "Request for Notice of Default and Sale" concerning any prior encumbrances. The person holding the junior lien has the right to redeem the property in the same manner as the trustor or mortgagor might from the obligations of the superior (1st) lien.

The recording of instruments affecting real property is of prime importance. The act of filing for public record is constructive notice to all of the contents of the instrument and its particular affect upon the real property concerned. There are numerous types of instruments besides the trust deeds, grant deeds, mortgages, leases and contracts of sale which are recorded due to their individual affect. To name a few: homesteads, assignments and releases of trust deeds, re-conveyances, probate orders, maps, notices of completion, assignments of leases, mechanic's liens, subordination agreements, attachments, abstracts of judgments, tax deeds, certificate of redemption and many others. The recording laws are permissive rather than mandatory except for involuntary liens and proceedings. An unrecorded instrument is valid as between the parties thereto and those who have notice (infra).

There is no specific time table for recording although it is of the utmost importance in giving notice of the condition of title.

The instrument is deemed recorded when it is deposited with and acknowledged by the Recorder who marks it "Filed for Record" with the exact date and time. Its contents are then photographed in most instances, the original returned to the person filing, or if not photographed (microfilmed) its contents are transferred to an appropriate book of record (*see* Chapter on "Investigative Sources").

There exists some finely drawn exceptions to the recording statutes. It is held a purchaser who takes title to land with knowledge of a previously executed grant deed, but unrecorded one, does so at his peril as he had "actual" notice of the situation and cannot claim his title superior. Further, if the land purchased is known to be in the possession of a person other than the seller of record, this is "constructive" notice to the purchaser of another existing claim, even though not of record. The inspection by the purchaser is to protect his rights as any prudent man is expected to do. This situation is not unusual in land frauds: Jones sells to Smith a parcel of land, but Smith neglects to record his purchase (Jones being aware of this); Jones then later sells the same parcel to Black, who, relying upon the Recorder's files alone, makes no independent inspection as to whom occupies or controls the land. Title remains with Smith. There is an existing remedy for such a fraudulent act contained in Section 533 Penal Code, "Selling Land Twice" which is a form of grand theft and punishable as such. However, if the original purchaser is not in *actual* possession and there is no physical indication of control or occupancy of any kind (buildings, power lines, etc. indicating some one having an interest) and is unrecorded, the fundamental rule of "first in time is first in right" loses some of its potency. Under the laws of California it has been held a purchaser in good faith and without notice who *records first* prevails over the unrecorded purchaser altering the rule to "first to record is first in right." But, the subsequent purchaser who records first must be bonafide to prevail.

Any instrument affecting the title to real property must be recorded in the county in which it is situated (lex loci). The standard form of a trust deed is lengthy, cumbersome and replete with highly detailed provisions. To avoid the necessity of repetitive recordation of these provisions, a "fictitious" or "reference" document is recorded and all subsequent instruments incorporate its provisions by reference. This gives constructive notice of its terms as to all later instruments which refer to it. A separate "fictitious" instrument must be recorded in each county.

Related to priority of recording are subordination agreements. Section 2953.1 Civil Code states as follows:

(a) "Real property security instruments shall include any mortgage or trust deed or land contract in or on real property"

(b) "Subordination Clause" shall mean a clause in a real property security agreement whereby the holder of the security interest agrees that upon the occurrence of conditions or circumstances specified therein his security interest will become subordinate to——the lien of another——security instrument which would otherwise be of lower priority than his lien or security interest

(c) "Subordination Agreement" means a *separate* agreement ——whereby the holder of a security interest——agrees that (1) his existing security interest is subordinate to, or (2) upon the occurance of conditions of circumstances specified in such *separate* agreement his security interest will become subordinate to, or (3) he will execute an agreement subordinating his interest to the lien of another which would otherwise be of lower priority

The subordination agreements are a necessary factor in present-day financing of real estate promotions. Purchasers often do not have sufficient funding to both pay the purchase price in total and the construction costs coupled with the fact they seldom use their own funds for purchasing anyway. Inasmuch as institutional lenders by the Finance Code (Sec. 1413 (d) must secure loans with first trust deeds or liens, the first trust deed securing the seller's interest in the property based upon his extension of credit to the purchaser ("purchase money trust deed") must be subordinated to the lender's security interest. In effect the seller is helping finance the purchaser's development. The safety and security of his credit extension depends upon the success of the venture.

There are two very important companies which play a large part in all real estate transactions if the parties are legitimate and want assurances of validity in the negotiations; they are the escrow people and the title companies. Escrow is a transaction in which a third party gets as an agent for both the seller and buyer, or for a borrower and a lender in carrying out the instructions of both sides and handling the disbursement of the necessary papers and funds. The escrow agent or company accepts deposits; prepares deeds and notes; obtains the title report; obtains the title insurance policy; makes an accounting of funds received and disbursed; and records the necessary instruments and documents. He is analogous to a stake-holder between two bettors.

The escrow operation has been accurately described as a short-termed trust arrangement. It has been provided for in Civil Code Section 1057 which says, "A grant may be deposited by the grantor with a third person, to be delivered on the performance of a condition, and, on delivery by the depositary, it will take effect. While in possession of a third person, and subject to conditions, it is called 'escrow' ". The sequence of events in an escrow are more or less uniform and static. They start with a preliminary title search and related report, the lender's statement (if involved), mutual instructions and the depositing of funds, disbursements of funds, transfer of insurance policies, recordation, issuance of the title policy and the escrow statement.

An escrow is termed "complete" when all instructions, both buyer's and seller's, are met. If it has been properly drawn and executed by all parties of interest it becomes a binding and enforceable contract. Escrows are normally terminated by performance and closing or mutual consent and cancellation. Specific performance must take place within the time period indicated in the agreement.

The examination of the escrow instructions and related instruments and documents by the investigator in a possible fraud situation is important for the developing of leads (see exemplars). The buyer's instructions at the outset disclose the actual amount of cash monies initially put forward and the remaining amount due within a specified time period and the amount of the encumbrances which is the total consideration of the sales agreement. The next element is the termination date indicating the full time period allowed for performance.

The source of the buyer's funds can often be ascertained from the leads disclosed in the instructions and by a good interview of the escrow agent. This, in essence, presents a problem in tactics as escrow instructions for the most part are considered to be confidential. Albeit, this source can frequently disclose hidden parties of interest, especially when paid in the form of a personal or a cashier's check. The bank then, becomes an additional source of information. The escrow agent during the course of his frequent contacts with the ostensible parties, even without any real effort on his part, becomes privy to many things which are inadvertently dropped during conversations and if he is experienced and knowledgeable, readily recognizes the signs or indications of sub-rosa purpose.

Following the section which discloses in whom title is to be vested and the legal description coupled with existing encumbrances, if any, there is set forth the conditions under which the escrow will close. This can include a variety of things from the obtaining of some permits to even the sale of some other property upon which instant purchase can be contingent. The encumbrance, a trust deed, is then explained as to total amount, interest, installment amounts and the period of time involved. The subsequent sections indicate the prorating of various costs and expenses and general instructions which are standard in all escrows.

The escrow statement is merely a recapitulation of the previous information in a properly contrived accounting form. There is one for the buyer and one for the seller and they correspond with the balances being equal. What is debited in the buyer's statement is credited in the seller's and what is credited in the buyer's statement is debited in the seller's.

The Civil and Penal Codes of each state and/or jurisdiction must be examined to ensure that all legal requirements of that jurisdiction have been complied with or not complied with, as the case may be, before undertaking any investigation. This is necessary to "plot the course" and evaluate whether or not an eventual prosecution would lie.

Real estate frauds have, apparently, existed down through the ages, for probably the same reasons they now exist, the main one being avarice. One of the earliest land swindles most people will recall was the purchase of Manhattan from the friendly Indians for about fifteen dollars. At that time, apparently both parties considered they were outsmarting the other, but history has proven the true victor.

Of the numerous methods of perpetrating land frauds, the first we shall deal with is regarding large land developments.

Most states today and the two Federal Agencies most concerned, the Federal Trades Commission and the Security Exchange Commission "the first for false advertising, and the second for fraudulent promotion deals" have gone a long way in curtailing such real estate sales schemes, however, some do still try and enjoy a measure of success. These operators will work both sides of the street. They will acquire a large tract via a small initial payment hooked by a promissory note secured by trust deeds or mortgages. When the income for sales begin to dip below the payments they must be maintained, they will sometime attempt a public offering of stock using this source for their note/mortgage or trust deed obligation. Frequently the Securities Exchange Commission, as they work interstate, and the Corporation Commission when receiving the application find things unhappily do not meet even the most minimum requirements for a safe security sale. The Real Estate Commission, of course, is apprized and the three agencies working jointly through their various injunctive processes, can and do, at least for a while, put a stop to their activities.

From a practical investigative standpoint, "a good offensive is the best defense." A fraud investigator should, upon becoming aware of the promoter's operations in his area, initiate even without reporting victims, inquiries as to the exact location of the tract; the utilities; its proximity to other centers of population; its accessibility; soil and topography studies; the identity and background of all the company officers; the manner in which company acquired the land to sell; a complete title examination of the land including the information from the escrow company; title company and detailed accounting from the original seller as to the approach used by the promoter; the history of the land use, the formation of the promoting company and its history of operations.

Further, all advertising matter and other means used to attract buyers should be obtained and recorded, not just for the present operation, but if there is a history of prior acts, the same information and documentation must be developed. This means the division of real estate, department of corporation or other comparable agencies, the Federal Trades Commission, the Securities Exchange Commission, county clerks and county recorders, title companies and banks and loan association or other previously affected areas must be canvased. This must also be accompanied by a formation from district attorneys or other agencies and victims who may have had prior experience with the same group. Again here, we are preparing the ground work or foundation to allege and *prove* additional similar acts and transactions.

To establish the base, a series of victims must be found who can "and will" properly testify that they did enter into negotiations with the promoters based upon the representations made by the promoters and their reliance therein, and that the representations were in fact materially false; and have the documentations to back up the allegations.

It is almost a one hundred percent by population count inherent desire to own some land in the country in which you reside. So powerful is the yearning that hundreds of thousands of people every year commit their life savings to buy land they have never seen and very often this is done on the spur of the moment. The land developers recognize this shield of human weakness and invariably turn this into a huge profit. Constantly there are several such schemes on the horizon attempting to extract your savings from you for land of a highly controversial value. Typical of these schemes is the case of Bill and Jane Anderson (fictitious names) who are engulfed in the loss of their savings as well as having to make huge payments on the land they bought: by mail and by phone call, they received an invitation to a free dinner and colorful brochures offering free gifts and a vacation in faraway places was afforded them. The federal government has passed laws to protect citizens against high pressured sales tactics of land developers, but they are unable to protect people against themselves. These people continue to be milked at an astonishing rate.

About three years ago the Andersons were invited by one of the nation's largest land developers to attend a free dinner and see a film on New Mexico property. They bought a lot that very evening sight unseen. However, their act was not unique in that this attitude has made land development an estimated six billion dollar a year industry. In interviewing the Andersons, an attempt was made to ascertain what made them buy the land that they did. They stated they had to drive through the snow to get to the meeting to which they were invited and they had a nice free meal. The meeting was held in a nice restaurant in a private room where podiums were set up and the sales manager acted somewhat like an auctioneer, beating the podium and using other hardsell tactics. He also had people at the meeting that he had sold to before using them somewhat as shields. They were also furnished with voluminous contracts in legal terminology which of course the Andersons were unable to have time to read or understand if they had read them. The promoter stated that of course they could take the papers home if they wished to read them, but there was a hazard in that they would lose out on the purchase of this property since the price might go up and there was quite a demand for the property. The Andersons also stated that despite the fact they were told to read the contracts, the light was somewhat dim in the restaurant and they had considerable difficulty in even reading them. They also were given a property sheet showing what property was available and while they were sitting studying the map a representative came over and urged them to make up their mind since people at the other end of the hall were deciding to buy and they might lose out. The representative stated that was all that was available that night and they had best make a selection as quickly as possible, so they gave them a down payment that night on a lot they had never seen. When asked why they bought without seeing the property, they stated they had seen the films, they had seen pictures of model homes and the lure of the great open spaces, fresh air, etc. really appealed to them and they were mesmerized into buying the property. Part of this mesmerization occurred when they were advised they could go skiing in the morning and come home and plunge in the pool in the afternoon and enjoy a real vacation type of living. This of course is appealing to everyone.

Prior to buying however, the Andersons asked what would happen if they decided they did not want the property. The salesman told them that he would resell their property at one of the same type of dinners and it would only cost them 10 percent commission.

Several months later, Anderson experienced financial difficulties and asked his salesman to resell his lot. The salesman again gave him a sales pitch stating that his investment had doubled and urged him to hold on, however, Anderson was unable to afford the monthly payments and insisted at that point and later attempts to reach the salesman proved fruitless and he was unreachable.

Anderson then, becoming desperate, called long distance to the tract and spoke with a representative who gave him a figure on his land which was more than he had paid for it. He asked them to resell it for him and they said they could not do it. He then called a real estate broker in the New Mexico area and one real estate firm would not handle the property, stating it was useless. The other offered him approximately one-half of what he had paid for it as a listing price. To date, the Andersons have not sold their property and they are stuck with the monthly payments by binding contract. The Andersons are typical of the average American citizen who trusts too many people. We all find it difficult to sit across from someone and recognize that person as someone who would cheat you out of anything. It is being learned daily that there are an awful lot of people selling land who are crooks, which is a nice way of describing them. They are out for the quick commission, they want to sell you that property and they will never see you again. They don't care if you waste your life savings, but until people are worried enough about their money and educated to the fact that there are individuals like this operating land sales, too many people are going to get into bad deals.

Almost in the same category as the case above is that of the individuals who are dreaming of a vacation home. A recent survey in the Boston area showed that 62 percent of 1,000 newlywed couples already were planning to buy a vacation retreat. Michigan seems to be the current hotspot, thanks mostly to the new snowmobile fad and the expanded interest generally in winter sports. Most developments promise ski slopes and snowmobile trails as well as sandy beaches.

While on summer vacation, two couples stopped at a Northern Michigan lake development and bought pieces of what they considered to be paradise in the north woods. One of the wives stated it was very attractive property. The golf course was right on the corner as you went in, and there was a little canal running into the lake. They said they would clean out the canal for the buyers and cut down the trees.

They asked if they could show the contract to their lawyer. The salesman said he could give them the sales price only if they bought that day, and the lots would probably be gone by the time they got back anyway. So without inspecting their sites, they put a deposit on two canal lots fourteen miles south of the nearest city in the middle of beautiful rustic vacation country.

However, they drove back later to discover the canal was more like a ditch and their lots were swampland. They had not yet received their deeds and so they began asking for their money back. However, to date they still have no deeds and they can't get a refund. The developer is a defendant in a law suit filed by the Attorney General of Michigan to stop illegal and deceptive practices which threatens to turn the state's vacation land boom into one of the biggest land scandals in years.

Most developers are law abiding and respectable, authorities say, even though some tread closely to the border line in their sales pressure tactics, but the boom still attracts more and more dishonest operators.

The great demand for vacation land is a nationwide movement touched off by a combination of factors—a growing population, more money, leisure time at all levels of income, earlier retirement age and increased longevity, greater interest in outdoor sports and the fact that the land supply never increases.

The way the unlawful developer operates is to buy an option on a large piece of land or put a down payment on a land contract, have a preliminary sub-division plat drawn up and start selling hoping to attract buyers fast enough to cover his expenses and pick up his own option and make his payments. If he can sell the first ten to twelve lots, then he has the money to build a road and pretty soon he can hire a surveyor and an engineer. However, if he is unsuccessful in doing this, many developers fall off that narrow margin and the resulted bankruptcys have left buyers with worthless options that are binding on no one but the defunct development firm.

In investigating this type of case, several things should be discussed with the complainant. (1) Did they physically see this specific piece of property and make sure the boundaries were clearly defined. (2) Were the documents checked by an attorney before they signed them so they knew exactly what they were getting. (3) Did they check the ownership of the property and its development status with the county registrar of deeds. (4) Did they ask the local health department about use restrictions and possible additional charges for water and sewer systems. (5) Did they check with the road department on possible charges for road improvement and maintenance. (6) Did they ask the county treasurer if there were any unpaid taxes assessments. (7) Were checks made with the respective authorities on the developers reputation. (8) Did they insist on a policy or commitment of title insurance.

Another ingenious type of land fraud was recently stifled with the conviction of the land purchasing firm and one of its officials being convicted of fourteen counts of using the mails to execute a fraudulent scheme. The land involved in this scheme included mountain property and adjacent property near an inland sea.

The evidence showed the purchasing firm official and the company filed a series of Superior Court suits in the respective county against the victim-owners, claiming the firm was the owner of the real property. They then mailed copies of the lawsuits to the victims with a letter implying the firm had purchased tax title and tax deeds to the real property involved from the State of California and the tax title was paramount to any interest possessed by the victims, all of which was untrue. In their letters, the defendants used the fictitious name of Pacific Land Title Research Company and indicated disclaimers and quit claim deeds were formalities necessary to insure a policy of title insurance. The victims were offered sums of $25.00 to $100.00 to sign disclaimers.

Evidence in the case showed that the defendants had acquired the land and resold it for amounts ranging up to forty-five times more than the price paid the victims.

As a result of the actions being filed and mailed to the property owners, the defendants fraudulently induced the victims to execute and deliver disclaimers and quit claim deeds to the company.

CHAPTER IX

INVESTMENT AND CORPORATE FRAUDS

ALMOST WEEKLY we read and hear of a respected high government official or respected citizen in the community being
indicted for some form of securities or corporate fraud. Many
begin these practices with a legal and ethical intent but too often
wind up enmeshed in practices unnatural to their at least super-
ficial integrity and become embroiled in one of many fraudulent
schemes intended to cover up their misguided practices.

Recently a judicial district judge and his partner in a bookkeeping collections and insurance agency each pleaded guilty to
twelve felony counts of violating a state corporations code. These
individuals had solicited investors to put money into their firm
and ten affiliate firms and then used the money to pay off demands from earlier creditors.

It was revealed they never told the investors that the companies were losing large amounts of money or that the state had
ordered them to stop selling securities, rather it was stated they
represented that the companies had tremendous assets.

In another recent federal case, an ex-securities exchange commission lawyer and a Pennsylvania business man were indicted
for alleged fraud in the disposal of one and one-half million dollars in stolen securities. They allegedly used the stolen securities
as collateral to obtain loans from a Bahamanian bank. It was also
reported that at least part of the securities were from a twenty-
one million dollar robbery at Kennedy Airport approximately
three years previously.

Another recent case brought forth the activities of three persons who were engaged in the illegal sale of securities. When ar-

rested the officials of that state called it "probably the biggest bogus security violation in the state's history."

They were charged with illegally selling between two point six million and three million dollars worth of securities to at least 850 investors. The investors were described as both large and small and mostly residents of a particular area. The securities were shares in an investment corporation and officials said the firm is now in bankruptcy.

The investigating officials said seven of the group were issued a limited permit to issue three million shares of the corporation at one dollar a share "to themselves." However, they violated the state's corporate securities law by selling shares to other persons without permission, even before applying for the limited permit. Some shares were sold for as high as $5.00 each.

The officials explained that resale to other persons constitutes a public offering for which a special kind of permit is required. To qualify the seller should show the state they have made "full and adequate disclosure" of facts of the firm, and the state must determine that the sale is "fair, just and equitable."

This procedure was set up to protect the public against fraud. Despite precautions, there was a considerable amount of traffic going on in non-licensed securities. Some of the businesses make money and no one complains, but it was stated "it is important for the public to know that permits are needed" to sell securities.

These individuals were also charged with false representation to the Commissioner of Corporations and to investors. A false statement to investors included representations that the stock would be traded publicly within two or three months, that the initial price would be as high as $20.00, and it would go to as high as $50.00 a share. Needless to say, none of these statements materialized and the firm was forced into bankruptcy.

In another interesting and unusual case, the founder and board chairman of the now bankrupt Sunday Mail was arrested on a warrant charging him with fourteen counts of grand theft and fifteen counts of corporate security violations. He was taken into custody by members of the police department and the state department of corporations.

He had formed the Sunday Mail, a publishing and advertising

distribution organization in 1969 as a private mail service and subsequently sold three thousand dollar franchises to at least 450 persons. It was estimated that total invested by dealers was $2,100,000.00.

According to this individual's advertising and sales guarantees, he told the franchise purchasers they could earn from $200.00 to $300.00 for one day's work every week. Instead, more than 450 persons complained that they received nothing for their investments.

One of the most prevalent and commonly used *modus operandi* in the security and corporate field is the "shell game." The so called "shell cases" are mainly responsible for a sharp increase in the past few years in the number of security and exchange commission orders which forced a temporary halt to trading in suspected stock issues, for the protection of investors. The ten day renewable orders usually suffice to deflate the promotion. The commissioner acknowledged the Security Exchange Commission's concern over the growing shell problem.

He said there were signs of organized crime heading and being involved in some of the cases. It was further stated that this is one of the products of an affluent society which provides a fertile field for the schemer and white collar crook. In several of the cases examined, they found that millions of dollars had been invested by the public and in corporations that had no managements, no offices, no assets and no income. The shell game now has been picked up by dozens of small time operators; it is the new thing in shady stock promotion. All promoters need to do is to buy, usually for a song, the corporate remains of a dormant enterprise that still has a corporate charter. The issues are sold in the over-the-counter market so there is no organized exchange to police the trading. And because the shares usually were registered and issued years ago, the registration and full disclosure of the Securities Exchange Commission were bypassed.

The raw material in this field is very plentiful. The corporate remains can be found throughout the southwest and far west which are relics of the uranium penny stock boom of several years ago and of older mining and oil promotions. For a time there was an active market in shells. Advertisements and financial papers announced "clean shells" for sale. As distinct from a dirty shell, a clean shell is one with no old legal claims, court judgments or financial liens against it.

The Securities Exchange Commission is working with some state commissions to reduce the number of corporate shells lying around to be picked up by promoters. Bills are pending in some western states which provide that a corporation's franchise expires when its franchise tax remains unpaid for a given period of time.

Investigative Suggestions

In handling any of the above corporate or securities frauds, the following leads are suggested:

1. Complete background checks of all suspects.
2. Check the corporation's status with the Department of Corporations in the respective state. Pay particular attention to the articles of incorporation and any and all permits which may or may not have been granted for their securities transaction, etc.
3. Check with the State Department of Securities for any information relevant to the corporation and/or the individuals involved regarding any permits necessary and permit granted.
4. Check all banking institutions with which the individuals and/or the corporations have accounts. It is emphasized that the daily transactions in the accounts must be examined to ascertain if other dummy accounts are being used and if check kiting was being utilized by the corporations, its officers or the suspects.
5. Contact a representative number of subscribers and/or stockholders to ascertain the guarantees, assurance, etc. which may have been presented by any of the suspects. Also, ascertain if any of the shareholders have experienced difficulties in dealing with any of the individuals involved and what they were.
6. Establish liaison with the SEC, Department of Corporations representatives, and other interested agencies regarding the activities and/or suspected illegal transactions.
7. Review the chapter on investigative sources for other applicable avenues of approach.

INDEX

A

Abortion shake, 50, 56, 57

Abortionist, 54, 56

Abstracting the accounts, 96

Accountant, 10, 20, 21, 68, 71, 86, 98–101, 109, 185, 187, 282, 286

Accountant embezzler, 107

Accounting, 79, 80, 84–111
loss, 184–88

Accounting clerk, 70, 71

Accounting clerk embezzler, 66–68

Accounting control system, 10, 101

Accounts Payable, 68, 69, 87, 88, 91–95, 185, 186

Accounts Receivable, 86, 87, 91, 93–95, 101, 193, 104, 185

Adjustor, 184–87, 190–92

Aeroclave device, 245–51

Alcohol Beverage Control Board, 285

Alphabetical exemplar card, 143

Alteration
of negotiable instrument, 117–19
of sales contract, 219

Ambrosia of the Gods, 253

American Arthritis Foundation, 251

American Banking Association, 109, 135, 136, 165

American Insurance Association, 196, 284

American Medical Association, 253

Appeal, 9, 19

Ardrey, R., 5

Area alarm method, 156–59

Arrest, 27, 29, 41, 43, 51, 56, 57, 73, 112, 142, 169, 224, 245, 259, 260, 269, 270, 323, 324

Arrest record, 37, 112, 141, 146, 260

Arson, 171–73, 175–77, 188, 196, 200, 284

Assault, 12, 112, 145

Assessment, 82, 171, 273

Assessor, 263

Assets, 21, 64, 81, 85–89, 100, 105, 193, 284, 323, 325

Assigned risk pool, 181

Attorney General, 208, 209, 229, 254, 320

Audit, 10, 68, 73, 99–101, 105, 107, 273

Auditor, 71, 75, 79, 95, 96, 256

Automobile Finance Act, 210

B

Badger game, 50

Bail, 52, 56, 59, 64, 77, 167

Bait and Switch scam, 205, 215, 216, 219

Balance sheet, 79, 86–89, 93, 94, 100

Bank officer, 66, 140–42, 160

Behavior pattern, 8, 80, 172

Behavioral research, x

Beneficiary interest, 63, 191, 262

Better Business Bureau, 204, 225, 228, 236, 284

Betting slip, 36

Bill of exchange, 115

Binder, 183

Bird-dog, 35

Blanket coverage, 182

Bonds, 8, 82, 116

Book value, 70, 184

Booking sheet, 29, 37, 146, 260

Bookkeeper, 71, 98, 108, 161, 165

Bookkeeper embezzler, 107